THE
ENNEAGRAM
ADVANTAGE

Publications by Helen Palmer

The Enneagram: Understanding Yourself and the Others in Your Life

The Enneagram in Love and Work: Understanding Your Intimate and Business Relationships

The Pocket Enneagram

The Enneagram: A Six-Tape Audio Class with Voices of the Nine Types (SOUNDS TRUE RECORDINGS)

THE ENNEAGRAM ADVANTAGE

USING THE 9 PERSONALITY TYPES
AT WORK

HELEN PALMER
AND PAUL B. BROWN

Harmony Books/NEW YORK

Published by Harmony Books, a division of Crown Publishers, Inc., 201 East 50th Street, New York, New York 10022. Member of the Crown Publishing Group.

Random House, Inc. New York, Toronto, London, Sydney, Auckland
http://www.randomhouse.com/

HARMONY and colophon are trademarks of Crown Publishers, Inc.

Printed in the United States of America

Design by Lynne Amft

Library of Congress Cataloging-in-Publication Data
Palmer, Helen.
    The enneagram advantage: using the 9 personality types at
work / by Helen Palmer and Paul B. Brown. — 1st ed.
    1. Enneagram.   2. Typology (Psychology)   I. Brown, Paul B.   II. Title.
BF698.35.E54P34   1998
155.2'64—dc21   97-25038
                                                          CIP

ISBN 0-517-70432-3

10 9 8 7 6 5 4 3 2 1

First Edition

To Janet and Sandy Levine.

Janet, whose vision of bringing spirituality to the work-place was the impetus for this book, and Sandy, for some terrific talks on how the Enneagram plays out in organizations.

Contents

THE
ENNEAGRAM
ADVANTAGE

An Overview

Although many of its definitions have been shrouded in centuries-old concepts of personality, the Enneagram is really not difficult to explain and understand. Originally developed as a blueprint for self-observation, the system describes nine different personality types and how they interact with one another. Each type is defined by an emotional habit, a characteristic pattern of thought, and a style of relating to others, which together produce a distinct point of view.

The origin of the word Enneagram (pronounced any-a-gram) is equally straightforward. In Greek, *ennea* is "nine," and *gram* means "something drawn or written." And that is exactly what the model is: A graphic representation of a nine-pointed star, with each of the points representing a specific personality profile.

Like all typing systems, the Enneagram is structured to show characteristics that people with the same profile share in common, but the focus is on normal and high-achieving people rather than on pathological disorder. In business organizations, the Enneagram advantage lies in knowing how coworkers think, feel, and sort the information that applies to their jobs. No one type is better than another, but each brings its own lens of perception to work and each type approaches the same job differently.

As suggested by its Greek name, the Enneagram is rooted in the ancient world, rather than in the analytic framework pioneered by Freud barely a hundred years ago. Since the beginning of time, people have invented templates to observe and understand the differences among us. Although separated by daunting barriers of mountains, oceans, and desert sands, world cultures have produced surprisingly similar systems explaining why people do what they do. Looking within to find what stood in the way of understanding themselves and others, the conclusion was unanimous: We get in our own way through habitual thinking, which prevents us from seeing other points of view.

The traditional explanation for different patterns of behavior lies in a revered ethical teaching called the vice to virtue transformation. Today the word "vice" is known as a defensive psychological survival strategy. The vice forms as a protective shield in early life to cushion emotional discomfort, and served a useful purpose then. But once we understand this childhood basis for the defensive core of our type, we can develop ways to transform, or convert, the vice into its opposite virtue.

Because it is an emotional survival strategy, vice also affects our relationships with others, ultimately interfering even with our ability to make a spiritual connection. In the ancient world, vice was seen as a source of suffering, and its healing was a spiritual achievement.

How we discover our vice, or ruling emotional passion, is a practical matter, but the Enneagram was originally designed as a road map to that discovery. The nine types each reflect a vice to virtue transformation. For example, a Perfectionist Type One's vice of anger can be converted to the virtue of serenity, while the underlying fear described by Loyal Skeptic Sixes is the raw material from which courage evolves. When you discover your ruling passion, you need to remember that it originally developed for a reason. While we want to learn more about our own point of view while working with other people, we also need to maintain compassion for all nine perspectives.

The conversion of vice to virtue is fundamental in the many world traditions that focus on personality as an agent of spiritual change. To name a few, Judaism, Buddhism, and Sufism (the mystical wing of Islam) have each identified the higher potentials of type. Another familiar example is the Christian concept of seven capital sins as the source of human suffering—with each vice creating a hunger for its corresponding virtue.

The vice of pride, for instance, swells when we feel important in the lives of others, and is painfully punctured when we feel rejected. But pride also directs a search for the virtue of humility to resolve the tension of seeking approval and feeling hurt when approval is taken away.

The silence of spiritual life, our prayers or meditation, may also be invaded by pride, if when we turn attention inward, we fear the loss of external support. Humility, then, is simply knowing exactly how others see you and being grateful for it, a condition that feels heaven-sent to those caught in the cycle of pride.

The traditional aim of transformation is to uncover your characteristic survival strategy, and to cultivate the opposite "virtue" or constructive way of being. Pride vanishes with the practice of humility, of knowing your real value to others. Likewise, the vice of avarice dissolves through learning nonattachment, and so on for all nine types.

The vice, or emotional survival strategy, is supported by a characteristic way of sorting information. For example, in the spiritual traditions that use type as a factor in human development, Enneatype Sevens were known as "monks of gluttonous mind," not because they overate, but because their attention constantly turned to pleasurable plans and fantasies. Likewise, type

Ones were called "monks of judging mind," because the vice of anger produces a focus on error and corrective thinking. The vice and its corresponding pattern of thought can only be recognized by self-observation.

The vice to virtue conversion illustrates a point of agreement between spiritual traditions, rather than showing how they differ from each other. Instead of being a matter of dogma or religious belief, the conversion is a basic ethical teaching that enables us to understand our actions and conduct toward others. In traditional spiritual communities, where systems like the Enneagram were first developed, conscious conduct toward ourselves, others, and the spiritual journey were seen as ethical choices.

The Enneagram Vice to Virtue Transformation

Type	Vice	Virtue
One	Anger	Serenity
Two	Pride	Humility
Three	Deceit	Honesty
Four	Envy	Emotional Equanimity
Five	Avarice	Nonattachment
Six	Fear	Courage
Seven	Gluttony	Moderation
Eight	Lust	Appropriate force
Nine	Sloth (Self-forgetting)	Action

It takes enormous reserves of time, energy, and attention to maintain an emotional survival strategy that served us in childhood but that may now be outmoded. The Enneagram can help us to observe how we habitually spend energy, and how to focus effectively on becoming more productive, proactive, and responsive in the workplace.

In 1988, I wrote *The Enneagram: Understanding Yourself and the Others in Your Life,* which described the nine Enneatypes in the context of spiritual ideas. *The Enneagram in Love and Work,* which followed in 1994, described the types in relationship. *The Ennea-gram Advantage* furthers our understanding of the nine points of view by locating the types in business settings and common work-place interactions—where most people spend most of their time and energy.

What Type Am I?

In the Enneagram system, no type is better than another, and each represents an effective life strategy, but they all differ radically in their point of view. While we will spend the rest of the book exploring these nine personalities in detail—concentrating on how they appear and interact at work—let's quickly sketch them here.

ONE: THE PERFECTIONIST

The world seems perpetually out of order. Something has to be done, and done with step-by-step precision. Reports, for example, should be comprehensive but just the right length. The feedback you give should be concise, without wasting precious time and effort.

You live with a severe inner critic who monitors every thought, word, and deed. The critic tells you that there's always room for improvement, and your self-imposed standards keep rising.

You may not even know that you're angry until you hear the polite, clenched, and rising tone of your own voice saying, "*Nothing* is wrong and I *never* get angry."

NINE TYPES OF PEOPLE

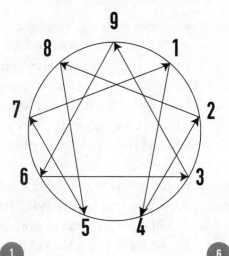

The Perfectionist
Diligent, Ethical, Practical, Angry

The Giver
Helpful, Empathetic, Manipulative, Prideful

The Performer
Efficient, Persuasive, Chameleonlike, Deceptive

The Romantic
Dramatic, Unique, Melancholy, Envious

The Observer
Private, Observant, Detached, Withholding

The Loyal Skeptic
Loyal, Questioning, Vigilant, Fearful

The Epicure
Optimistic, Futuristic, Scattered a Gluttonous

The Boss
Territorial, Confronting, Protective, Trustful

The Mediator
Ambivalent, Agreeable, Stubborn, Self-forgetting

Maximizing Your Opportunities: Jobs that emphasize organizational structure and require meticulous attention to detail are attractive because quality control is embedded in your thinking. There's pleasure in good work and a job well done, so you drive yourself harder than most. Attention is drawn to improving procedures, correcting errors, and producing those small daily victories that occur when everything falls into place "just right."

Minimizing Risks: You're not attracted to jobs where decision making is based on fluid or partial information. The inner critic goes wild without guidelines, so you want to stop and check. On-the-spot decisions increase the risk of error and personal accountability. You may freeze in the crosscurrents of multiple points of view or differences of opinion.

YOUR BOTTOM LINE: "Perfection requires heroic efforts. I'm not there yet."

TWO: THE GIVER

Your focus is on giving care and receiving close, personal feedback, so you find identity largely through relationships. A power behind the throne who manages by persuasion or manipulation, you generate approval by being pleasing and indispensable.

Several different "selves" develop, each adapted to meet the needs of others. You have a self for the boss, a self for the team, and other selves for family life. Your challenge is to recognize the difference between "giving to get" and altruistic support.

Maximizing Your Opportunities: Positioning is important. Your best selves emerge through association with front-runners who are counting on you. You work *with* a boss, not *for* the boss, because you're managing the boss's life. Attractive people in need of help are TWO bait.

Minimizing Risks: Environments that give little positive feedback are difficult for you. It's hard to keep going if you don't get some show of gratitude for having met other people's needs.

YOUR BOTTOM LINE: "They couldn't make it without me."

THREE: THE PERFORMER

The world loves a winner, so you project a successful image, becoming the role model of your profession. You know you can make anything work if you throw enough energy at it.

Emotional life gets sacrificed along the way, but you decide, "Don't think about it—just do it." You're in control as long as you're fast forward, but inactivity is terrifying. Performers depend on immediate results and positive feedback, and it's horrifying to think, "What if this doesn't work?"

Maximizing Your Opportunities: You want a status job where there's plenty of room for advancement and where you can excel. Work should reward long hours and star performance. People who don't want footprints on their back get out of your way.

Minimizing Risks: Jobs with a ceiling are unattractive. You like quick turnover and fast results, so creative projects requiring introspection and long periods of trial and error are grueling.

YOUR BOTTOM LINE: "You're only as good as your last victory. No cookies for losers."

FOUR: THE ROMANTIC

You may have two jobs, the one that pays the bills and your real job as an artist. You want work to create an avenue for meaningful expression, and you won't sell out for superficial prosperity.

Attention constantly shifts to the best of what's missing.

What's far away and hard to get looks tantalizing, and in comparison, there's not much on your own side of the fence.

Your efficiency may be tied to mood. It's difficult to stay interested when you're feeling melancholy. Projects can languish during crises or when you're involved in a love affair.

Maximizing Your Opportunities: You prefer a creative job that calls for a unique, even eccentric approach. You're drawn to emotionally charged occupations, running the gamut from working the trading desk at a wire house to handling the night shift on a suicide hot line. You keep asking yourself, "Why shouldn't professional life reflect authentic human values?"

Minimizing Risks: Mundane jobs in ordinary settings are crushing. Similarly, you need to avoid bureaucratic positions requiring anonymity and emotional detachment. Equally deadly are jobs where you have to work in cooperation with others who are more skilled, more valued, or better paid. You feel demeaned by plebeian work, the definition of which is known only to yourself. Gardening can be plebe work. So can being a CEO.

YOUR BOTTOM LINE: "Something's missing. I wish I had it."

FIVE: THE OBSERVER

From your detached point of view, a great many activities seem pointless. Why do people run around wasting energy on trivial pursuits when it's so delightful to retire and think? Since privacy is paramount, you treasure withdrawing to a protected place, safe from unwanted intrusion.

Doing with less simplifies everything. You have fewer needs to deal with, fewer obligations and office interactions. Doing with less also liberates more time and precious energy for study and thought.

Maximizing Your Opportunities: Your ability to detach and analyze brings order out of chaos. Emotional detachment also makes it possible for you to work alone for long periods of time in single-minded pursuit of answers. You're attracted to the kind of jobs that protect your time and energy. When possible, you prefer limited windows of contact—and tend to reinforce your guard with a barricade of secretaries, E-mail, and fax machines.

Minimizing Risks: Any job that requires open competition or direct confrontation is anathema. It's risky to put yourself on the line when you have limited resources of energy. Open-ended meetings, spontaneous decisions, off-the-cuff brainstorming, and emotional interactions are draining.

Your Bottom Line: "Mind over matter."

SIX: THE LOYAL SKEPTIC

You act with strength under adversity but are prone to doubt when it's an easy win. Doubt, coupled with imagining the worst-case scenario, prompts you to ask, "What if this situation turns dangerous?" and "Yes, but shouldn't we think this through again?" Ironically, anxiety peaks with visible success because notoriety attracts competition. However, you go full out for an underdog cause or in a turnaround situation, particularly in collaboration with allies.

Maximizing Your Opportunities: It's easy to work in hierarchical environments with clear lines of authority. You know what to expect and exactly what you're up against. Self-employed positions are also attractive, because you are your own authority. Your determination to deal with hard questions makes you a natural troubleshooter and a highly valued analyst.

Minimizing Risks: High-pressure jobs requiring spot decisions can lead to analysis paralysis. Under pressure, thinking replaces doing, sometimes producing procrastination. High-profile competitive jobs with ambiguous guidelines feel like a setup for failure.

YOUR BOTTOM LINE: "Question authority."

SEVEN: THE EPICURE

You see a world filled with opportunities and options, there's always new data to absorb and fascinating plans to make. Buoyed by a sense of your own worth, you feel entitled to success, and that enthusiasm rubs off on others. Where most people see limitations, you see positive new ideas.

Life's OK when you can see the possibilities. You're a brainstormer and networker who sidesteps conflict. This wizardry is both brilliant and distracting. It can produce original ideas, but also lets you slip away from sticky commitments.

Maximizing Your Opportunities: When initial stages of a plan require multi-option thinking and a positive future vision, that's where you shine. You'll be attracted to new beginnings, and to the parts of a project that require synthesizing crosscurrents of new information.

Minimizing Risks: When implementing a plan requires routine work that does not support a spirit of adventure, you are less than interested. Critical supervision or closed-end jobs cause you to reframe the rules and network yourself into a better position.

YOUR BOTTOM LINE: "You're OK. I'm OK. Isn't everyone?"

EIGHT: THE BOSS

The focus is on control. "Who has the power, and will they be fair?" You take charge and fend off the competition, rather than risk being controlled yourself.

Anger is the emotion of choice, and trust in others is built through confrontation. You know that people blurt their true thoughts when they're angry and during a confrontation you are trying to discover if people are manipulative, whether they fight fair, if they're honest, and whether they wimp out.

Speaking your mind clears the air, and tests coworkers to make sure it's safe to surrender control. Justice for all is a major theme, and you're highly protective of "our side," "my people," and "our team."

Maximizing Your Opportunities: You're known for your aggressive, take-charge leadership, but you can also empower others. Leadership positions are a natural, because you combine tough-minded, tender-hearted support with just the right amount of force to move a massive project forward.

Minimizing Risks: You're not great in jobs that depend on diplomacy and following orders, and you are especially sensitive to power plays and covert manipulation. You want clear lines of redress for grievances, rather than depending on the goodwill of superiors.

YOUR BOTTOM LINE: "My way or the highway."

NINE: THE MEDIATOR

You want consensus and a peaceful workplace, so you weigh the pros and cons. You see all the good points and all the bad points of a decision, which keeps you on the fence. You can identify with everyone else's position, and that may derail your own agenda, making you wonder, "Do I want to do this, or was it someone else's idea?"

Once involved, it's hard to say no, so you may stick around longer than you really want to. Rather than get angry, you'll dig in your heels and get stubborn.

Deadlines are a call to action, and you're highly productive when you get rolling. The trick is to hold your own position, when it's all too easy to focus on what other people want.

Maximizing Your Opportunities: Seeing all sides of a question makes you a natural mediator. People around you feel accepted, because you can see the world from their perspective.

Minimizing Risks: High-image jobs requiring continuous self-promotion are risky. So are settings that call for rapid turnover in procedures. Shifting priorities distract your attention, and conflict tears you apart.

YOUR BOTTOM LINE: "Keep the peace. Don't make waves."

If your initial reaction after reading the nine snapshots is to say: "I'm not sure yet which one I am," you are not alone. After all the Enneagram's nine-pointed star is enclosed in a circle, which is meant to show that we have access to every viewpoint. Still, each of us has a primary type. The following Enneagram Type Quiz is designed to help you identify yours.

ENNEAGRAM TYPE QUIZ

This self-assessment quiz describes nine different personality types. None are better or worse than any of the others, but they do see the world differently.

The following paragraphs—labeled "A" through "I"—are simple descriptions of the nine types. They are not intended to be a comprehensive portrait of an individual's personality. As each paragraph may describe you to some degree, please select those that seem most applicable.

In making your selections, consider each paragraph as a whole, rather than taking individual sentences out of context, and then ask yourself: "Does this paragraph as a whole fit me better than any of the others?"

SUGGESTIONS:

If you find it difficult to choose between two or more of the "snapshot" paragraphs, think about how someone close to you would describe you.

Also, because personality patterns are usually most prominent in young adult life, you may want to ask yourself which one of these descriptions would have best fit you in your twenties.

A

I am a person who seeks balance and harmony in my life and on the job. I work best in a well-ordered and predictable environment with clear responsibilities. I can be very adaptable to what the organization or other people need, but I will tend to resist change if it comes at too fast a pace.

It's important to me that people get along well, and I can be very uncomfortable with conflict. I don't like to get angry and I'll usually try to avoid a fight, but once in a while I may blow my top.

I'm good at accepting all kinds of people and many different points of view. People usually feel very comfortable talking to me. Because of these qualities I can be an excellent mediator. I often find myself in a peacemaker role for individuals or presiding over whole groups in the role of chairperson.

It's important for me to try to clarify my own point of view and agenda; otherwise I can end up feeling controlled or pushed around by the opinions and agendas of others.

Another challenge for me is to manage my energy and focus on priorities. I can get lost in the details of a project, or I can get lost in the big picture and feel overwhelmed by everything at once. It helps for me to have feedback and support. When I'm on the right track I can be steady and very productive.

B

I'm good at thinking ahead, planning for positive outcomes, and synthesizing ideas from many different sources. I'm interested in all kinds of subjects, and generally look forward to new experiences. Life seems like a wonderful adventure. I like to find ways to enjoy my work and the people I work with, but I don't like routine.

I tend to be optimistic, and I have a talent for seeing the possibilities in any situation. I'm good at consulting, motivating, and talking with people, but I can become frustrated if others seem to be negative thinkers or don't share my enthusiasm. Sometimes people consider me overly positive or unaware of what can go wrong.

I'm especially good at creating new visions and getting things started but I have a tendency to lose interest after a while. It's usually OK with me if other people carry out the vision to completion.

My style of working doesn't always fit into a regular schedule or the traditional organizational structure. I work best when I have the room to be creative and I can try out new ideas. I prefer to have a lot of leeway in how I get the job done, and I'm uncomfortable with someone looking over my shoulder or giving me constant direction.

C

I consider myself to be a strong and capable person. I usually have strong views, and I'm willing to say what I think, even if that involves conflict with other people. I want others to be direct with me as well, and I don't like it when people avoid the issue at hand.

I often find myself in a leadership role, even if I haven't planned it. Somebody needs to take charge of the situation, and I'll step forward if it seems necessary. On the other hand, I appreciate good leadership and can take direction well when it's given in a way that's fair. I trust my instincts and will make decisions based on a gut-level sense of what needs to be done. I want ideas to lead to action, and I don't like it when people get stuck in talking about concepts or theories.

I can be very generous and protective toward my colleagues or my staff. I may be tough on them myself at times, but I'll stick up for them if anyone tries to treat them unfairly. I'm very sensitive to injustice and will move heaven and earth to redress a wrong.

Because I tend to be assertive and forceful, people may at times find me intimidating or bossy. I don't necessarily need people to like me, but I want to be treated with respect.

D

I am a supportive person who is known to care for people at work. I'm also an effective communicator, and I take pride in my ability to get along with anybody. I can engage people with a positive image and a friendly attitude, and I am appreciated by others for this.

Conflict or criticism makes me pretty nervous unless I'm sure people will still like me afterward. Balancing my need for positive feedback with maintaining an independent course of action can be a big issue.

I am especially good at seeing the potential in others, and I want to bring this out. But I have to be careful with my tendency to get overextended in giving to people, taking care of their needs and neglecting my own. I may at times have strong emotional reactions that can throw me off course.

I'm usually more comfortable working in partnerships or teams, and it can be hard for me to take the spotlight or the primary leadership role by myself. I like a lot of people contact, and I prefer not to work alone for long periods of time. As long as I feel good rapport with others, I'm generally flexible about how we get the job done.

E

I have very high internal standards for doing things correctly, and I can be very critical of myself and others in an effort to get the job done the right way. It's important for me to maintain a high level of personal integrity and honesty, and I can get pretty bothered or uptight if other people seem to cut corners or do not take the time to do the job well.

Other people may see me as overly judgmental or perfectionistic, but I try to be fair-minded. I strive to be responsible, and if I say I will do something, I'll do it and do it well. I expect other people to be responsible also, and I can get resentful toward my coworkers if they don't keep their agreements or pull their weight.

I have a strong sense of order, and I prefer to work in a very organized manner. I like to have clear rules and structure for how the work gets done, and I don't particularly like unexpected changes in procedure.

Work comes before play, which can make it hard for me to relax or take time off. Sometimes I worry too much about the details of a project. I can accept criticism if it's given fairly, but I am my own worst critic.

F

I am very task- and goal-oriented, and I consider myself a high achiever. Success is important to me, and I will work very hard in order to be successful. I want to avoid failure of any kind, and I really don't like setbacks or poor results.

I like to jump right into action, and I may get impatient if other people slow things down or get in the way. It's hard for me to understand why people are sometimes so cautious, or need to work out all the details ahead of time.

It's important for me to present a winning image, and I'm usually confident of my ability to perform well in any situation in which I find myself. I see competition as a good thing. I generally support equal opportunity for everyone, but I expect people to work hard and produce.

My attention is drawn to the bottom line. I'm very practical about what works, and I'm willing to change rules and procedures in the interests of efficiency. My tendency to work hard and stay on the go usually takes priority over my personal life. It's a challenge for me to slow down and take the time for relaxation and relationships.

G

I consider myself a loyal person who is committed to the organization and to seeing the work done well. I'm willing to take the time to think about strategy and to understand things thoroughly before taking action. I'm particularly good at anticipating problems and developing solutions.

I tend to operate well when I have a good conceptual framework, and I can be very uncomfortable with people who don't want to think things through ahead of time. On the other hand, my need to figure things out can sometimes lead to procrastination.

It's important for me to know where I stand with people, particularly my boss. I don't like uncertainty or ambiguity in my work relationships, and I will push for clarity. I prefer either a well-ordered, hierarchical chain of command or a team-based approach. But in either case, I want to know what the rules are. If there's conflict, I want it out in the open where I can see it; otherwise I may spend too much time worrying about other people's motives.

I am usually perceptive about other people, although it may be hard for me to trust these perceptions. I can get nervous making presentations, even when I know I'm good at it. I strongly prefer positive visions or personal praise to be tempered with a realistic assessment of the situation.

H

It is very important to maintain my individuality. Although I'm good at creating the appropriate external image for my job, I stay in touch with my inner feelings as well, even if I must share this side of myself with my coworkers.

I like to find meaning in my work, and I may become dissatisfied with mundane tasks. I generally seek to understand things deeply and emotionally. At times I feel critical of my colleagues, especially when they appear superficial.

Emotional authenticity is crucial to me, and I try to find ways to express my creativity both in my work and my personal style. I have a very good aesthetic sense and will often attempt to improve the look of the products as well as the physical environment.

I'm often considered empathetic and caring. However, I find that it's easy for me to feel disappointed in people when they don't look deeply at themselves. Because of my strong inner feelings I can be moody at times. This may create problems for people who are afraid of their emotions.

I

I consider myself an excellent strategist and theoretician, and I am generally regarded as an expert in my field. It's important for me to be knowledgeable and understand things thoroughly. I like to study and accumulate information. I'm usually very perceptive about ideas and concepts, but this may not translate into knowing how to relate to other people.

It's very important that I have my privacy and time to recharge my batteries. I often experience being with other people as draining, although when I have time to prepare, I can be an excellent teacher and communicator.

I'm a good observer and prefer to stay on the edge of a group where I can see what's going on. I'm usually cautious about jumping into an activity or project and participating with other people since I'm concerned about conserving my time and resources.

I'm happy to work alone for long periods of time, and I don't like to be intruded on. I don't need as much emotional contact as other people do, and at times people have considered me withdrawn or unsupportive.

I tend to be both self-reliant and self-motivated. I find my inner world to be rich and interesting, and I'm hardly ever bored while spending time by myself.

SCORING KEY

This is the order in which the preceding personality descriptions correspond to the points on the Enneagram.

- Paragraph A: Point 9
- Paragraph B: Point 7
- Paragraph C: Point 8
- Paragraph D: Point 2
- Paragraph E: Point 1
- Paragraph F: Point 3
- Paragraph G: Point 6
- Paragraph H: Point 4
- Paragraph I: Point 5

Confirmation Checklists

Another way to approach your self-assessment is to look at the following "descriptors." These are the words and phrases that best describe the nine types.

Having gone through the Enneagram Type Quiz, see how your choice matches up with the following checklists.

POINT ONE: THE PERFECTIONIST

- Attention goes to error, to what needs correcting
- Judging mind. Things are either right or wrong
- Powerful inner critic monitors thought, word, and deed
- Contained or righteous anger; under constant tension
- Worried about getting things right; unusually sensitive to criticism
- Striving for perfection
- Responsible
- Postpones pleasure

- Repression of impulses/desires
- Focus on being good
- Rigid, overly controlled
- Independence valued
- Virtue is its own reward

POINT TWO: THE GIVER

- Attention goes to the needs of significant others
- Price in giving/helping; "People depend on my help"
- Gives to get approval and acceptance
- Sometimes feels taken advantage of
- Hard to express own needs
- Self-presentation alters to please significant people
- Manipulative. Indirect approach to meeting of own needs
- Likes to be the power behind the throne

POINT THREE: THE PERFORMER

- Attention goes to accomplishing tasks. Leisure activities are also results-oriented
- Focus on goals not means. Product over process
- Primary identification with accomplishment and success
- Seeks approval and acceptance based on performance
- Image is important. Looking good. Super Mom
- Inattention to feelings. Emotions get in the way of work
- Fits own image to a work role. Prototype of the job
- Anger at obstacles to tasks
- Impatient. Feels constant pressure to perform

POINT FOUR: THE ROMANTIC

- Attention goes to what is missing
- Push-pull phenomena; what's available here and now; what's distant and hard to get
- Feels special and elite. Suffering sets you apart from others
- An abandonment theme. "I'm not lovable"
- Empathetic, especially for the suffering of others
- Romantic and artistic
- Resists being evaluated. "I am different"

POINT FIVE: THE OBSERVER

- Marked need for privacy
- Attention goes to observing rather than participating
- Intellectualizes
- Detached from feelings
- Limits intrusion from a world that wants too much
- Minimalist. Reduces needs; limits desires
- Self-sufficient
- Hoards time, space, energy, knowledge
- Compartmentalizes
- Looks superior (aloof), but feels inferior

POINT SIX: LOYAL SKEPTIC

- Attention goes to potential difficulties, danger, interference
- Active imagination; amplifies questionable areas
- Safety and security concerns
- Doubting mind, contrary thinking
- Questions people. "Bullshit detectors"

- Sees implications, inferences, and hidden meanings
- Questions authority
- Ambivalent about success; discounts it, or fails to complete project
- Procrastinates because of fearing the outcome

POINT SEVEN: THE EPICURE

- Attention goes to what is positive and to future possibilities
- Optimistic; sees multiple options
- Difficulty with commitment
- Does not want limits
- Pleasure-seeking; life is an adventure
- A glutton for experience and enjoyment
- Has many interests
- Active—lots of projects and overbooked
- Experience is more important than success
- Feels entitled; narcissistic
- Charming and disarming

POINT EIGHT: THE BOSS

- Attention goes to power, dominance, and control of territory
- Concerned with strength and protecting the weak
- Denies own vulnerability and weakness
- All or nothing polarities; things are black or white
- Believes in absolute truth, justice
- Aggressive, intimidating, impulsive
- Wants stimulation and excitement
- Direct and confrontational
- Expresses anger ("gets pissed")

POINT NINE: THE MEDIATOR

- Attention shifts to secondary activities
- Nonessentials may get equal attention with the essential
- Sees all sides of an issue
- Peacemaker/harmonizer; overly adaptive
- Pleasing and caring; has difficulty saying no
- Participates. Joins in
- Wants the comfortable solution, avoids conflicts
- Ambivalent
- Indirect anger; passive aggression
- Contains own energy and anger

THE STRUCTURE OF THE DIAGRAM

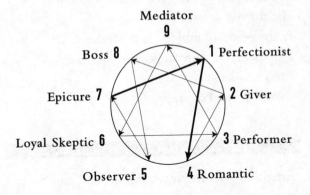

It takes many years of time, energy, and experience to build a personality, and once formed we remain true to our type. Why then, people ask, do I recognize myself in some—or all—of the other perspectives? The answer is that each position is rooted in a common human experience. We've all felt an Epicure Seven's joy in having pleasant choices, and we've all felt the melancholy of a Romantic Four. But it's important to note that we never "turn into" another type of person. Performer Threes, for example, will always be go-getters, sometimes feeling the happiness of a Seven or the melancholy of a Four, but they will always remain true to the Performer profile.

Each of us has one basic emotional pattern that creates a lifelong lens of perception. However, any single strategy is insufficient in coping with the complex demands of life, so to ensure flexibility, we shift patterns in a predictable way to deal with stress and to enjoy periods of security.

While much of the Enneagram's psychological value lies in its description of the nine types, its predictive power is in the network of interconnecting lines that you see in the diagram on page 28. Those lines indicate that each type has three *distinct* responses:

First—our familiar day-to-day thoughts and feelings that we consider to be "my type," the home base that we think of as "me."

Second—Because we are flexible beings, as the arrows indicate, we take on the strategy of the type ahead during times of risk or stress. For example, a corporate downsizing requires mobilizing for action and gearing up to deal with the situation. Although the word *stress* carries the connotation of a negative response, representatives of the types often report breakthroughs when they were challenged. In times of difficulty, we take on either the positive or negative characteristics associated with the type in the direction of the arrows.

Third—During periods of security, our guard drops, and we relax into the behavior patterns of the type behind our own. Again, we can take on either the positive or negative aspects of the security position.

When you feel secure, for example when landing a good job, you'll tend to move against the arrows. A job with prospects for advancement is likely to produce a relaxation of our emotional survival defenses. The following diagram shows how this works for the Performer Three.

A Performer Three will always be image-minded, but once

DYNAMICS OF CHANGE: THE ARROW FORMULA

Type 3: The Performer

Stress response for 3:
Throws energy at details in order to stay busy.
Sticks to known procedures that have worked in the past.
Looks for a way to bail out
and to find a new success.

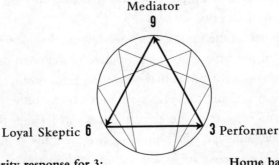

Mediator
9

Loyal Skeptic **6**   **3** Performer

Security response for 3:
Experiences the
emergence of feelings.
Becomes aware of
personal priorities that
were suspended by overwork.
May lose confidence in
own ability because of these
unexpected emotions.
Learns to wait long
enough for own creativity
to surface.

Home base for 3:
Becomes a role model by
projecting of personal
feelings. Focuses attention
on product and results, at
the expense of personal
feelings.

he understands his focus, he can tone down his emphasis on status and appearance. Likewise, he can modify his driving need to get the job done regardless of consequences, remembering to recognize the input and concerns of colleagues involved in the project.

Because different types of people view the same project through a specific lens of perception, recognizing those differences can accelerate your improvement in key business areas such as:

- communication skills
- motivation
- time management
- negotiation strategies
- training and development

The Enneagram can help you to recognize your own type, and provide the information you need to cope with on-the-job issues that you face on a daily basis. In addition, it can help you better understand work associates, family, lovers, and friends by providing insight into people who perceive life very differently from yourself.

Without this understanding, you might easily see those people as uninformed or simply obstinate. But misperceptions and blunders can be vastly reduced when you know your own profile and can see the validity in other points of view as well.

HOW THE ENNEAGRAM CAN HELP YOU WORK WITH OTHERS

In a recent Enneagram class at the Stanford University School of Business, the students at first blush all looked like versions of Performer Three. Social personas nailed down tight, they seemed to embody the appearance and aspirations of corporate America. Then the class started and as the students began to interact, their differences emerged. Eventually, we discovered that the types were represented in almost equal numbers in that class, just as they are in the working world.

From the boardroom to the boiler room, every profession has its fair share of people doing the same job in apparently the same way. But beneath surface appearances, different types of people are tackling that job from radically different perspectives.

In the next nine chapters, we will look at the way each

Enneatype functions on the job and how interactions between the types play out in practice. We will view these interactions from two perspectives. In the first half of each chapter, we will be looking through the lens of the type. The rest of each chapter is devoted to how each type appears to colleagues in five specific aspects of work: communication style, motivation, time management, negotiation, and training and development.

COMMUNICATION STYLE

The way you communicate with others is related to your lens of perception. Each of us is on the lookout for relevant information that supports our point of view, and often, without knowing it, we tailor our response accordingly. For example, Romantic Fours, who rely on close personal associations, will notice signs of developing rapport. Once those signals seem confirmed, a nonverbal vocabulary of assumed mutual understanding permeates their communications. For example, simply asking a Four questions such as, "I know what you did, how did you feel about it?" or telling them, "I know what you mean, but here's what I would be feeling in that situation," provides the connection that draws a Four's attention. The conversation needn't be overly emotional or personally revealing, but feeling statements make Fours feel understood. Observer Fives, on the other hand, preoccupied with privacy and detachment, are far less likely to respond to relational cues, and Outgoing Epicure Sevens, who favor adventure over emotional contact, are inclined to steer the conversation away from feelings.

People of different Enneagram types reveal their typical communication style not only in words but in facial expressions, body posture, hand gestures, tone of voice, closeness to others, eye contact, and a host of other nonverbal signals. Giver Twos, for example, move energetically toward others, inviting approval, whereas reserved Observer Fives withdraw behind an impassive facial mask.

MOTIVATION

A single company typically houses several different motivational approaches, because what works on one side of the corridor doesn't necessarily suit the needs of a manager down the hall. Each manager eventually hits on her own chosen approach and applies it to her department, often selecting a motivational technique that mirrors her own outlook.

Yet employees are not unilaterally motivated by the same incentives. Perfectionist Ones are motivated by the manager's approval of the quality of their work, whereas Giver Twos want to know, above all, that you approve of them as people.

The situation is compounded by the fact that consultants may recommend different motivational systems. Some favor a competitive bonus system, while others promote the value of cooperation as a motivating force. But managers who are aware that one shoe doesn't fit all have a real advantage. They know, for example, that while Performer Threes and Boss Eights flourish within a competitive environment, other types are turned off by emphasizing performance over people.

Different types of people are motivated each in their own way. Even classic incentives such as public recognition can paradoxically demotivate Loyal Skeptic Sixes or Observer Fives, who dislike titles. Observers, for example, are highly motivated by incentives such as a private workplace and being allowed to create their own time schedule. Time alone is intrinsically rewarding to Fives, who love to withdraw and think, and they perform best when protected from the office interactions that are a prime motivator for people-oriented Giver Twos.

The intrinsic motivations that move different types of people forward will operate regardless of the motivational strategy favored by their employers. Boss Eights will always be energized by fighting for justice and Perfectionist Ones will work hard for the sheer pleasure of a job well done. None of these intrinsic motivators may be apparent to managers, but the advantage of knowing what different types of people need to stay interested and to work well is obvious.

TIME MANAGEMENT

Time is a constant. Everyone's wristwatch moves at the same speed. There are exactly sixty seconds in a minute, sixty minutes in an hour, and exactly twenty-four hours in a day. Yet different types of people each have a subjective perception of time's passage. Although we all say that we spend time, waste time, and frantically try to save time, we mean these phrases very differently. No type uses time more effectively than another, because time is a constant and we all have the same amount of it. But each Enneatype inwardly calibrates time in its own way.

Time carries us along when we're engaged. We say, for example, "Has it really been a year since I last saw you? Time flies so quickly." When time drags by we think "I can't stand another minute of this."

In organizations, time is an asset that must be managed carefully. In the workplace, "time is money" is an absolute given that factors into every decision. There's also an operating assumption that labels such as "important," "urgent," "priority attention," and "please take your time" carry the same impact for everyone.

But they don't. Imagine people of different Enneatypes receiving the same memo from their boss stamped URGENT. A Six considers it a good use of time to think about the hazards involved in carrying out the directive. A Seven would see that as a waste of time, preferring instead to spend time creating a plan of action. Twos and Fours might say they were using time wisely by reviewing the emotional impact of the memo on coworkers, whereas Fives would consider such affect-laden conversation a poor use of time.

NEGOTIATION

In the business world, most communications involve negotiation; sometimes they focus on major organizational decisions, such as settling a strike with a labor union, but more typically they deal with minor matters, such as dividing up tasks and assignments.

Each Enneatype will structure a negotiation based on its own lens of perception. If you're a Mediator Nine, for example, you will naturally notice all the merits in each party's demands, and because you perceive areas of common agreement, your negotiating style will tend toward consensus settlement. But if you're a Romantic Four, you are probably a dramatic negotiator, conscious of what you might be losing if you give in to the other side, and feeling quite emotional about it. If you're a Boss Eight, you may be so focused on the merits of your own case that you fail to recognize the validity of another position, and so on for all nine points of view.

By focusing directly on the interpersonal dynamics of a negotiation, input from the Enneagram can help both sides achieve the results they want. Obviously you may not know in advance with whom you will be dealing, but knowing your own type's natural inclination allows you to step back and observe the differences between your own approach and the strategies that other people bring to the bargaining table.

TRAINING AND DEVELOPMENT

Training is not about intelligence. It's about the different ways that people take in information. If you are a trainer or give frequent presentations, there's a natural inclination to assume that all the participants in your class are more or less aware of the same data.

But if you looked through another type's lens of perception, you'd see certain information etched in bold that doesn't occur to you. For example, through a Performer's eyes you'd see an efficient route to the goal that bypasses most of the steps and procedures that stand out to Perfectionists. Likewise, you'd see Observer Fives taking in each module of the training as a separate unit of information, while the Nines in the class are preoccupied with expanding each module into a comprehensive picture.

As a trainer, you're likely to structure class materials based on the way that you take in information, and you will deliver feedback in a way that is characteristic of your type. But how should you provide feedback to people who don't see the world the way you do? The idea of type-specific learning provides an easy way for trainers to shape materials for maximum benefit.

In preparing the materials, you need to ask yourself: How do different types of people sort the information they receive? What are the barriers that different types encounter in learning new skills, and how can these be circumvented? Trainees have to be seen as individuals with specific needs, motivations, and ways of achieving competency, because different types of people learn the same task differently.

Trainers who know their Enneatype will be aware of how they give feedback and how the various types receive it. They'll know, for example, that Performers are likely to crash and burn under criticism, although they hide that fact beneath a smooth, professional facade. Likewise, if the trainer is a Performer Three himself, he'd do well to know that the Perfectionists in his group will discount him as ill-informed unless he corrects errors and comments when mistakes are made.

In the following nine chapters on the Enneatypes, you will see how the five key factors of communication, motivation, sense of time, negotiation, and training and development are crucial to business success, underscoring the advantage of applying the Enneagram system in the workplace.

A CAUTIONARY WORD

One of the problems with using the Enneagram is that it's all too effective at categorizing people. It is one of the few systematic explanations of why people do what they do designed for normal and high-achieving people, and it condenses a great deal of psychological wisdom into a compact system that is relatively easy to understand.

The benefit of this approach is clear. If we can type ourselves and recognize the people who are important in our lives, a lot of information about the likely hot spots in our relationships is immediately available. The downside of that knowledge is also obvious. We may naturally tend to put the people we know into one of nine boxes, trying to figure out how they think and what they need and to predict their likely reactions.

If we can reduce everyone to being a type, if we think we've got their number, we could hope to make cause-and-effect predictions. We could say: "Sevens always do that," or "Quit being so Sixish," or even, "Since she's a Nine, I'm sure she'll say this when I say that." This desire to predict each other's thinking flows from our natural human tendency to categorize. We have to make distinctions to function and to communicate. We cannot *not* categorize.

Powerful systems like the Enneagram are invariably seen as an attempt to put people in boxes by categorizing the human condition in simplistic ways. Yet if there's any truth to the idea that type creates a subjective lens of perception through which we view ourselves, our job, and each other, then we're already in a box and need to find a way out.

Yet we all recognize all nine perspectives, because each is rooted in a natural response to the human condition. For example, we all zero in on the goal—just like Threes—when we face a deadline, and most of us are melancholy and Four-like during the final scene of a sad movie. But unless we are a Three, we don't walk down the street seeing the environment and the people we meet through a lens of perception focused on tasks, goals, and results. Neither would we describe our world as "a sweet and melancholy place"—as Romantic Fours are likely to do—unless we are in some special circumstance, like witnessing a movie.

Perhaps the most telling illustration of why we recognize all nine viewpoints is that the habitual way of sorting information ascribed to each type is by far the most efficient way of dealing with particular kinds of data. For example, the corrective thinking pattern of Perfectionist Ones is precisely the mind-set that we all adopt in proofreading a report. Likewise the locked-in, dead-ahead mental focus of a Boss Eight typifies the pattern that we all adhere to when dealing with adversity.

Adding to the flexibility of the basic type pattern, we shift position to align ourselves with secure or stressful outer conditions. This is another way of saying that each type is actually a composite of three distinct components: a dominant aspect—or home base—which identifies our worldview, and two additional aspects that emerge when we feel either threatened or secure.

The degree to which we identify with our type will also vary. Sometimes we are so preoccupied with our own lens of perception that we cannot focus on anything else. Yet often enough we have the flexibility to see the situation in a different light, allowing ourselves to be persuaded by someone else's point of view.

Still, despite the accurate insight that typing confers about our style of managing, communicating, and working with others, it can set up a self-fulfilling prophecy in which we begin to treat people as caricatures of their Enneagram profile. It's a small mental shift from "knowing" about type to seeing others "as" their type. These preconceptions can make Eights appear too controlling, Sevens seem uncommitted, and Nines look spaced out—regardless of their actual behavior.

It's very easy to misuse valuable information even if we're thinking and acting with positive intentions. For instance, the Enneagram does not help an employer to draw up a list of "do hires" and "don't hires" for a particular job. This is because a mandate of "Do hire a Mediator Nine" for a job resolving disputes makes no sense whatsoever if the Nine can't make a decision, even though he can see all sides of the question. "Don't hire a people-oriented Giver Two" for an adversarial position is equally naive if the Two in question is extraordinarily gifted at facilitating discussion between warring parties.

Neither will it work to put together an "ideal team" based on the fact that Fives make good strategists, Threes are terrific salespeople, and Eights are natural leaders. Teams are formed and people are hired on the basis of their skills and past record, rather than some silly notion of rushing out to hire a Boss Eight when a business is facing adversity, or assuming that Observer Fives are the only people skilled in research. Personality systems like the Enneagram do not account for every nuance of skill, talent, intelligence, or kindness that permits us to treat each other wisely.

So why should managers and coworkers be concerned about type? If an accurate set of labels won't eliminate the risks involved in hiring, and can't guarantee successful teams, why bother uncovering type—either our own or someone else's?

In organizations, the Enneagram advantage lies in knowing how our coworkers think, feel, and sort the information that applies to their work. For although no type is better than another, each does view a job through its own lens of perception.

Likewise, there is no better way to make teams cohesive than by learning to anticipate each other's decision making. Teams thrive when the intrinsic motivations that drive different players are seen and understood. Consider these comments.

"You're singling me out for criticism. You're doubting my intentions. You're running on to the next job without considering my input." The list is endless, but most of the items on that list are type-related behaviors that look very different when viewed through that type's lens of perception. Criticism, for example, may be motivated by the deep respect Perfectionist Ones can feel for someone who's "almost perfect." Ninety-nine percent is not acceptable when an employee's capable of more. And who would suspect, unless you looked through a Loyal Skeptic's lens, that doubting oneself and others is the way to steadfast commitment?

Every successful manager will benefit by knowing how their type's managerial style comes across to others, and how to effectively influence, intervene, train, and support different types of people. The goal is to know the strengths and limits of your own point of view so you can lend yourself to other people's perceptions.

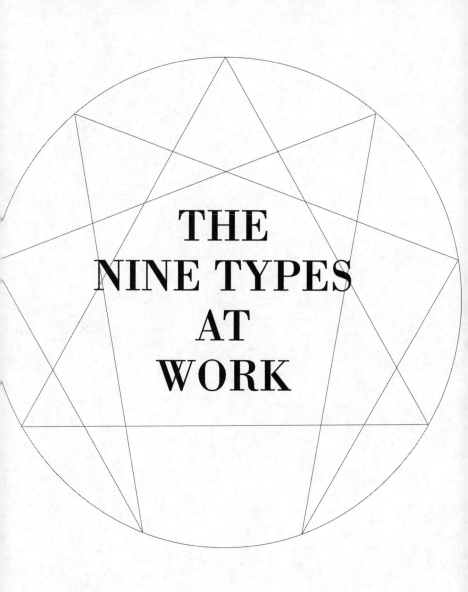

THE
NINE TYPES
AT
WORK

Point One: The Perfectionist

Alias: **Judge, Reformer, Paragon, Purist, The Organized Person**

Motto	*Find the rules and master them.*
Mental Model	*Good people improve themselves.*
Lens of Perception	*Notices error.*
Way of Sorting Information	*Unconsciously comparing events against inner standards of perfection.*
Blind Spot	*Accepting the gray zones.*
Growth Edge	*Knowing there is more than one right way.*
Spiritual Path	*Forgiveness—error is part of the learning curve.*
Vice	*Anger.*
Virtue	*Serenity—accepting black and white as parts of the same whole.*
Inspired By	*The quality of perfection.*
Managerial Style	*Leads by moral example. ONEs model ethical idealism, inspiring others to embody those precepts. Their actions seem beyond reproach.*
Appearance to Others	*Formal, neat, well-mannered, and appropriately behaved.*
Typical Conflicts	*"I'm right, you're not"; digs in under criticism, falls back on rules and the letter of the law.*
One-Minute Resolution	*Remember it's all right to be angry.*

The Signals ONEs Send

Positive	*Virtue is its own reward. The buck stops here.* ONEs *exemplify right action and effort for its own sake, without expectation of praise.*
Negative	ONEs *always see room for improvement, making others feel that they never get it right: coworkers sense a* ONE's *silent judgment without knowing what they've done.*
Mixed	*When* ONEs *think they're being clear and precise, coworkers may be hearing a list of changes they ought to make "for their own good."*
Security Response at Point Seven	*Here's where a* ONE's *inner critic dissolves, and positive plans emerge.*
Stress/Risk Response at Point Four	*Here anger turns to sadness and melancholy. What's the point of struggling in a world filled with error? Under stress,* ONEs *examine the difference between what they "should" do and what is personally meaningful to them.*
Work Best In	*Organizations with clear guidelines and in jobs requiring detail, such as accounting, finance, science/technology.*
Have Problems Working In	*Fields where the rules of the game constantly change, such as marketing technological products; entrepreneurial start-ups, where decisions are made with partial information.*
Where Business Wants Its ONES	*Hospital operating rooms, nuclear reactor inspection teams, umpiring the seventh game of the World Series.*

ARE YOU A ONE?

Perfectionists are dedicated to self-improvement. Tiny mistakes stand out in comparison to the way things "should be," and a minor slip that most people wouldn't notice can bother you for days. It's upsetting when you hear coworkers say, "That's good enough for now" or "We'll fix that later"—aren't they concerned about quality or about customer complaints? Don't they feel accountable?

On the other hand, you are more than patient with colleagues who try to improve themselves. You respect the effort involved, because the desire to get things right and make the world a better place is the hallmark of an ethical character.

Your sensitivity to error is largely due to a critical inner voice that's been with you since childhood. The inner critic sounds much like the classic voice of conscience, an inner surveillance system that monitors what you think and say and do: "Yes, that was well done," or "That wasn't good enough—you'll have to try harder," or, more frequently, "That was bad—you should do it over again." You naturally assume that coworkers have a similar running commentary going on in their heads, so when they bend the rules, it looks like they're deliberately cheating.

Those coworkers, however, may see the situation differently. What they see is your dedication to perfection, down to the details, and it's the details that become a problem. Work that's good enough from their perspective doesn't meet your high standards, leaving a wake of criticism.

Witness Linda, a newly appointed marketing v.p. preparing for her first day at the new job—it's only Sunday morning, but she couldn't wait to get started. She somehow manages to look tidy and businesslike, even dressed in weekend sweats, and here she is, boxing file folders in reverse order, to make sure they'll be unpacked in the right order on the shelves of her new office.

This promotion has confirmed her conviction that honesty, effort, and principled attention to details pays off. Linda's strength, she believes, lies in the old-fashioned virtues of hard work and personal integrity. To keep on track, she creates precise guidelines and holds herself accountable to them. She's very appreciative when others do the same.

The truth is that this promotion is a mixed blessing. She felt great when she first got the word, because it vindicated her as a good person. But instead of thinking, "Hey, it's great I've been promoted," and calling friends for a victory celebration, she's elbow-deep in boxes and beginning to worry.

"What if I'm not as good as my predecessor?" Linda makes a note to check with whoever last held this job to find out what's really going on. It feels urgent to fill in the holes in her marketing education. "What if my first campaign isn't as good as the one they're doing now?" The thought of being criticized is so painful that Linda sits down and buries her face in her hands.

The contingencies and unknowns of what she's facing are overwhelming, and now that she has a prominent position, the chances of a grand-scale mistake have just increased enormously. The annoyance of it all starts to surface. She hates critiquing herself in anticipation of being criticized by others. But the fact that she is the one imposing these impossible standards on herself just doesn't register.

As she pauses for a sip of tea from the thermos she's brought along, Linda finally feels a flood of relief. For a long, lovely moment her responsibilities drop away and her mind stops judging. It's the same serene feeling she gets during the rare times that she goes on a long walk out in the country. Nature has a calming effect, and her inner critic goes away. The sky's in the right place, the trees don't have to be improved, and everything's fine just the way it is.

HOW ONES SORT INFORMATION

In the spiritual traditions that use type as a factor in human development, ONEs are traditionally called "monks of judging mind" because they focus on eliminating error and correcting flaws. If you looked through Linda's lens of perception, you'd see how a small mistake can rivet her attention. For example, a 5 percent margin of error in a report magnifies until it seems like a giant hurdle.

Linda's way of dealing with information rests on the conviction that there's ultimately one correct solution for any problem. When the one right way is discovered, other options should simply vanish, so Linda keeps working to eliminate that last 5 percent. Unlike Epicure Sevens, who entertain a multitude of options, or Performer Threes, who focus on positive feedback, Linda sees the errors that obstruct her search for the one right way.

> *If it's not 100 percent right, then it's wrong.*

Linda ups the ante even further by comparing her own best effort against a gold-seal standard. She's elated about the promotion and coasts on the feeling that she was selected for good cause—until the critical inner voice interferes. The inner critic functions like a prosecuting attorney in a courtroom drama. Linda watches her own mind build a case as her thoughts alternately challenge and defend her.

"Yes, you made the cut, but now you have to make good." Her mind defends her: "But I did make good." The case intensifies as her thinking shifts from judgment to praise and back again. "You may be good, but your predecessor was better." It's like a tennis match, with Linda in the middle. "You can't make good if you keep judging yourself." "I'm trying not to judge." "No, you're not." "I *am* trying." "You're not doing it right."

Here she is, comparing herself to the gold-seal standard of an experienced veteran, and criticizing herself for being a critical person. But all of this is happening in her head, unbeknownst to the people who support her.

ONES AT WORK

Perfectionists excel at refining systems, and this has always been Linda's strength. Her quest for perfection originated in childhood, where she remembers being obedient, responsible, and stung by criticism. To protect herself, she learned to self-correct so that her mistakes wouldn't be noticed, a habit that made her precise and detailed in her thinking.

All that hard work also taught Linda that a job well done is a private source of pleasure. She looks forward to a full schedule, to losing herself in the momentum of her projects, and to going home feeling well used at the end of the day.

If you're a ONE, you'll relate to Linda's high ethical standards and her attraction to a job well done. You'll also feel secure in a workplace that provides clear guidelines and a strict demarcation of responsibilities. However, because you shoot for a perfect product, you may feel challenged by an organizational culture that depends on constantly shifting information. It's just plain traumatic to make decisions when you don't have the right information.

John, a research analyst for a large pharmaceuticals corporation, describes his frustration at trying to do the right thing when the rules keep changing.

I love the intellectual rigor of science and the precision of laboratory work, but predictably, just when I'm getting results, my company's priorities shift, and I'm back at the drawing board.

The fact is that it's infuriating to have a great idea put on hold. But who am I to get angry when the problem's not my responsibility?

John, a ONE, feels he can't legitimately express his anger unless he's absolutely in the right. In a perfect Catch-22, anger—the vice ascribed to ONEs—is a "bad" emotion that was punished in childhood. John has difficulty even knowing that he's angry unless the situation is wrong enough to be an ethical violation. John continues:

Years ago I would have said that I never get angry. Irritated—yes. Annoyed, peeved, and fussy—definitely so. But angry? No, because nobody likes angry people, and I'm trying to be a good guy.

Inside, it didn't seem like I was ever mad—although I got feedback that I was tense and critical. That's because I didn't read my tension and my voice getting pinched as signs of being angry. Inside, I'd feel energized, on track, like I was getting the lab organized, but I wouldn't have called that anger.

Then one day I blew. Totally over the top—I must have shouted for an hour. We were halfway through a promising experiment, and sure enough, word came we had to retool. For some reason it was the last straw, and I could feel the fury rising. There was amazing clarity in it. I had almost total recall of all the other times I'd been angry about retooling and said nothing—and the truth is, it felt wonderful!

It turned out that John's coworkers were thrilled when he blew up—not only because they completely agreed with him, but because they didn't have to guess about what he thought. Of course they recognized his anger, even if he didn't, but John always said what he "should" say, until his rage boiled over.

ONES are incredible team players when everyone's pulling their share of the workload. They take on a great deal of responsibility and are committed to fair play, but they do need recognition and won't ask for it. The fact is, it feels dreadful to heroically continue doing the right thing when others remain oblivious. Why are there so few rewards for honesty and effort? It's not fair.

All of this enormously hard work is compounded when you notice the mistakes that team workers are making. If they don't pick up the slack, you feel it's your responsibility to carry the burden. So of course you're annoyed.

In your spiritual path, anger is something you have to work with, rather than avoid. It's very helpful to notice when your thoughts turn critical and to name what's happening. Step back from what has made you angry and note: "I'm judging now." Your anger may be entirely justified, but that's not the point. The point is for you to become aware of *when* you start judging, before you bury your anger. Then you can find a way to deal with the situation.

Withholding puts you in a bad bind: You can't be openly angry, but the situation's unfair. That bind leads ONES to pull back their effort. What the team sees is someone who was initially capable and forthcoming, who then stopped participating for some unknown reason.

A FINAL THOUGHT

It would not be altogether flip to say that your path to renewal lies in healthy hedonism and pleasure seeking. You're already committed to disciplined work and the extra effort it takes to succeed, but pay equal attention to what's going right.

Remember Linda, the new v.p. of marketing? She has to

remember why she got promoted in the first place. All she wants is to be as conscientious and productive as her predecessor. But she keeps aiming for perfection, instead of accepting that she's a perfect beginner.

SECURITY AND STRESS

Dynamics of Change for Point One

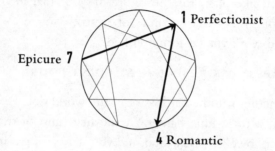

SECURITY RESPONSE AT POINT SEVEN

ONEs are dedicated workers, and you can take pleasure in a job well done when you're not shooting for impossible goals. During periods when you feel secure, you're less inclined to judge yourself. It's like going on vacation and waking up one morning to find that the inner critic's voice has dissolved. Projects move quickly and easily, seemingly of their own accord, when you're not distracted by small mistakes and when you're less preoccupied with a perfect outcome. You know you'll perform well enough, and doing well is a whole lot easier than being perfect.

One of the fringe benefits of being a perfectionist is that it feels so great when everything falls into place. ONEs have small daily epiphanies, when just clearing your desk or organizing a perfect calendar fills you with a sense of accomplishment. There's a natural rhythm that emerges when work is on course, and by yielding to that flow of events, you navigate detours and interruptions that would normally feel threatening.

In secure periods, you just plain worry less, and then the discipline that you've worked so hard to develop can carry you forward. You can take time off to rejuvenate without worrying that the office will fall into chaos in your absence or that you won't want to go back to your job if you relax.

Without much being said, the work picture looks fuller and more promising. Now you can see your options by entertaining Seven-like plans for the future. It's not that error escapes your attention, but during times of security, you're also aware of the good work you've accomplished.

STRESS/RISK RESPONSE AT POINT FOUR

Sometimes all the hard work in the world doesn't lead to success, so you try a little harder. At the first signs of stress, the critical inner voice gets very loud, and you start seeing error everywhere. Eventually your irritation spills over, often directed at coworkers who don't seem to be pulling their share of the workload. Oddly, you don't think of irritation as anger, because anger is a "bad" emotion. It's okay to feel irritated or frustrated or annoyed, none of which reads to you as being angry. But the message that you're angry definitely gets through to the people you work with.

Why is it always up to you to clean up the mess, notice mistakes, take on responsibility, feel the tension? Why don't coworkers see the mounting chaos and intervene? How can they ignore this? In a negative spiral, your anger gives way to Four-like resignation. Hard work wasn't enough, and what else is there?

Moving into the stress response at Four leaves you feeling: "I played by the rules. I don't deserve this. It's not fair." It helps to find a safe place to complain. Once your anger is recognized and expressed, the workload just seems easier to manage.

ONEs under stress can learn a lot by asking the forbidden question: "What do I want?" Perfectionists are more than aware of what "should" be done, but paradoxically, when what you "should do" stops working, you have an opportunity to discover work that gives you pleasure.

COMMUNICATION STYLE

When making a presentation, ONEs will transmit facts to their audience, rather than speak in generalities. They strive to make complex notions orderly and are uncomfortable when a discussion wanders in tangential directions. They produce well-documented information, conveyed in point-by-point fashion, building steadily to an unambiguous conclusion. Given their type, it's not surprising that they take this approach: A clearly communicated position reduces the risk of error.

In aiming for a perfect product, they like to spend hours preparing, dissecting, and comparing one opinion to another to construct an unshakable analysis. That's understandable. However, highly structured communications work best in teaching situations, but sound preachy in conversation. Because ONEs think in terms of right and wrong, it's difficult to grasp the gray zones of nuances, possibilities, flights of fancy, and remote associations that flood the conversations of some other communication styles. So an interesting dynamic develops. ONEs can be sterling speakers when they're passionately committed, infusing listeners with the force of their convictions. But speakers who are swept away by their own beliefs can also come across as true believers who don't leave room for alternative opinions.

ONEs can mentally blank out during the question-and-answer period, especially when a question generalizes the discussion beyond the specific information that they've just presented. Communications are most meaningful when ONEs feel secure enough to voice those incomplete thoughts, hunches, and improvisations that form the subtext of an interesting presentation.

Nonverbal Communication

ONEs are generally silent until they've considered the point they want to make, but their mental debate produces a thoughtful, worried expression. The constant pressure to "get it right" builds internally, making them appear tense and preoccupied, much like a bloodhound straining to find the correct scent.

As their inner tension builds, others feel judged without a word being said. The message reads: "We're not there yet; we're not trying hard enough; we have to do better." The unspoken admonition to keep trying is wearing on types like Nines, who try to avoid conflict, and Sevens, who like to "go with the flow" of new ideas rather than limit themselves to a single course of action.

If a ONE begins to boil inside, their suppressed anger can radiate through the room to the point where others feel uneasy about the unacknowledged tension.

All of this can relax with a little appropriate humor. Make it clear that you're not laughing at the issue or at the ONE presenter, but rather at the intensity with which ONEs attack the issue head-on, as if there were only one right way to get the job done.

COMMUNICATING WITH ONES

- ONEs are very critical, which can be either useful or become overly negative. Try to welcome criticism while placing it in a positive context. Criticism supports the overall positive vision, or when it is balanced with appreciation.
- Speak with authority based on your own sense of what is right. Be sure to acknowledge your own mistakes, yet stay on course.

- Give room to debate the pros and cons of an issue. ONEs will do this internally in any event. Make it part of the process so that it doesn't block their participation.
- Draw out the ONEs' grievances. Support their expressing resentment even when you don't agree. Ask them to focus on the matter at hand, rather than a long list of past grudges. Respond in a rational manner and help them redirect their frustration into a positive framework.
- Be as specific as you can. ONEs have a hard time with generalities. Make sure that you are well prepared and have a good grasp on what you plan to say before speaking.
- While acknowledging their good intentions, help them to see that there is more than one right way to accomplish a goal.

MOTIVATION

ONEs want to do good in the world. They set unusually high standards for themselves and suffer over small mistakes that most people wouldn't notice. Because they are so focused on correction, those moments when everything falls into place "just right" become the private epiphanies that keep the day glowing.

Expect that focus on error. ONEs have what can best be described as a "comparing mind." Internally, there's always an ongoing mental comparison between the way life is and how perfect it could be. So to them, it appears there is always room for improvement.

For example, a sales manager for a paper supply company will notice that his boss doesn't process funding requests as efficiently as he could. Where any employee might notice the same mistake, he feels caught between wanting to fix it and not wanting to appear critical. A mental chalkboard springs into place, and the sales manager places the boss under surveillance. "Look, he's doing it again. He's processing the requests one at a time. If he would look them all over first, he'd find numerous items that we all need, and could buy them in bulk, saving the company some money. Look, it's happening again. This has to stop!"

The sales manager will even suffer when the coffee machine leaks and stains the carpet in the employee lounge. Somehow it's his fault and his mental chalkboard gives him a demerit. "I knew we shouldn't have put it there. Why didn't I speak up when it was being installed?"

But conversely, Perfectionists also know how satisfying a job well done can feel. It's a source of pleasure that may not be apparent to other people. Motivated by the private desire to be the best possible person in their own eyes, ONEs are attracted to working for a worthwhile cause, and gratified by building personal skills.

Seeking perfection, they are drawn to work that models integrity and builds a strong ethical platform into their career. For example, a teacher will be scrupulous about professional conduct and codes, seeing her responsibilities as a mission rather than a nine-to-five routine.

Easily shifting into the stance of teacher and preacher, she will try to convert others to her own perfect ideals. Obsessively concerned with details, she will quickly notice when others relax the rules and feel responsible to correct the error. When standards slip, a ONE is going to find herself caught between rising resentment and her desire to work harder to pick up the slack, a bind that creates further resentment.

> *This urgency to do things right can pave the road to burnout when the job doesn't get done or problems mount. At those times, a ONE feels as useless as a sponge in an ocean of indifference.*

When work that was initially motivated by a desire to make things right becomes frustrating, burnout quickly follows. Our teacher's attention will fixate on the inefficiencies and indifference of others, and an emotional holding pattern develops to contain her anger at being a participant in wrongdoing. Caught in a cycle of wanting to do good and feeling ineffective, she holds her tongue to hold her job, but the trade-off is flaring resentment over the details still within her control.

Weary Perfectionists are motivated by the private moral victories that come from doing the right thing, and by feeling ethically superior for having done so.

A ONE's growth edge lies in knowing when judging thoughts take over, when the focus on error magnifies so that everything seems flawed. ONEs will know they are progressing when they see the difference between noticing problems that can be rectified and focusing on error simply out of habit.

MOTIVATING ONES

- Combine strong values and ideals with a practical sense of what works. Join them in establishing a positive vision and high standards for excellence.

- Be honest and fair. ONEs will work hard for the right cause or the right leader if they feel that the situation is fair. They may justify holding back their contribution if the game is seen as stacked in another's favor, or if the leader is seen as lacking integrity.

- Make sure that ONEs have contact and feedback from people whom they respect. Don't let them get bogged down in adversarial relationships with people who don't meet their standards. They don't need to be in harmony with everyone, but they do need one or more selected individuals they can count on.

- Take the time to create and maintain structure and clear channels of authority. Any areas of ambiguity should have good boundaries. ONEs want accountability, guidelines, and an orderly work environment.

- ONEs are afraid to make mistakes. Let them know that mistakes are part of the process. Help them lighten up on having to get it right. Encourage them to take risks, trying out a new approach when appropriate.
- Be sure to structure positive feedback and appreciation. ONEs need appreciation but they may not ask for it directly. Resentment about not being recognized may be displaced onto trivial office issues.
- Help ONEs set limits on their responsibilities. Be clear about who is responsible for what. Let them know that they won't be blamed for the mistakes or shortcomings of other people.

TIME MANAGEMENT

ONEs live under the gun of time. It's the feeling that there's never enough time to produce a good product and that good people don't waste time. Accounting for time creates back-to-back slots in their appointment books—a prisonlike schedule of "shoulds" that tends to eliminate free time for fun. They believe pleasure should be deferred until after the work is done.

A severe internal critic offers a running commentary on their actions. The inner critic operates much like the classic "voice of conscience" and is such a familiar presence within the mind of ONEs that when others do less-than-perfect work, it looks as if they are deliberately cheating.

Ironically, that critical voice is a major source of procrastination, causing ONEs to spend time evaluating every step against impossible standards of perfection. ONE-like procrastination is about being afraid to make a mistake. ONEs can't help noticing flaws, which makes it difficult for them to produce quick-and-dirty estimates or a thumbnail sketch.

This focus on eliminating error slows progress. For example, a perfectionist writing a report notices a wrong word choice or a badly formed sentence at the moment it happens and immediately wants to stop and edit, which blocks the flow of concentration. It's hard to keep a flow going, even if all that's required is a rough draft.

Each point in a ONE manager's report—say, about the feasibility of opening a new location—has to be considered and deliberated. "Is this statement central to the argument? Should this thought be left out?" For a ONE, it's difficult to drop a single point that has content value, which results in each paragraph being a work unto itself. It takes time to create several coherent, neatly documented paragraphs, and then it takes even more time to give them exactly the correct amount of weight in the central argument. ONEs can lose sight of the big picture by spending time on a single facet of the discussion.

HELPING ONES MANAGE TIME

- Perfectionists may get bogged down in trying to get all the details done right. Let them know when it's "good enough" and encourage them to move on.
- Keep the focus on goals and results. Help ONEs move their attention off procedure and managerial concerns when necessary.
- Support ONEs in delegating responsibility to others. If they overload themselves with work, it might not get done on time or completed at all. Encourage them to see others as capable of taking on responsibility. Don't set them up to save the world (or the project) by themselves.
- ONEs can get jammed up when their judging mind is overly active. They will be more productive in the long run if they also take time out to relax and to release ten-

sion. Taking time off supports their being more efficient at work.

* Help them manage their criticism of other people. Communication and teamwork will suffer or slow down if others feel constantly judged. Encourage them to give appreciation as well, and to maintain the positive vision.

NEGOTIATION

ONEs may enter a negotiation feeling compromised. They know a perfect person wouldn't be in this situation in the first place. Words like "trade-off" and "settlement" have no place in a world dedicated to excellence, and the very idea of compromise carries the negative connotation of compromising ethical standards.

It's imperative to get everyone on the same page before negotiations begin. The most commonly reported mishap occurs when ONEs construct a painstakingly correct case on a faulty perception of the facts—the way things "ought to be"—rather than the way they are. Set up a search-and-discovery period so that both sides start with the same information. Exploratory meetings are unusually helpful in forestalling the decision-making crisis that can ensue when unexpected information is introduced.

A ONE's unshakable case moves in a logical stepwise sequence, so it's extremely disorienting to change, say, step five without accounting for every other step in the logical staircase leading to the goal. When struck by an unexpected turn of events, ONEs may fall back on the rule book, entrenching in a legal technicality or a definition of fair play.

> *ONEs do not change their minds quickly. A logistical error can throw a whole opinion into confusion, so that the solution has to be rebuilt from scratch.*

An effective negotiating strategy is to enter ONE territory. You will be respected for careful documentation and planning. You look good when you're polite, prepared, and fair. You look bad if your research is faulty and especially if you get angry or expect special treatment. So stay civilized and don't wing it.

In case of a stalemate, try a trade-off tactic. ONEs think in point-by-point detail and may be open to trading a point to get a concession in return. Sometimes the trade-off tactic serves to break a logjam by reducing the number of items on the table, thus simplifying the decision.

TRAINING AND DEVELOPMENT

ONEs need very strong context. Trainers need to stand up on the first day of class and announce the specific categories of learning to be covered, the precise level of proficiency required, the time frame, and the exact grading criteria.

> *Perfectionists want to be dead sure they know what's required. If they don't know the rules, they feel they're being set up to fail.*

It's important to stress that a personal learning curve is the correct way to achieve competency. Trainers should emphasize that mistakes are the best source of learning, that a miss is as good as a hit in terms of information.

ONEs think they should be experts straight out of the gate and tend to freeze under pressure. Oddly, they demand strong context so they know the goal of the training and then pressure themselves to reach the goal prematurely. Perfectionists don't learn well on their feet and dislike winging it. An unknown outcome makes them pull back and think about what could go wrong.

Frame learning as rules to be followed. If the rules say it's important to relax, then ONEs will relax. If the rules say that learning requires a loose, open way of paying attention, then ONEs will learn the appropriate procedure. Block out the material in manageable chunks with identified skills. ONEs like to proceed one step at a time and go home with a specific technique they can practice.

When obvious mistakes occur, trainers should instantly reinforce the idea that a good learning curve looks like two steps forward and one step backward. Encourage questions that ONEs might normally feel inhibited about asking by saying something like: "Now you've hit the point of the learning curve where it's time to review. Please keep asking questions. Your questions help us in updating our training manuals. It helps others when you identify points of confusion." The idea is to invite a ONE's critical analysis into the training so he doesn't freeze at making a mistake.

ONEs are mindful of the trainer's level of expertise. They notice imprecise directions, contradictory information, deviations from the schedule, and any inability to handle questions. They are particularly aware of appropriate dress, good manners, and especially the trainer's respect for participants. Trainers earn a silent cheer from every Perfectionist in the room if a beginner's question can be reframed as a teaching tool.

THE CASE OF THE ONE CFO WHO FOUND OUT WHAT HE WANTED

The situation is all too common. Following a twenty-year career in a Fortune 500 company, a Perfectionist ONE controller opts to follow his Nine boss when she becomes president of a start-up funded by venture capitalists. He's hired as the new firm's chief financial officer.

There are minor problems from the start. Used to having a large staff, the new CFO is slow in responding to requests for financial data. And there are a lot of them. The board, dominated by representatives of the venture capital firm, wants constant updates, both to keep their partners informed and so that they can be prepared at a moment's notice to take the company public. Six months after he is hired, the board notifies the Nine president in writing that they are not getting either sufficient or timely information. She promptly passes a copy of the note to the CFO.

Stunned by what is in essence his first-ever poor performance review, the Perfectionist ONE hires a second assistant and starts making it a point to come in an hour earlier each day. He's not happy about his workload—it's far heavier than he thought—but his added effort seems to satisfy the board. The complaints stop.

In the meantime, the stock market begins to boom. The board decides it's time to gain additional funding and coincidentally, gain a nice return on their initial investment by selling their shares as part of the public offering.

To expedite the process, the board tells the Nine president to fire the financial director and replace him with a CPA from the outside accounting firm that audits the venture capital group.

Yes, the chairman of the board tells the Mediator president, the CFO has developed his skills and has responded to their complaints, but for the offering they want a finance person in place who is familiar with SEC filing requirements and will inspire confidence in potential shareholders.

TYPICAL INTERACTIONS

Nine-like, the president is torn by competing loyalties. She can see everyone's position. Almost every one of the board members comes from the venture capital firm that hired her, and they want to cash out their investment as quickly as possible. She understands that. They risked their money backing her, and they expect to be rewarded.

As president, she also sees the importance of going public. It will mean increased credibility in the marketplace and make it far easier to raise money in the future. But she's conflicted by her long-standing relationship with the ONE CFO, and she detests conflict.

"He had a clean twenty-year record at our old company. He would have been secure if he hadn't followed me here. Am I responsible for his leaving our old business? Did he choose for himself, or did he feel pressured by our friendship? What about his family? How will they manage? Will they be angry at me?"

The Nine tells her secretary to hold all calls as she tries to figure out what to do. Is there a way to keep the CFO on in another capacity? What's her leverage with the board? If there's nothing to be done, how can she cushion the blow? It's very easy for her to slip into the ONE's position and see herself through his eyes.

Faced with having to deliver bad news, the Mediator Nine plays for time. "Maybe the stock market will fall apart, and we'll cancel the offering. Maybe he'll figure a way out for himself." She feels her attention scatter at the prospect of a confrontation.

The ONE CFO has indeed picked up signals about the impending crisis. When the board first complained, he reluctantly changed the reporting procedures he had used for years. Thinking about the requirements of a public offering makes him see red. His Perfectionist inner critic starts to activate. "Why wasn't I told? If I was smarter, this wouldn't have happened. A skillful person would be on top of this."

He doesn't want more responsibility. If the company goes public, he will be forced to spend time with outside shareholders, and the thought is infuriating. But his inner critic berates him: He should try harder. He should sacrifice. He shouldn't quit.

By now his critical mind is in high gear. "How unfair! I shouldn't have to start over again at my age. This isn't my fault."

His anger is rising, but he doesn't know whom to blame. "I

made a mistake coming here. She brought me, that was her fault, but I shouldn't have listened to her."

He can't express his anger without a legitimate target. He needs the president's help, but it's too humiliating to ask. He needs the board's help, but he's never met them. He's angry at himself. He's angry at the president's lack of foresight. He's angry at the venture capitalists, and he's angry at fate. Just at that moment, his telephone rings. It's the Nine president, asking that he come to her office.

When he arrives, the president looks at him and thinks of their twenty-year history. She knows this man's family. She was at his daughter's wedding. A photograph of their joint farewell party at their old Fortune 500 company sits on the bookcase behind her desk. All she wanted was to keep the peace, and instead here they are, unable to speak. She can't distance herself from what he's feeling. Maybe she should be the one who quits. He is so filled with anger that it's making her stomach turn.

Without a word being said each has triggered the other's type. Unable to contain himself, the Perfectionist ONE has to spend his rage, while the Mediator Nine, desperately trying to avoid conflict, is mired in indecision.

THE TIDE TURNS

With 20/20 hindsight, the Nine president looks back, seeing the times when she had an impulse to improve the CFO's chances for survival and could have intervened but didn't.

She could have sought him out when the board first discussed the possibility of going public. She could have warned him when one of the venture capitalists asked her: "Just what kind of experience does our new CFO have in taking companies public?"

In retrospect, the Mediator Nine sees the checkpoints where she could have made a difference and swears to herself that next time she'll stay awake. Nine-like, she smoothes the waters by offering the CFO a well-intentioned gesture.

"This situation is beyond my control, but I'll get you the best severance package I can," she begins. "I'll use my contacts, and obviously I'll let you know when a job comes up as the company expands."

The ONE explodes. Twenty years are about to be tossed out the window, and who's to blame? "The board doesn't know me and you don't care." He hears his voice get pinched and accusatory. "Why didn't you speak up? Why didn't you insist?" Now he's ranting. He hears the fury in his voice as he rails on; he sees the president absorb the pounding.

She can't look at him, and mindlessly she shuffles the papers on her desk. The helpless action catches his attention, forcing him to stop in midsentence. She's hunkered down behind the desk, looking as trapped as he is. She hates this, too.

The insight is revelatory. If it's circumstantial, there's no one to blame. No one's at fault. Without realizing it, his inner critic lets go and he feels an unaccustomed welling up of relief. He can forgive himself for not being perfect.

RESOLUTION

The truth is the CFO doesn't want to gear up to the new level of SEC requirements, not having worked with them before. He has been so busy attacking himself for what he should do that he never asked himself what he wanted. Eventually in self-defense, he criticizes his longtime friend and fortunately is relieved to discover he doesn't want more hard work and additional worry. He wants to stay with the skills he already has.

> *Perfectionists take criticism very personally. What's worse, if bad things happen, they believe it must be their fault.*

Now the only question is the best way to part. They set up an appointment for the next day to discuss terms of the CFO's settlement package. He knows she'll try to help him and he knows he'll try again somewhere else.

Self-observation
Knowing the difference between genuine needs and what we think we should want is a good discrimination for any type of person. But against the backdrop of severe self-criticism, going with what he needs is a big relief to our CFO.

It would help if he could recognize when his mind begins to criticize and then ask the question: "What do I need that is being blocked by my 'shoulds'?"

Point Two: The Giver

Alias: **Cheerleader, Supporter, God's Right Hand,
The Power Behind the Throne**

Motto	*Every successful person relies on a good Giver.*
Mental Model	*People depend on my help.*
Lens of Perception	*Other people's needs.*
Way of Sorting Information	*Keeps a running inventory of the likes, dislikes, hopes, and dreams of others.*
Blind Spot	*Twos don't know their own needs.*
Growth Edge	*Separating self-worth from other people's approval.*
Spiritual Path	*Distinguishing between genuine altruism and giving to get.*
Vice	*Pride in being indispensable.*
Virtue	*Humility—knowing your objective worth to others.*
Inspired By	*The freedom to act for yourself rather than through others.*
Managerial Style	*Every interaction is a relationship. TWOs consider it important to develop key people, meet client needs, make useful alliances, and focus on staff development. TWOs think, "How can anyone argue with a manager who has their interests at heart?"*
Appearance to Others	*Warm and ingratiating, TWOs move toward people with an attitude of helpfulness. They talk about others' needs, but not about their own.*

| Typical Conflicts | *Coworkers can think they are the TWO's favorite and then suddenly get dumped. Maybe they forgot to respond properly.* |
| One-Minute Resolution | *Notice what the TWO wants and provide it, without mentioning the fact that they need you.* |

The Signals TWOs Send

Positive	*Others feel appreciated and special.*
Negative	*The message reads: "Come to heel or make it on your own."*
Mixed	*Support is withdrawn and information is finessed.*
Security Response at Point Four	*Here real needs can surface, and TWOs discover their own creative agenda, instead of backing other people.*
Stress/Risk Response at Point Eight	*An all-out battle. The TWO has had it with helping; even manipulation didn't work; so now the gloves come off.*
Work Best In	*Jobs where there's a high interpersonal component: human resources, health care professions, service industries, sales representatives.*
Have Problems Working In	*Jobs that are isolated from positive contact with people: lighthouse keeper, forest ranger, computer programmer, tax auditor.*
Where Business Wants Its TWOs	*Facilitating a fund-raising drive, representing them at local chamber of commerce luncheons, dealing with the media.*

ARE YOU A TWO?

Givers see the potential in people and how it could be developed. You render support with a personal touch, instead of just giving advice. Sometimes a soft, appealing manner works: "May I call to offer my help?" Or you may give more aggressively: "Listen up—you need my help!" But regardless of how you connect, your other-directed focus of attention creates a blind spot about what you want in return.

You may also notice you're pulled in a number of different directions. You'll be the eager go-getter to please a Performer Three, and the detail guy to suit the tastes of a Perfectionist One. By molding yourself into what other people need, you become an indispensable ally, ensuring your place in their thoughts and future business plans.

None of these different selves are faked, but the people you work with may each feel they know you well, when in fact they only know an aspect of your personality. These same coworkers may not realize that fitting yourself in as a source of help shields you from the risk of rejection.

But being a Giver can also be exhausting. A TWO might easily wind up wondering: "Which of my many selves is the real me?" Witness Bill, an assistant manager, scanning the store layout one more time, making sure everything's in place for their biggest sale of the year. He's satisfied with his arrangements.

As he looks around, Bill double-checks the company's most precious asset—the people who work for him. Internally he reviews what he's discovered this morning: "John doesn't seem very upbeat today—I'll take my lunch at the same time he does and try to find out why. . . . And Amy seems kind of standoffish. It's not good for morale, and that attitude could carry over to the selling floor. Still, she probably just looks young and vulnerable to customers."

He rapidly scans his other impressions until he gets to Jane. She's really been coming through for the team, and his calendar shows she has a birthday next week. A festive celebration could please her and give morale a boost.

But as good as the assistant manager is with the people below him, he's even better at getting along with higher-ups: the store manager, the regional manager, and the vice president in charge of their division.

Unconsciously, it seems, he has developed a plan for being helpful to all these people. Each is looking for something to make his or her life easier, and in each case he can see a convenient way to provide it. In Bill's mind, he plays a useful role in these unfolding plans. He imagines himself as an instrumental figure, a confidant whose advice is well respected.

How twos Sort Information

In the spiritual traditions that use type as a factor in human development, TWOs are traditionally known as "monks of prideful mind," not because they always feel good, but because they see themselves as dispensing goodwill to others. If you looked through Bill's lens of perception, you'd see his staff's needs, because his pride depends on meeting those needs. Unlike Nines, who take on other people's agendas as their own, Bill is selective about whom he helps, and he believes the sales team couldn't make it without him.

If you're a TWO, you'll understand Bill's focus on supporting other people's potentials. Everyone has some redeeming feature, so why dwell on unflattering liabilities? His management style capitalizes on knowing the conditions under which each employee works best. He listens carefully to their stories, notices what they like, and pays attention to complaints. All of this seems generous and altruistic to Bill—a good way to do business. What he doesn't see is his pride in dispensing goodwill.

His TWO way of sorting information resembles a Rolodex with a card profile on each staffer. He can instantly flip to any card and recall small matters, like John preferring to work with his door closed and Jane needing a cheery greeting. More important, he naturally slips into the appropriate self to offer the help he knows his people require. Although the items on his mental Rolodex cards are work-related, Bill's convinced that people work better when they feel personally attended to, so he adjusts into a suitable self to get his message across.

The mental Rolodex is constantly being updated about family matters, health concerns, and the hopes and dreams that Bill believes impinge on performance. If an employee does perform poorly, Bill will likely couch his intervention as an acknowledgment of the problems of the moment. He also remembers what to avoid: Don't barge in on Phil if the report has to get done on time. Don't bring up the subject of boyfriends with Lisa.

This supportive approach is an effective management strategy, but Bill's mental Rolodex could also be used to manipulate. For instance, his manner, while not ingratiating, does shift work relationships to a more personal footing. And while Bill knows a lot about everyone else, his own needs are never expressed. Bill does have a blind spot about what he expects to get for his efforts. His management style is relational, but to be available to so many, he rarely reveals himself.

TWOS AT WORK

TWOs want to be indispensable, and this has always been characteristic of Bill. As a child, he remembers sliding into the right look and figuring out the right approach to please his parents, teachers, and other adults. But this willingness is neither calculated nor designed to put Bill on the throne of power. He would much rather be the power behind the throne than the visible leader upon it.

For instance, he was thrilled when his boss said, in front of the entire staff at the end of a successful sale, "We could never have pulled it off without Bill making everything work so smoothly." He felt powerful as the eyes and ears behind the scenes, because he knew the boss was counting on him.

Similarly, Bill won't necessarily think he's "managing up" by making friends with his boss's boss. To him, making friends and easing the way for others is just something he's good at. Still, this cultivating of people is not indiscriminate. TWOs like Bill deliberately choose their associates, and they tend to be attracted to high-potential people on the way up.

Givers typically thrive in people-centered organizational cultures. They happily minimize the anonymous work of reports and procedures in favor of human interaction. Those who do find themselves confined to work in isolation typically look for a swift way out, like this MBA student who found herself punching numbers for statistical reports in a marketing research lab.

> *The story of how I got into marketing research is that I fell in love with my statistics professor, and found ingenious ways to get close to him. I made a complete study of what he liked, and especially where he spent time. I'd even go to his office to ask questions, although I might already know the answers, and eventually wound up majoring in statistics.*
>
> *I graduated with honors, but the truth is I hated statistics. The hook was the emotional juice of knowing he cared about the outcome, and as I look back, I am still amazed at the total split between working at a job I couldn't stand, and loving the job because it was in his laboratory.*

Our MBA was blithely ignorant of her needs until she got cut off from contact. She was simply inspired by her professor, studied up on his interests, and eventually made his field her major focus. All of this seemed like a good way to choose a career at the time, but she confused what she needed with what her mentor valued.

KEEP THIS IN MIND

TWOs need an emotional hook. Does someone significant care about your work? Is there an association with a respected member of the profession? Are you sympathetic to the other players on the team? You want more than intellectual content; you want emotional connection to the content, and that tie comes from the passion that others have for the project.

A team of equals may present a bind. You want to be inspired by someone who brings out the best in you, and that's not easy when everyone is more or less on the same level. You can feel competitive with peers if you're deprived of special attention. Watch out for wounded pride when you have to wait, move methodically through obstacles, and suffer being overlooked.

Your spiritual path has to do with humility—knowing your real value to others, instead of getting hooked on approval. At first it's humiliating to think that you need assistance when your survival strategy depends on being instrumental to the team. You may find it embarrassing to cooperate as a peer, but given your track record, you'll repay coworkers who offer the help you need. Try speaking up for yourself instead of exerting your influence indirectly through others. Back up your own position in the same way you normally support your favorites.

A FINAL THOUGHT

While you sincerely want to be of service, your assistance may actually weaken the people you support. The stage is set for future resentment if they become dependent on your goodwill.

Remember Bill, the assistant store manager who takes such good care of his staff? He is dedicated to their welfare, but may wind up in a fury if they don't take his advice. The flaw in his reasoning is assuming that everyone on the staff is needy and that he has the solution, which may keep them in a pleasant holding pattern that eventually becomes wearing.

Goodwill is a natural factor in business relationships, but clients aren't children needing constant support, and neither are Bill's favorite salespeople. He finds it hard to separate what's good for another from what's good for himself, when his own welfare is tied to relationships. Yet he must distinguish between genuine altruism and casting himself as the beloved giver.

SECURITY RESPONSE AT POINT FOUR

TWOS generally prefer to funnel their creativity and leadership through an associate, but being perpetually second in command doesn't foster complete self-expression. Paradoxically, when times are good, you no longer need to mold yourself to others. Now you can discover who you really are, though that can be unsettling.

When skills and creativity are properly recognized, TWOS naturally move into the intense emotionality of the Romantic Four. Then you have to face questions of meaning and purpose: What is the real value of work? Is it personally satisfying? It's humbling to realize how easily you can sell yourself out for a pat on the back, neglecting your full potential by overattention to others.

Secure TWOS are less afraid of rejection and can produce highly individualistic work. Now is when you can achieve a unique, Four-like expression. You enjoy working alone and need less approval for what you accomplish. In this frame of mind, you will back yourself in the way that you customarily support others.

Rather than being a place of depression, the Four position allows Givers a chance to stand on their own. However, the low side of being seen as powerful in your own right creates a dilemma for TWOS: "Should I promote myself or serve others?" From a Giver's stance, these may seem like mutually exclusive choices, but if a Giver receives the right context, his own success need not seem to conflict with the well-being of others.

STRESS/RISK RESPONSE AT POINT EIGHT

The first signs of stress stimulate the basic defenses of your type. Being left out of the loop is terrifying, so you position yourself to heighten your importance. You've done your best, you've worked tirelessly for others, and still it didn't work. Suddenly you're on red alert for cues and signs of who's in favor, and you find yourself being super nice to everyone.

If your outreach doesn't work, pride deflates like a balloon that's suddenly punctured. Givers inflate with approval ("They couldn't make it without me") and deflate with rejection ("Poor me"). Bad times are marked by disapproval. It just seems incredible that you've put everyone else first, yet nobody cares.

In a negative spiral, the giving strategy turns into outright manipulation. You know what people need and hold them hostage until they pay their debts. Having become a central figure on projects and indispensable to staff, TWOS are primed to strike. Records are lost, schedules are scrambled, and important matters slip through the cracks. Nothing gets done, which proves your

SECURITY AND STRESS

Dynamics of Change for Point Two

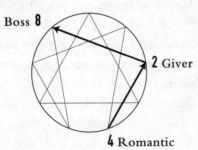

indispensability, and in revenge, you may ally with former competitors.

The shift into Eight is usually marked by explosive anger. "How could you? And after all that I've done? How ungrateful!" You still have an underlying desire for reconciliation and apologies that would reaffirm the relationship, but TWOs moving to Eight become remarkably uncooperative, tenaciously hanging on to whatever they can get.

A positive aspect of this shift is that it can help you find the up-front power to go public on your own. Your leadership extends as a protective mantle to others as you leave the position of second in command to sit on the ruler's throne.

HOW OTHERS SEE TWOS

COMMUNICATION STYLE

When communicating, TWOs are testing the situation for signs of affirmation. They are energized by your nod, a smile, a yes. They interpret this as recognition and respond with their best efforts.

They are seductive communicators, projecting an upbeat, attractive persona that makes people feel recognized and supported. They make others' interests and insights seem valuable, and because their time is obviously important, their coworkers feel singled out for special attention.

This palpable interest in coworkers' activities sends the message, "We're in this together. You can depend on me." Those signals are reinforced through gestures of encouragement and admiration, all of which are genuinely flattering.

With a finely tuned radar for positive feedback, TWOs gear their presentation to please their audience, pitching a sale based on personal appeal to customers. Projecting an energetic stance that woos and convinces, they scan the crowd, looking for a responsive connection to inspire their performance. An entire program can be inwardly dedicated to forming a relationship with a receptive person in the hall, but a good program is ruined if a key figure looks bored. Even when making a technical presentation, TWOs have a tendency to offer information relationally rather than rationally. How other people see them and receive them can be just as important to TWOs as shared intellectual agreement.

> *Givers inhale appreciation like oxygen. Indeed, implicit between the sentences of a conversation is the question "Do you like me?"*

Hard questions are softened to cushion personal rejection. If they can't deliver the right answer, TWOs put on a pleasing smile and speak in a textured purr. Staffers might hear something like: "I have good news and bad news. There's been a change in our funding, so the project we talked about is no longer feasible, but my office door is always open." A consultant might be told: "Even if the contract doesn't work out, I'm sure we'll be seeing you again." When the skids are well-oiled others may not even realize they've been dumped.

The downside of communicating with TWOs is that coworkers feel guilty about failing to meet an unspoken agenda, namely to affirm a TWO's indispensable help. It can be stunning for others to realize that these implicit expectations were operating all along. The TWO's message was "We're in this together," but suddenly that message changed to "Look what I did for you. You wouldn't have made it without me."

What happened? At first Givers provide unwavering support, and suddenly they seem to pull the rug out from under the person they previously encouraged. People who have been successfully manipulated by TWOs may need some time to discover exactly what they were expected to deliver and didn't.

TWOs are strongly other-oriented, which means they shine the spotlight and focus their attention on others. This effectively shields them from being seen for themselves. Because their needs and wants remain in the dark, you don't notice them or fulfill them. To prevent this from happening, communications with TWOs must include an airing of the Giver's needs. Find out up front: What does a TWO expect? What does he want to get in return? It also helps to periodically review the needs of the relationship, not just assessing practical aspects such as salary and responsibilities, but also the level of interpersonal commitment.

Nonverbal Communication

Acutely sensitive to emotional fluctuations, Givers communicate through several different personas. They are likely to think, "I can be helpful here," and they present themselves in the way they think will be most useful. Such adaptations produce the right mannerisms, the right pacing, and the right energetic tone, each unconsciously engineered to make people feel comfortable, to relax the tension, to make even bad news palatable.

TWOs can be standoffish until they know who they have to be for a colleague. They monitor what that person does and does not like and adjust accordingly, waiting to communicate when the timing and mood are right. All of this maneuvering makes others grateful for such careful attention, but the same approach works to a Giver's advantage, when wanting to influence someone's decisions through flattery.

COMMUNICATING WITH TWOS

- Maintain personal warmth and a friendly tone as much as possible. Conveying personal interest and appreciation is important in delivering your message.
- Draw out their expectations to avoid miscommunication or disappointment. Because they are so attuned to pro-

viding what other people need, TWOs may assume that others will do the same for them.

- Encourage them to make "I" statements rather than simply reporting on what people need from them.
- Set limits on how much they do for you. TWOs may try to become indispensable by doing too much or by taking on tasks that are not in their job description.
- Criticism may be perceived as personal rejection. Focus on the specific issue or error, while providing reassurance that they are valued as employees or coworkers.
- TWOs communicate through their body language and tone of voice. The way they say things is often more important than the content. Help them understand their impact on other people. Remind them that not everyone likes as much personal contact as they do.

MOTIVATION

Giving is sometimes motivated by pure altruism, sometimes by simple human decency, and sometimes by selfishness. This is true of everyone, including TWOs. When first hearing descriptions of the nine Enneatypes, some people mistakenly think they are TWOs simply because they are basically kind, generous, and helpful people. Yet a One may help so that you "get it right." A Three may help so that you just "get it done." A Six may help so you don't "get in trouble." A Seven may help you just to have a new experience, etc.

TWOs help because it allows them to establish an emotional bond, making them feel valuable to you. What TWOs give is less important than *why* and *how* they are motivated to do it. The potential trap for Givers is obvious. By conveying empathy and concern, TWOs become dependent on the approval of others, and without the protection of that approval they feel insecure.

For TWOs, a good relationship to authority is the best motivator of all. They don't have to be motivated when they feel accepted and inspired by the people around them. Givers are talented, vivacious go-getters who initiate readily when permission is given for their personal talents to surface. Oddly, TWOs who are clearly in charge may still see themselves as just responding to someone else's needs, so a good project may die when positive approval is withdrawn or attention turns to someone else.

Skillful in positioning themselves, TWOs who feel powerful in the Givers role become weakened and embarrassed when they have to receive in a direct way. They are protected in a giving stance with all eyes focused on the designated leader, who is of course artfully controlled from behind the scenes. Givers deal in "influence" rather than in direct control. They do their work through other people.

Although they may be highly competent and creative, it can be difficult to raise them to leadership status. Their preoccupation with nurturance makes them more comfortable in roles such as administrative assistant to the chief executive, or the number one aide to a high-profile corporate officer. Since TWOs exercise power indirectly, they may be supporting themselves when they appear to be highly motivated to help others. If personal security depends on the success of a boss, then TWOs are ensuring their own future by taking charge of their boss's career. The boss will be put in touch with the people he needs to meet, he will be made aware of potential competition and will be well represented. It's like a relationship in which the TWO partner energizes the other, each taking overt pride in the other's accomplishments while privately enjoying being the impetus behind that success.

Givers describe themselves as shape-shifters, able to mold themselves to please the people and causes that deserve their help. For example, a TWO nurse will volunteer time to assist the overburdened head of surgery handle all his paperwork. She will remember the children in the oncology ward and, in concert with the head nurse, arrange for special favors to be on their trays at Thanksgiving. She is highly motivated to create a supportive and responsive work environment that allows others to fulfill the abilities that she saw within them early on and helped nurture. At the same time, our nurse may be aware that she is offering strategic help that aids her own ambitions.

> *Helping others to achieve their goals is a source of satisfaction and fulfillment that may not be apparent to other people.*

When TWOs are frustrated by lack of response, when our nurse feels no acknowledgment for the sacrifice of time and energy invested, when too much goes out and too little comes back, she can overextend to the point of exhaustion. When her efforts are ignored, or ironically, when administration becomes overly dependent upon her, even she will eventually burn out.

Caught in a cycle of seeing what others need and feeling rejected, TWOs typically withdraw all support. At an all-time low, our hospital nurse is motivated by her own needs, by the private victory she feels in supporting a favorite, and by the standoffish pride of seeing others flounder. But low periods also produce the right conditions to renew a TWO's intrinsic motivations—the humane and altruistic giving that genuinely supports others. It takes very little to reenergize a Giver's enthusiasm. Simple gestures of acceptance like saying: "The boss really liked my report, thanks for sitting with me and giving your feedback."

Resist the temptation to sympathize or offer overt help. At the same time realize this is your best opportunity to show your appreciation for the Giver separate from what she gives. Be aware that you're dealing with damaged pride. Better to pick up her empty coffee cup from the desk and drop it off full on your way back from the lounge rather than ask her, "Do you need anything?" "Do you want a cup of coffee?"

Highly attuned to what others need, TWOs must learn to give to themselves. It helps to observe when an opportunity to take control appears and to resist volunteering, "I can arrange the meeting." Or "You can count on me." When the urge to move in and help arises, the key question will be: "Is what I intend to offer, something I should give to myself?"

MOTIVATING TWOS

- When possible, give TWOs the attention and warmth that supports their participation and maximizes their contribution. Personal rapport opens the door to productivity. A few minutes of personal contact goes a long way.
- Structure lots of personal interaction. TWOs generally work better with a partner or as a member of a team.
- TWOs tend either to overestimate their own importance or to be insecure about their self-worth. Help them to clarify their role and responsibilities, establishing their value without the pressure of proving themselves.
- TWOs often feel threatened by conflict or disagreement. Remind TWOs that people will still like them afterward. Create enough safety so they can speak their mind. Let them know they don't have to be nice all the time.
- Twos are especially sensitive about appearing foolish. Don't expect them to go out on a limb or welcome risk taking. Give them time to learn new things. They learn well if they have good role models.

TIME MANAGEMENT

Givers live on relational time. They feel a strong need to respond immediately when a request comes from someone who's important. Qualifiers such as "This is a low priority, finish what you're doing first" or "This can wait until Monday" are empty phrases, when what counts to the TWO is meaningful time working with people who matter.

Even a minor request from someone significant draws a TWO's attention away from his own deadlines and priorities. It's easier to drop whatever he is working on and respond immediately to the new request, rather than thinking about it all weekend.

Time seems to fly during emotionally charged interactions, while impersonal tasks take forever. TWOs can be patiently bored in a meeting not because they're incapable of paying attention, but because content without contact feels like a waste of time.

But those same dull meetings come alive again when a favorite boss or executive is presenting the facts and figures. If a close associate comes under fire, Givers will enter the debate with a passion, later being surprised at how quickly time went by.

A TWO's inner sense of time is focused on emerging relationships between participants in a project, regardless of the project's content. From the perspective of personal time, projects are a blip on the larger emotional curve of how people feel about each other, because it is those feelings that endure through time.

Givers can do a full-time job while staying abreast of their favorite person's progress. It doesn't seem incongruous to keep a running mental tab of several different schedules, or to wonder how friends, or important people, are faring at other events while TWOs are sitting in a meeting of their own.

Highly efficient in the interests of a relationship, TWOs like to promote others and perform so as not to forfeit approval from important people. As a result, they look remarkably independent, but internally they know how much of their time is spent anticipating other people's needs.

For example, a salesman finds it easy to hit his quota when he sees himself in liaison with the boss, the department, or the company. It's even easy to run a sales meeting when he sees himself as a member of a team who just happens to be in the limelight. But procrastination often sets in when he is out there on his own, cut off from contact.

Givers are can-do, capable people who support others, an attitude that makes them particularly nervous about looking foolish in public. For example, a planning executive will put together a deftly reasoned, innovative program outlining in detail where the company should be positioned in the marketplace five years from now, and he will vigorously present that plan if it is to go out over his boss's signature. However, if he writes it under his own name, he will find himself tuned to check out his boss's thinking, because he is apprehensive about public visibility. He may procrastinate because, as first author, he fears public rejection.

HELPING TWOS MANAGE TIME

- TWOs often make assumptions about what other people need and then try to fill those needs. Help TWOs discriminate between what other people actually require and their own need for contact.

- TWOs tend to fill up the space with advice or helpfulness. Remind them to step back so that other people can step forward, even if there is a temporary delay.

- Encourage TWOs to focus on their own work. They will tend to be overly concerned with the feelings and needs of the people around them. It's easier to pay attention to other people than themselves. Help them make personal boundaries, and let other people handle their own problems.

- Although they are high-contact people, TWOs can benefit from time spent alone that enables them to restore their calm and their focus.

- In situations that are stressful or chaotic, TWOs are at risk for getting sick or burning out. They tend to absorb other people's feelings and upsets. It's important that supervisors and coworkers support TWOs in finding effective ways to take care of themselves so they can stay on the job.

NEGOTIATION

Skillful in strategizing behind the scenes, TWOs are likely to research personal information about you. They want to know who you know and the caliber of your reputation. For TWOs, a reputation may have less to do with credentials or business success than how you treat your bosses, employees, suppliers, and loved ones. They are likely to call a key secretary or a disaffected employee or someone they know who likes you a lot.

Their strategy is focused on relating to you as a person before they negotiate the issues on the table. They know your profile and will tailor their approach for maximum impact and persuasion. If you're seen as a tough guy, you'll be met with a tough-guy stance. If you're known as someone who's considerate of employees, the TWO will align with that position.

It helps if you help a Giver to save face. Mindful of image and approval, they will respect you for respecting them in public. You may be on opposite sides of the table, but TWOs still want you to like them, and why shouldn't the debate look interesting enough to turn heads?

Pride leads TWOs to believe they can win anyone over, so negotiations may not feel adversarial. You will be handled adroitly in hopes that the interaction goes smoothly and the final handshake leaves a wake of positive comments from all sides. However, if the outcome looks disappointing, damaged pride pushes TWOs into a 180-degree turn and suddenly you're facing a wounded tiger who will not compromise. Be prepared. TWOs moving into the stress of Eight will attack.

Like Sixes, TWOs are fierce underdog defenders. Motivated by the need to help a cause or person in whom they believe, Givers can publicly represent just about anybody as long as it isn't themselves. Jan, a successful consultant, described herself as "great in negotiating a fee for someone I believe in, but dismal in naming my own figure." Givers are excellent at determining someone else's worth, but feel put upon to set a price on their own value. Unfortunately, TWOs may assert themselves only when they feel victimized. They may justify moving into an aggressive stance by claiming injury and victimization. Rather than allowing the negotiation to escalate, call a break, because TWOs more than any other type vent their anger and then want to be friends.

TRAINING AND DEVELOPMENT

A TWO's key strategy is adapting to please, so their behavior is geared to a specific audience. If they find themselves in a training class filled with smart alecks, they're tempted to contribute their share of wisecracks. If it's a studious group, Givers shift to horn-rimmed-glasses mode. They tend to blend with group expectations, asking similar questions, adjusting to what other participants like or don't like, and reporting the same problems with learning. Don't assume that the persona you see in the training room is the one who will show up at work.

All of this wanting to fit in is geared to gain approval and ward off rejection. TWOs take pride in keeping up appearances, they need a lot of reassurance, and if the plan is to have them flying solo, they'll have to be protected from looking foolish. Trainers are the authority figures in the room, so TWOs want validation and recognition from them. They want to know what the trainer expects, and will ask for guidance. The wise trainer will make warm personal contact with TWOs, which opens up the learning process.

To get the best from a training, give TWOs a real or imagined model to follow. They are disinterested in detailed rules or procedures. Unlike Ones, they don't operate "by the book"; they can, however, easily adapt to personify the role model that trainers present. TWOs mold themselves to the expected role. They want to know how to look and behave in performing their task. The mechanics of the job follow once they feel solid in the role.

Video clips of people on the job are especially helpful, because TWOs want to know the implicit requirements as well as explicit skills. "What should a competent person look like performing this task?" For example, if you're training Givers as executive secretaries, they will assume responsibility for learning task competency, but will be eager to learn from you details such as whether they're expected to protect the boss's time or to allow others access to him.

Paradoxically, although they don't seek direct recognition, they have a large need for personal contact. Since it's difficult for them to acknowledge these needs directly, it may be confusing to trainers who do not supply enough approval. You don't have to gush, but trainers must reinforce approval because TWOs move quickly from warmth to resentment, making them appear inconsistent or unreliable. But Givers can be quickly brought back by friendly contact. Unlike Eights or Ones, they do not get locked into a fixed position. More than any other type, an angry episode is quickly forgotten.

THE CASE OF THE TWO DIRECTOR WHO FOUND THE VIRTUE OF HIS TYPE

The ongoing strike has been a no-win situation for both sides, and negotiations are not going well. So far the company has remained open through the use of replacement workers, but profits are down substantially and the firm is falling steadily behind on filling orders. The union has gained some concessions on higher wages and guaranteed employment, but the gains have been far less than expected. Both the company and the union have been compromised by the fact that many of those who crossed the picket line were union members. Now, negotiators are closing in on a face-saving out for both parties. Legal realities will determine the public outcome of the strike, but personalities will shape the agreement.

Two new players appear toward the end of these protracted, bitter negotiations between management and labor. The company's director of human resources is a Giver TWO. He had hoped to enter as a fresh face, but the union played the same game by importing a well-known negotiator of its own, a Four. They have come to settle the question of strike-breaking, both by some members of the striking union and by replacement workers: the issue has already drawn national media attention. During another strike on the other side of the country, the union's negotiator successfully argued for firing scabs, and the union expects him to repeat the same winning argument here.

TYPICAL INTERACTIONS

The Giver TWO director of human resources recognizes his opponent from television newscasts. He'd been impressed by the man's passionate rhetorical style and hopes this won't turn into a battle of words. The director is a pretty good speaker himself, but this negotiation isn't about posturing or making a point for the cameras. For him, it's a question of jeopardizing personal relationships. He has friends both among the workers who crossed the picket line and among the strikers keeping a raucous presence outside the main gate, and he feels torn between the two factions.

Up until this point, Giver-like, he's been a behind-the-scenes influence in moving the negotiations toward settlement, wielding power indirectly rather than taking the spotlight. The director prides himself on being one of those people who can get along with anybody. He moves easily between groups who ordinarily don't talk to one another, acting as a bridge between conflicting parties.

He contrasts his own helpfulness with that of his counterpart, whom he has pegged as a soapbox orator, someone who doggedly preaches "us against them." It hurts the Giver's pride to know that the union negotiator probably sees him as someone without principles. Yes, he thinks the scabs should keep their jobs, and he also wants the approval and goodwill of the strikers. What's wrong with that?

From his side of the table, the Romantic Four is coming off a series of public appearances in which he continued to refine his eloquent rhetorical style. But he also has a deep personal commitment. He's third-generation union and embodies his message in a typically Four-like way, by placing the conflict on the grand scale of historic precedent. This isn't just a straightforward battle between one union and a company, but rather a symbolic conflict between the power of solidarity and the evils of corporate America. The fact that unions have been weakening throughout the country in the face of participatory management doesn't faze him. Even if his brothers and sisters in the union have not yet learned the truth, he knows that "participatory management" is just another way of trying to weaken the little bargaining power employees have left.

The human resources director he now faces typifies the way that management saps a union's strength. To him it is clear that the director is a sell-out, a sycophant who has never suffered. He casts the director as a person of privilege, compromised by social status.

From the other side of the bargaining table, the TWO director sees a skilled and deadly actor wrapped in a union banner. For him, the union is an outdated machine—witness this fanatic who has risen to command center stage. The director knows the situation is tricky. The company has remained operational, showing a modest profit all through the strike. Why, he wonders out loud in the crowded negotiation room, should he turn around and punish the scabs, the very people who have kept the company up and running?

The union's response is quick, clear, and unequivocal. The scabs have to be punished to placate the rehired strikers; otherwise there can be no agreement. Standing to defend his cause, the Romantic outlines the key issue in impassioned strokes. The scabs must be fired or the strikers will have sacrificed for nothing. Union strength depends on numbers, and these deserters have profited from their betrayal of the union's power base.

On his feet, the Four begins to sense himself as the man who could reenergize the entire union movement—the right person in the right place at the right time, a lightning rod for history. The clarity of his conviction silences the room. Still immersed in the rhetorical moment, he sits down to a note placed at his position on the table. It's from the TWO director, requesting a private meeting.

THE TIDE TURNS

The director knows that he and his counterpart must break the stalemate or negotiations will crumble. Taking the initiative, he risks the Four's disdain and says: "You know you've lost. The company is up and running. We can hang on indefinitely. No, we aren't making as much money as before the union went out, but we are profitable. Meanwhile, you pay out strike benefits every month with no dues coming in. How much longer can you afford that?"

The TWO hates being disliked, but goes on anyway: "I'm proud to know people on both sides of the line. Like you said, we really wouldn't have hired some of those 'scabs,' except for the strike. But good people crossed the picket line so their company could survive. In fact, I influenced a few of them to cross, and I won't let them down now."

Both men feel defeated. This is a definite no-win situation.

The union Four asks, "What's your proposal?"

The TWO responds immediately. He's used to sensing what people need and, Giver-like, knows that the union man needs to be rescued.

"Let's announce a settlement on the ten o'clock news," the TWO says. "The company will agree to take back everyone who struck at the salary structure we've already worked out. Then, when the dust settles, we'll decide on a case-by-case basis which scabs will be offered permanent employment."

The Four feels a fiery shot of victory. At least he's saved the union presence. Membership won't die. He gets the director of human relations to agree that the shop steward has to be in on the rehiring. "Some of those scabs have to be axed": it's a small vindication of his place in history. The TWO makes no response.

Both men shake hands mechanically, agreeing to a news release omitting mention of the rehiring dilemma. Surprisingly, the Romantic Four feels content. It's not a historic turnaround, but the members will understand he's done his level best.

The director, on the other hand, suddenly realizes he's about to enter TWO hell. He'll be sitting on a hiring board with management delegates, supervisors, and the shop steward, making person-by-person hire-or-fire decisions and taking body blows for each unpopular call. There will be no strings he can pull and no way to influence the outcome.

RESOLUTION

The director spent about a week in the throes of humiliation. He hadn't realized how much power he wielded by being in the Giver role until it was taken away. Now he just didn't want to be around people. It wasn't about the outcome of the strike, because the truth was that both sides had gotten something, and even the press had been complimentary about the sanity of the decision.

When he looked at it honestly, it was about himself. It was about having to appear in public stripped of the power that made him feel secure in the eyes of others. But what else could he have done? Skilled in working the power structure, he had used his advantage with the different factions in the company to bring about the best possible settlement. The director has no guilt about what he did, but he suffers because his pride makes him want to be all things to all people.

The Giver director has three choices. He can go underground until he feels needed again and get off the hire-fire board as fast as he can. He can stoically hide his humiliation, pretending that he doesn't mind having his vote publicly judged. Or he can do something that most people never do. He can reach into the blind spot in his thinking and—without necessarily knowing it—take a step in the right direction for his spiritual welfare.

Self-observation

TWOs, like every other Enneatype, need to know there's a way to transform an outmoded emotional survival strategy. The director suffers from the vice of pride. So even though his actions are honorable in his own eyes, he feels rejected when other people disagree.

However, if he stepped back to observe when he feels touched by humiliation, he'd be able to tell the difference between coworkers who like him because he meets their needs, others who are simply indifferent, and—revealingly—those who like him as a person, although he never gave them anything. That discrimination is called humility—knowing your true value to others—a virtue that is quite different than giving to get approval.

Point Three: The Performer

Alias: **Achiever, Promoter, The Instant Expert**

Motto	*I am what I do.*
Mental Model	*The world values a champion; no cookies for losers.*
Lens of Perception	*Tasks, goals, and results.*
Way of Sorting Information	*Convergent thinking: any idea that ever worked in another setting is aimed at the current goal.*
Blind Spot	*Failure.*
Growth Edge	*Developing access to feelings.*
Spiritual Path	*Investing hope in the work process instead of your own role in the process.*
Vice	*Deception—exaggerated self-image of your own abilities.*
Virtue	*Honesty—knowing your actual abilities.*
Inspired By	*Hope.*
Managerial Style	*"If you don't want footprints on your back, get outta my way." This is the American corporate style of machinelike production, go-go-go success, and quantity over quality. Staff has to scramble to keep up.*
Appearance to Others	*Energetic, optimistic, can-do leaders who embody the image of their profession.*
Typical Conflicts	*Other people feel exploited. THREES direct, delegate, and assume leadership without consulting: Someone's either on board or out.*
One-Minute Resolution	*If you work with THREES, coordinate your intervention with a natural pause in their schedule. To get their attention, the magic*

> *words are, "This isn't working," followed by a constructive suggestion. If you are a THREE, remember to ask yourself, "What am I feeling?"*

The Signals THREES *Send*

Positive	*High-profile, positive image and dedication to results is uplifting. THREEs inspire hope in others.*
Negative	*THREEs project an artificial crowd-pleaser image that changes from group to group. It sometimes seem as if they don't care about others, especially about others' feelings. Things and goals may appear to matter more than people do.*
Mixed	*THREEs relate through a role, which can be confusing to coworkers. They're allies when alliance is called for, supporters when the job requires them to assist, and competitors when the roles switch.*
Security Response at Point Six	*Here personal feelings arise. There's time to stop and think, which paradoxically brings up questions and anxiety. Six is the place of discovering work that is chosen, rather than expedient.*
Stress/Risk Response at Point Nine	*Since a THREE needs to keep as many balls in the air as possible, down time is a big stressor; attention spreads to details so that the THREE can stay occupied.*
Work Best In	*Competitive environments with a ladder to climb and a clear system of rewarding effort. Salary, titles, and decision-making roles are incentives.*
Have Problems Working In	*Jobs that require periods of apparent inactivity with no clear game plan. THREEs do not like to sit around and talk about ideas, revise a decision, or get slowed down by questions.*
Where Business Wants Its THREES	*Marketing, sales, and advertising; during a rapid expansion phase of any business; situations that require efficiency, streamlining, and rapid turnaround.*

ARE YOU A THREE?

THREES are the prototype of the hard-driving American worker. Totally dedicated to the task at hand, you're at your best in a grueling race to the winner's circle. You believe that the world values a champion, so you go for the gold in the fastest, most efficient way possible. There are always several projects afloat at the same time, and you're already focused on the next task well before the current one is completed. You prefer days crammed with activity, so you wind up cutting as many corners as possible, and the fear of failure keeps you moving very quickly.

Slowing down to relax is threatening, especially if you're supposed to sit around and talk about feelings. Emotions are messy, unproductive, and incompatible with getting the job done. So when feelings come up, you shift gears and accelerate into the next task. You can make anything work if you throw enough energy at it.

However, the people you work with may interpret your workaholic streak as heartless. But those same coworkers also seem happy to stand around wasting time while the competition moves in. It drives you crazy to think of being second best, so you figure out what coworkers need to hear, project the right image, and sell them your game plan. Once they're sold, you run for the goal—first, fast, and looking good while you're doing it.

Adept at projecting an image that woos and persuades, THREES usually land on their feet. Witness Peter, a real estate developer and a prototypical THREE, whose image and dedication to success saved the day when the project he was working on had come to a complete halt.

Peter's team thought they had put together a syndicate to buy the last bit of undeveloped land along the river. But now—on the day before Thanksgiving, no less—the lead bank has sent a fax saying, "Our position has evolved. We are going to have to review your request further."

Peter is devastated. Without this bank's support, the project is dead, but there is no way he'll let that show. A winner's facade is his stock in trade, so he blocks his feelings and goes into fast-forward. He assembles the team and, without having a clue about what to do, tells them: "Don't worry. I have a plan. Get ready, because this is going to be big. Enjoy the holiday, and I'll see you bright and early on Monday."

There has to be a solution somewhere, and he doesn't dare rest until he finds it. It's a brick wall, but he keeps at it all night, and when the right idea hits, holiday or not, first thing on Thanksgiving morning he calls the head of the smallest bank in the syndicate and explains what has happened.

The call is crucial, so before dialing Peter imagines himself facing the banker across the desk and moves into total belief about himself and the project he represents. Any lingering doubts are wiped from his mind as he focuses on the string of positive points he has to convey. Each point has to hit home, and he knows he must move from one item to the next with absolute conviction. He believes this is the solution, and will convince the banker that his plan will work.

"You know," Peter says casually, "in our situation, we can always pull in a couple more banks or get each of the remaining partners to kick in a couple more dollars. But I have another idea. Why don't you use this as an opportunity to make a splash? Instead of taking a small role, why don't you guys jump out in front? Become the lead bank—and put your name on the project."

They have the bare bones of the deal sketched out long before the Thanksgiving Day parade is over, and Peter begins strategizing how to sell the new version to the team.

HOW THREES SORT INFORMATION

None of what Peter says is an outright lie, but he does finesse the particulars. In spiritual tradition, this pattern is tied to vanity, and he would be the type of monk who deceives himself and others about the real extent of his abilities. Like each of the eight other types, the THREE does to others what he does to himself. He has to believe in his own ability in order to persuade others, and because he's a proactive leader, he doesn't wait around long enough for questions or doubts to surface. In fact, he's moving so fast that he has time only for positive feedback that helps him get where he wants to go. It's not that he chooses to ignore negative indications, they just don't make it onto his screen.

Every THREE will define success differently, but each definition aims at winning in a competitive environment. In academic life, that would mean being published in a professional journal. For the salesperson, it's being called up onstage in some exotic locale during the annual trip designed to honor the company's best performers. The key in each instance is that your colleagues see you as successful.

When a viable project appears, THREES move into a way of sorting information called "convergent thinking." If you looked through Peter's lens of perception, you'd see the syndicate deal etched in bold. You'd also realize that the deal has become so fixed in his attention that he's now seeing his assets, his associates, his professional contacts, and his entire personal history in terms of the development project.

When the syndicate deal picks up speed, Peter's attention narrows to just those critical items that can get the job done. Once the project lodges in his thinking, he stops seeing people as people and begins to mentally "recruit" their skills. He hears every conversation in terms of potential assets for the project and begins to enroll support from everyone he meets. His other projects are shuffled to accommodate the new priority. He sorts wildly through his memories of every remotely similar situation and every partial solution that has ever worked in any other deal. In Peter's mind, any pertinent information from any source whatsoever converges on the syndicate project, while irrelevant data just slides away.

THREES AT WORK

Threes are focused on results, and this has always been Peter's strength. He recalls teachers and other adults prizing him for what he could do, but his emotions didn't seem important. Because he saw that performance brought attention, Peter set goals, suspended his emotions, worked hard, and won. Over time, he paid increasing attention to earning the status, prestige, and material benefits of public success, so he didn't notice the sacrifice of his feelings.

If you're a THREE, you'll understand the phrase "I am what I do." Like a skilled actor, your manner and appearance shift as you move through the different events of the day. You look very different in the boardroom than when you visit the boiler room, because your image changes to enhance results.

Image can be deceptive. It's tailored to produce an impact rather than express your needs. In your mental model, people value a winner, so it's natural to project an image that makes the right impression. If your success is bolstered by appearances, you may "become what you do." You start to think in the interests of your task, slipping into the appropriate vocabulary, mannerisms, and look that represent the task well.

Beneath surface appearances, you also take on the emotions that your job requires you to feel until you become a living prototype of your profession. All of this benefits you on the job, because people place their confidence in your expert demeanor.

But when you go home from work, it may be hard to face a whole Sunday with nothing to do.

> *Good vacations have a productivity coefficient, i.e., you can't just have fun playing golf. You have to work hard at improving your score.*

THREEs flourish in work that offers practical rewards such as bonus plans, profit sharing, and promotion. So they're often unhappy in organizational cultures that run on bureaucracy. If you're a THREE in a job with a ceiling, you'll find yourself reinventing your career, as did Lisa, the publisher of a home crafts magazine:

> *To me, time away from my desk feels like punishment. I go on a long-overdue vacation, and instead of watching the waves, I'm out on the beach with a portable computer and a ton of manuscripts. I'm checking my voice mail several times a day and have made sure everyone knows my hotel fax number "just in case."*
>
> *The truth is, my heart's in my work, and I've developed an extraordinary small publishing company that lets me write, edit, design, and sell—all at the same time. I should also say I'm an escapee from ten years in corporate life, where I was paid an obscene amount to perform the same work year after year. So now I work night and day for much less money and no vacation, and I love it.*

If you're like Lisa, activity makes you feel in control. THREEs coming home from vacation are more likely to rattle off how many countries they toured, or the number of golf courses played or the professional journals they got to read, rather than how good it felt to relax.

KEEP THIS IN MIND

THREES on teams have to deal with the difference between a solo performance and taking pleasure in group wins. Convinced that coworkers are equally preoccupied with job advancement, THREES have a natural tendency to compete—but not always on behalf of the team.

Remember Peter, the successful property developer? He was a solo player, and it did work out for him. He took the whole bank syndicate problem on his own shoulders and sent the team home for Thanksgiving, but why didn't he consult with them?

Peter's competitive, solo-player focus is evident in the current Silicon Valley scene, where new products are rapidly introduced and immediately shoved into every conceivable market. Expansion plays to a performer's strengths. When times are good, you want to expand the product line and move into new territories: "Let's keep it going." When times are bad, THREES deceptively paint the picture as looking bigger and better anyway.

The problem is, you can be so focused on the potential opportunities that there's a reluctance to slow down and go back to the drawing board to see how the product can be improved. There is a reason why most hot high-tech companies flame out.

In the meantime, coworkers may be feeling exploited by your determination—especially since you begin to direct, delegate, and assume leadership without necessarily consulting them. From your point of view, your measure of worth lies in meeting the immediate crisis. But you are infinitely more effective when you can wait, consider questions, listen to feedback, and take time to reconsider.

Your spiritual path has to do with honesty—just being yourself instead of projecting an image. You've taken the whole burden on your own shoulders, instead of trusting in the work process that carries you forward. You've taken leadership on your shoulders, instead of placing hope in the people around you. The team will carry their share of the load if you can slow down and listen.

A FINAL THOUGHT

You know how to work, but you may have to learn about feelings. Your survival strategy is to brush feelings away because they slow you down and interfere with work. You may even see emotional people as crippled by their feelings. Why don't Loyal Skeptic Sixes just quit being afraid? Why can't Romantic Fours lighten up? In your haste to get the job done, you may see feelings as a problem to be solved, whereas other types are enriched by emotional connections.

> *You can either get the job done or get emotional.*

Your lens of perception highlights positive feedback cues. You see what's working and where your advantage lies, while discounting negative signals. There's no time to get bogged down in inefficient distraction, so you forget what you feel about it and just do it. Feelings vanish in the same way that negative feedback slides off: "Later—I'll deal with feelings later. Right now I'm too busy."

An action orientation filters out information that has the potential to slow you down. Your attention is on the next step, and halfway through that step, you're figuring out what's needed for the next and the next, with no stops in between. The work itself may be deadly boring, but oddly, grinding labor keeps you focused on the next rung on the ladder. You can rest after the next career move or the next raise in pay.

Over time you climb the ladder, seeing others as you see yourself—as efficient performers. Once perched on a high enough rung, you may look around and realize that you're uncertain about what you feel. It's vital to remember that you're a human being, instead of a "human doing," and to treat yourself honorably, knowing that your worth as a person is greater than your dollar value.

SECURITY AND STRESS

Type 3: The Performer

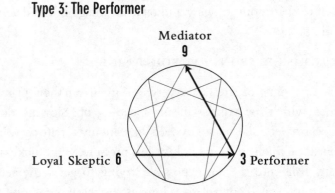

SECURITY RESPONSE AT POINT SIX

Ironically, good times can produce an identity crisis. Who are you when you're not working? What's there to talk about? The feelings that naturally surface when you relax may be confusing: "What am I supposed to be feeling? Do I have the right emotion?" Sometimes your emotions seem fraudulent: "Maybe I'm faking this. Maybe this is just part of my image." Your strength lies in your task orientation, which favors doing over feeling, so it takes a long time to discover where you stand emotionally.

When you act from the low side of your security point Six, you worry about losing your prestigious image. Will people still like you if you're just being yourself? The fact is, coworkers will be endeared by your new Six-like doubt and self-questioning. Suddenly you don't look so relentlessly self-confident, and you're less inclined to set a backbreaking pace that pushes everyone else. When you feel secure, you move a little slower and question your course of action, instead of producing like a machine.

It's very scary to just be yourself. You never meant to be deceptive, but now you can tell the difference between your genuine responses and the image that automatically emerges when you seek positive feedback. Knowing yourself and others as people instead of producers allows you to absorb their thinking, lend yourself to their point of view, and take advantage of the diversity around you.

STRESS/RISK RESPONSE AT POINT NINE

At the first signs of stress, every type digs in on their primary defenses, which for THREES means speeding up. Slowing down produces anxiety, and inactivity feels like enemy territory. Where another type might feel grateful for less pressure, you quickly toss as many balls into the air as possible, trying to get some action going. Doing equals control, so as long as you're on the phone and in motion, you can outspeed anxiety.

Externally, you may look energetic and engaged when you're under stress. The positive spin you put on your activities still operates—but now you're talking about what's in the works for the future, instead of immediate projects. Internally, as stress deepens, there's a mad scramble to line up new prospects. Some of the balls drop, but the ones that stay in the air get a huge amount of your time and attention.

You'll recognize your shift into the position of the Mediator, NINE, when you start drawing up elaborate billing records to justify your time and attentively read background materials you usually ignore. You seem perpetually loaded down with trivia, but can't let any of it go, because it could conceivably lead to important work.

But Nine also allows you to tell the difference between staying busy and choosing a real priority. In the past, work gave you a sense of control, but in truth you were being controlled by a compulsion to work. Now's the perfect time to go back to the drawing board and discover what you want. You'll never lose the ability to mobilize, but instead of thinking, "I am what I do," find your identity in doing what you love, like Lisa, the magazine publisher.

HOW OTHERS SEE THREES

COMMUNICATION STYLE

When it comes to putting across a concept—be it a new, multi-million-dollar project, or the need for a better office copier—Performers sway the crowd by promoting goals and results.

However, in presenting materials to coworkers and associates, THREEs package and communicate their ideas so as to minimize potential risks, difficulties, and hazards, just as they would do in a sales presentation.

And just as they would during a sales pitch, Performers make chameleonlike adjustments of vocal inflection, vocabulary, and body language to keep the audience engaged. THREEs intuitively adjust their public persona to ensure maximum positive feedback. They have an ability to sense what the crowd likes and give the audience what it wants.

In fact, THREEs play an audience the way a musician plays his instrument. They can rouse emotions without actually feeling those emotions themselves. When feelings are called for, a skilled Performer can shift her voice and adjust her pace until she has the crowd in her hand.

Not surprisingly, THREEs can appear to be different people on different occasions, depending on their audience. Colleagues may see this as deliberate deception, but after all, THREEs think, the same car can be sold in several different ways, depending on the taste of prospective buyers. Why shouldn't a presentation be tailored?

The energy output used to get an idea across is calibrated to appeal to those different buyers, but the message is consistent: "This will work for you." THREEs' enthusiasm and "can't-miss" approach attracts people who like reassurance, and the confident statement "Join my team and you'll wind up in the winner's circle" more often than not invites people to line up.

> *Selling a positive image is one way to look successful, and it often translates into a self-fulfilling prophecy.*

Performers can bowl their listeners over with their drive and energy; there's practically no time lag between idea and action. Coworkers may be skeptical about the way THREEs go about things, but it's hard for them to resist being swept up in the wake of a goal-directed THREE who's committed to making her vision a reality.

Once in gear, however, the THREE can perform robotically, coming across as superficial and impersonal. The sales quota and the applause meter replace real feelings and commitment. Communications focus on bottom-line results, but the subtext reads: "Compete, earn, and win. Nothing else matters."

This does not go unnoticed. Colleagues frequently comment that in her eagerness to move forward, a THREE often glosses over important facts, sometimes drowning an audience in a rapid flow of ideas. THREEs accentuate positive solutions, rather than raise hard questions. Much is promised, apparently without risk.

Performers are market-conscious people, selling themselves as a prototype of their own successful enterprise. The audience sees a star, someone who looks fully committed 100 percent of the time. The look of a presentation is extremely important. Are the brochure graphics outstanding? Is the sales force handling the questions well-groomed?

All this hustle is disconcerting for those who may like the THREE as a person but dislike one of her business decisions. The best way to communicate dissatisfaction to THREEs is to make sure that you protect their image. A good line sounds something like: "I really respect your capabilities, but we disagree on this point."

Nonverbal Communication

Colleagues will also notice that one-upmanship creeps into the conversation. Within minutes of being introduced, they've heard about a THREE's credentials, status, and probable earning power. People feel energetically "put in their place," and their place is less important in the light of a THREE's accomplishments.

Similarly, THREEs typically promote their current interest at another's expense. For instance, a Performer's coworker who is really interested in rock climbing is likely to hear: "I was into that last year, but listen to what I've got going now!" A Performer's energy pumps up when attention turns to her activities and dies when it's somebody else's turn.

THREEs want eye contact so that they know how they're coming across. There's a positive "this is great" feel about the interaction while it's happening, but still, people aren't sure whether the THREE likes them or not. Conversations are usually a progress report. If a new acquaintance has something to offer a THREE's current project, he'll be greeted with a flush of interest; otherwise, he'll get a fast handshake.

The communication is entirely different when the THREE is on a project with others. A coworker's personal interests are suddenly important, not because the THREE shares them, but because his welfare is now directly linked to the THREE's performance.

COMMUNICATING WITH THREES

- Speak in the language of results and accomplishment. Emphasize action over context and theory. Keep a focus on the bottom line.
- THREES tend to rush ahead. Challenge the thoroughness of their analysis and planning. Be willing to say "stop" in order to anticipate problems and incorporate additional input.
- Demonstrate the many ways in which others contribute to the project's success. Be firm in presenting other points of view, showing how other ways of doing the job can work.
- Time is precious to THREES because their self-worth is tied to productivity. Recognize their concern about not wasting time and try to communicate quickly and efficiently.
- Build in regular checkpoints and feedback sessions to promote quality control.
- Raise questions and concerns in a way that sounds constructive instead of negative. Frame criticism as leading to better results or improved performance.

MOTIVATION

THREES are motivated by tangible evidence of success. They respond to the classic incentives of salary and material status symbols, and will buckle down to the sheer challenge of earning a title. All this activity is rooted in the human need for approval in the eyes of others, but the hurry habit also produces powerful moments of pure purpose when effort drops away and the work seems to be doing itself.

Performers say that such times are intrinsically rewarding—a high state of energy and excitement that's worth working for—

even if it didn't produce tangible success. That intrinsic reward of being caught up in the forward moving energy of worthwhile activity is at the core of what motivates THREEs in the workplace. There's nothing more pleasurable than diving into the concentration tunnel that leads to a useful goal.

Without becoming too philosophical, it's safe to say that while everyone is motivated by approval needs and by having to earn their way in the world, THREEs, more than other types, feel compelled to work so as to avoid fears of failure.

Many THREEs work continuously and enjoy losing themselves in activity. For example, an executive secretary may be thinking of heading down to the cafeteria, but will use the trip to knock a couple of items off her "to-do" list. Along the way, she may become so preoccupied with new items for her list that she could easily bump shoulders with a colleague and continue down the hall without noticing. Focused on her tasks and the flow of activity, she loses outer awareness of herself and her surroundings.

The same THREE secretary will become angry and accusatory if her forward momentum is thwarted, because slowing the pace threatens her need for success. Unlike other types who might enjoy a modest workload, an enforced slowdown invites this secretary to look for greener pastures or moonlight at a second job to keep herself occupied.

> THREEs *are solo performers. They're out there alone, aimed at* *stardom, and there's no hope for losers.*

Our executive secretary depends on her own initiative rather than trusting the process or placing hope in the efforts of others. She will work efficiently provided she has a ladder to climb. She may have started out in the general secretarial pool, but will quickly decide to work toward being an administrative assistant, climbing as high as she can go.

But her urge to achieve paves the way to disappointment when goals are delayed, when hard work isn't enough, and when projects are mired in problems. When her efforts are reduced to a paycheck and a series of robotic tasks, THREE-like, her attention will fixate on other people's laziness. Caught in a cycle of wanting to succeed and feeling hopeless, she will then perform just well enough to hold a job, becoming emotionally distant.

But an absence of challenge also produces conditions that rekindle a THREE's intrinsic motivation—the hopes that spring from finding a new direction. Infinitely adaptable, THREEs don't stay down for the count. They do not have to be encouraged to work, since the need to produce is embedded in their type. For them, the important motivational factor is more about finding hope in intangibles such as goodwill, creativity, and emotional depth, rather than seeing their value in material rewards. THREEs don't have to be motivated, but they do need to question why they work so hard.

MOTIVATING THREES

- Engage their enthusiasm with a clear road to success. Define what success means to you or your organization so that THREEs can align themselves with your purpose and goals.
- Support them in being able to move quickly into action. Structure planning and review in between getting things done rather than all at the beginning. THREEs are impatient with too much delay.
- Provide a system of regular rewards and recognition for good performance. THREEs like to be given credit in a highly visible way.
- THREEs appreciate good role models. Provide confident, competent, and clear leadership.
- Help them to harness their competitive spirit to the over-

all success of the organization. A superior posture may alienate coworkers.

- THREES depend on their accomplishments for self-worth. Be sure to provide personal support when they encounter problems or make mistakes. Let them know that they are valued even when things aren't going as expected.

TIME MANAGEMENT

THREES live on professional time. They perform in a "think-do" pattern, by prioritizing and acting immediately without considering options. Private goals are less important than those that come to public attention. THREES believe people are hired to work, and therefore the more work done the better. Time is a finite resource that is allocated to production. They refine goals into separate tasks, each with an assigned time frame—for instance, large projects consist of sequential blocks of time, and each thirty-minute unit of time should produce a specific result.

A THREE newspaper columnist might think: "During lunch, I can finish the story based on yesterday's interview. Today's interview will take an hour, an hour and a half tops. The El Greco exhibit just opened, and it's on the way to the interview. I can see everything at the gallery in forty-five minutes. That will work. I should call the paper's arts editor to see what he needs on the exhibit for the Sunday edition. I can block out today's story in the cab ride back to the office, and still be able to meet my six o'clock deadline."

Inwardly, a Performer defines time as the space between now and the next deadline, but typically other tasks are brought into play before the first job is finished. Any time lags, or downtime, is frightening, because a Performer's identity is tied to public recognition. The inner sense of time is organized around the most pressing priority. Once focused, THREES barrel toward the goal in fast-forward. First is best, and quantity can be advertised to make it look more impressive than quality. Quantity is visible and unequivocal. It does not require the downtime and the time for introspection demanded for a quality product.

THREEs also relish a deadline, which, of course, is an objective measure of progress at any given time. There's an operating assumption that any time frame can be met with a clear priority and a THREE at the helm. Over time, THREEs have learned to hold back, because their rush of enthusiasm often upsets an established pace, leaving tracks on the backs of people who don't move along quickly.

> *When THREEs are running short of time, they mentally reassign available hours carved from other commitments. This manipulation of time either gets the job done or produces a result that was obviously thrown together in haste.*

Focused on public approval, Performers are generally outgoing and friendly except when they're interrupted at work. The day has been organized by allocating just enough time to accomplish a list of specific tasks, so they have a quick rise of impatience turning to fury if the schedule's delayed. They hate to wait in line or to have an associate delay progress. It's a standing joke among colleagues that THREEs will drive a twenty-mile detour and keep moving rather than face a ten-minute wait in stalled traffic. Action is a THREE's form of control, so a stall is not only wasteful, it's nerve-racking.

Performers are genuinely bewildered by colleagues who say they need time for themselves or who let their feelings interfere with the timetable. Similarly, they don't understand what could be fun about looking forward to a weekend of "nothing special." What do you have to show for time spent just hanging out? After all, from a THREE's perspective the net result will just be wasted time.

There's limited tolerance for people who don't finish projects on time, yet, ironically, performers waste time when they have to go back and redirect a faulty course of action. Rather than face the fear of failure stirred up by slowing down and attending to quality, THREES will circulate between several projects when they're stymied, projecting the image of a busy and successful worker. By hiding in activity, they set themselves up to fail if the work lacks rigor and has to be redone.

HELPING THREES MANAGE TIME

- Support THREES in slowing down when necessary. When their minds begin to race they can learn to say internally: "Speeding, this is speeding." Breathing deeply and relaxing the body will help establish a somewhat slower pace and lead to better results.

- Remind THREES that not everyone moves into action as quickly as they do. When you need other people on board, it's often necessary to slow down and listen to their concerns in order to achieve goals.

- THREES speed up and try to do more when they get panicked or overwhelmed. Help them understand that working harder or faster is not always the solution. Show them how to step back, locate the source of the problem, and make the necessary adjustments.

- The need to keep a successful image makes it hard for THREES to admit mistakes. It may seem easier to race on to the next task or shift to another project. Help them take the time to review errors and to value the learning process. Appreciate them as people, not just for what they produce.

- THREES tend to overcommit themselves and may spread themselves too thin. Help them be realistic about what they can do in order to forestall burnout and exhaustion.

NEGOTIATION

Even if a THREE sales rep has lost her major account, she'll present it as a partial victory. "Sure, we lost our biggest client, but look at all the things we learned from that experience. See how we all came together to try to keep them on board. Now we're focused and ready to make our next presentation."

Not surprisingly, THREEs can fake it at the bargaining table. They radiate suave preparedness and utter self-confidence. Image firmly in place, they project the message: "I can lead you to victory. Depend on me."

Unlike TWOs, who want personal attention, Performers want others to admire their results, rather than who they are as people. It doesn't matter whether other negotiators like them; what matters is respect for their performance. A THREE who negotiates legal contracts for a major California telecommunications company candidly puts it this way: "It's like playing to a jury. It doesn't matter if they like who I am, but they have to buy my client's pitch."

Master strategists, THREEs can shift position very quickly. Unlike Perfectionist Ones, who move in a clearly defined direction, or Boss Eights, who take over the session, THREEs can change course in mid-sentence. "Let me rephrase the option—put a different emphasis on the problem. You misunderstood my offer, I really said something else."

Like actors stepping into the mannerisms of a role, they are convincingly forceful, dramatically aloof, or pleasantly appealing, all in the interests of getting the job done. In negotiating with THREEs, stick with content. Don't be cowed by choreographed press releases and support materials such as endorsements from high-profile professionals. Just stick to content because you're getting very close to a weak point in their argument when THREEs resort to showy techniques of persuasion.

TRAINING AND DEVELOPMENT

THREEs like to learn on their feet. They have a limited tolerance for detailed learning and abstract theory, since their attention immediately moves from idea into action. In fact, they frequently develop their game plan while they're on their feet and talking. As a result, they have little tolerance for hours spent on background material, analysis, planning sessions, debriefing, and the like.

THREEs prefer hands-on practical problems to solve. They walk into a training session thinking: "If they do this right, I'll leave here with new skills that will help me do my job faster and better." Trainers should arrange manageable chunks of learning with a clearly defined end result. THREEs depend on concrete positive feedback, so each stage should be marked by an explicit public reward, such as listing their name in the company newsletter.

However, trainers need to remember how competitive THREEs are, and avoid any form of ranking during the sessions or THREEs will internally shift from concentrating on personal skills to outperforming others.

In general, THREEs are experiential learners. They like concrete goals and tools to achieve practical results. Stick with to-do formulas such as "If you face A, then do B." Stay away from abstract analysis, but emphasize how solution B can also be used to solve other problems the THREE might face.

Trainers should model a good use of technology in presentations. THREEs are strictly business and like to learn from people who match their own expectations of marketplace success.

Although they are quick studies, Performers do not learn well unless they feel confident of success. In a difficult phase, trainers should deliver criticism carefully, remembering that THREEs don't really hear negative feedback or respond to criticism. Reframe a miss as a partial hit or as a successful interim step to keep THREEs on task.

In group learning, frame the goal as a cooperative effort so that THREEs don't position themselves as the leader. If the goal is cooperation, then model cooperation as a task with a defined result. Trainers will have the impression that THREEs are ahead of the class, so make sure that quality control hasn't been sacrificed in the name of THREE-like efficiency.

THE CASE OF THE OVEREXTENDED THREE

The THREE entrepreneur never thought it would come to this. When she founded Super Sales four years ago, the business took off faster than she ever could have imagined. Three years of marathon selling have led to a company that now has $5 million in annual revenues. True, Super Sales has yet to record its first profit, but that, she knows, is just a matter of time. Every once in a while she even takes a moment to imagine what she'll wear when *Inc.* magazine asks her to pose as its Entrepreneur of the Year.

That pleasant daydream quickly becomes a nightmare as she reads the registered letter on her desk. It is signed by the Five CEO of the factory that produces 90 percent of the goods she sells. The key paragraphs jump out as if they were written in fluorescent ink.

> *Super Sales now owes us $1.3 million, most of which is more than 120 days overdue.*
>
> *We are planning to open a sales division. In an attempt to collect our debt, we offer to purchase the equity in your company by forgiving the $1.3 million in debt you owe us and converting Super Sales into our new northeastern division.*

TYPICAL INTERACTIONS

The THREE entrepreneur feels fury edged with panic as she rereads the note. She crumples the letter into a ball, then thinks twice about throwing it away and leaves it on her desk. She's invested her life force in Super Sales. She closed her first sale from the kitchen telephone, perfecting her pitch between cups of coffee. Now the noose is tightening.

They've probably been planning to create a sales division for over a year, she realizes, or they would have closed her down earlier. She pauses and then slams her hand down on the desk. "They kept extending me credit so I'd keep selling. In fact, I've been working for them for all this time!"

The insight stops her cold, but even now her mind drifts to her daily schedule. Anything is better than standing still. But now the next call—the proverbial next call, a salesperson's rudder through thick and thin—is meaningless. Why keep going if the results benefit someone else? Her body starts reacting. Her hands get sweaty and her heart pounds, but she still isn't sure what she's feeling. She has never been here before. Is this what failure feels like?

The phone rings. She regains equilibrium in the familiar gesture of reaching for the receiver and putting on a smile. She slips full tilt into Performer mode when she hears an old customer's voice. Incongruously, despite the devastating letter wadded on her desk, she closes a $50,000 order. Then reality registers: "Hold it! This deal is mine. They won't get it! I won't surrender *my* company."

Riding on her anger and the energy of the order, the entrepreneur dials the Five CEO's private number at the manufacturing company. As usual, she gets his secretary, and she struggles to keep the edge out of her voice. In the past, she was invariably put on hold, but this time her call goes right through.

Sliding into his customary conversational tone, the Five CEO hopes this won't bog down. He takes on these tricky negotiations because he can handle emotion with professional neutrality. Besides, he thinks as he waits for his secretary to transfer the call, the decision to make this acquisition was not a particularly difficult one.

Buying Super Sales is a practical marketplace decision. The benefits of vertical integration had been obvious for some time. Personally, he doesn't care for the THREE entrepreneur. Their interactions have been strictly one-way affairs. She can back him into a corner even on the telephone. He never has time to think because she moves so fast, and it pleases him to think she won't be pressuring him for credit extensions any longer.

In a detached, even voice, he comes right to the point after saying good morning. "Are you calling in reference to my letter?"

On the other end of the line, the embattled THREE strategizes: "What's his opening move going to be? I just closed a fifty-thousand-dollar order and he wants to dump me. He's probably delighted I'm now working without pay."

But in fact the Observer Five isn't gloating. To him, this is a business matter. The current arrangement is no longer feasible and they have to negotiate another. The equity buyout is a reasonable solution. Her company owes his firm more than $1 million, after all, and he wants to move into retail.

The THREE's voice is neither cooperative nor compliant. She has decided to be absolutely direct: "Why did you keep me dangling? So I'd keep running on hope? I created this company. I've just made another fifty-thousand-dollar sale. If I was selling for you, how much commission would that be?"

The Five's legal training kicks in when he hears the innuendo of unfair trade practices. For the first time he realizes this equity buyout could be more complicated—and costly—than he anticipated. The Performer's voice is rankling with the prickly edge of litigation. He knows the figures, he is aware that her net worth is negative, but she is sending a message about all the work she has done in developing her client roster. Can she stick a price tag on goodwill? How much is her reputation worth?

The CEO's long pause brings the Performer THREE into focus. She feels her argument click into place.

She aims her comments straight into the CEO's fears. "I'll have to think about the letter. I need legal advice." She feels it's best to leave him hanging. "I'll get back to you when I'm ready."

The Observer Five immediately tells his secretary to hold all calls. He needs time to assimilate this disturbing news, to reposition the negotiations. Suddenly the whole deal is in question. Has he overlooked something? How much cash do you pay for the goodwill associated with someone's name, when their company is technically insolvent? He is in nebulous territory. He believed he heard frustrated hope in her voice. Is his company accountable for leading her on? Does she really have a case? He suddenly imagines them both in court, flanked by lawyers, arguing the finer points of intent.

THE TIDE TURNS

The CEO feels emotionally blackmailed in having to account for intangibles such as goodwill. He wishes the entrepreneur would drop this emotionality and get on with her life. After all, the buyout is nothing personal.

From her side, galvanized by rage, the entrepreneur can't wait to get moving. Within minutes her legal appointments are in place. She wants an immediate resolution to save her professional status, while the Five retreats from confrontation, wanting a way out.

When there's nothing left to do but wait, the Performer

THREE reviews her resources: "Could I go to a competitor with my track record and client list as a bargaining chip?" That would threaten the CEO.

She loves running a company—her company—and is furious at being used and discarded, but is it worth the tremendous effort it would take to gear up again? Is she wasting energy to prove something to herself? To show the CEO up?

She is proud of her achievements, but work is her whole life. Her needs rarely enter the picture. Does she honestly want to continue to sacrifice twenty-four hours a day to keep the company going? Years ago that image drove her; now she isn't so sure. She can't remember when she last had a vacation.

She makes a cup of coffee and sits down. To be honest, she doesn't know what she wants. But she does know what she doesn't want. She realizes that she doesn't want to go it alone any longer.

Priorities are also suddenly prominent in the Five's thinking. The entrepreneur has actually been very successful in her blunt, pragmatic way. The point about her long-term client connections was especially telling. He imagines her taking customers to a restaurant and spending hours on the road, all the while making calls on the car phone. Although he finds her intrusive, her customers obviously respond well. People like her are a sales magnet; she has a kind of energy that he knows he's missing—and that is a business asset.

The word *asset* sticks in his mind. She has parlayed her personality into a career asset.

Now he understands the reasoning behind a suit. All those hours for so little return. He wonders if her motivation would die if she worked for someone else. Thinking about the Performer's feelings has softened his detachment. He can't afford to ignore her efforts, and unexpectedly, he doesn't want to.

Knowing he's on the right track, and personally unattached to the outcome, he switches on the Dictaphone and composes a memo to his executive team recommending that "as part of the equity buyout, we negotiate a role for the entrepreneur."

The key sentence of the memo reads: "Her value as a major sales asset is proven by client goodwill and by her personal reputation in the field, as evidenced by building sales to five million dollars annually. We should work hard to keep her."

RESOLUTION

The Performer resolves a key THREE issue—self-deception—when she evaluates her position honestly. Strongly identified with professional status, she has become her work. The shock of the letter helps her sort out appearances from real needs, helping her realize that she loves the image of running the company, but she also wants a life apart from her career.

The message from her side of the negotiations has to do with vindicating her efforts. She probably would have earned more on commissions over the years had she worked for someone else, but building name recognition attracted her THREE-like entrepreneurial spirit.

Now, instead of jumping quickly into litigation, or repeating another uphill start-up, she can choose the CEO's more satisfying offer. All of this depends on her ability to distinguish between what she feels and how she wants to look in the eyes of others.

Self-observation
A good way for the entrepreneur to stay on track would be to ask herself: "For whom do I work? For myself? For what I believe in? Or to look good in the eyes of others?"

By making it a point during each day to ask, "What am I feeling?" she can discover the difference between emotionally satisfying work and working to enhance a public image.

Point Four: The Romantic

Alias: **Muse, Elitist, Connoisseur, the Special Person**

Motto	*Fill the half-empty glass.*
Mental Model	*The grass seems greener on the other side of the fence.*
Lens of Perception	*Something is missing.*
Way of Sorting Information	*Unconsciously embellishing what you can't have. By comparison, what you do have seems pale.*
Blind Spot	*Taking satisfaction in what's here.*
Growth Edge	*Finding simple happiness.*
Spiritual Path	*Appreciating the ordinary.*
Vice	*Envy—must have what others have to be happy.*
Virtue	*Equanimity—balancing emotional highs and lows.*
Inspired By	*Authentic emotional connection.*
Managerial Style	*Flair and a distinctive touch. It's not worth doing if it's been done before: "We're not just making a new computer, we're creating an outrageously great machine." "This is not merely an ad campaign. These ads will change the way people feel."*
Appearance to Others	*Ranges from tasteful and special to flamboyant and bizarre. Never anything ordinary.*
Typical Conflicts	*Hurt feelings about being misunderstood or underappreciated for making a special contribution.*
One-Minute Resolution	*If you are a FOUR, remember it's all right to be one of many.*

The Signals FOURS Send

Positive	FOURs understand others and their feelings. They are willing to stick when the going gets rough.
Negative	Others are not enough. The FOUR is still disappointed and still needs more.
Mixed	Other people look more interesting when they're distant, less so when they're available.
Security Response at Point One	FOURs achieve clarity of vision and precision in follow-through without emotional encumbrance.
Stress/Risk Response at Point Two	FOURs give themselves away to gain approval.
Work Best In	Jobs in which creativity and individuality are prized. They gravitate toward distinctive work—advertising, performance arts, product design.
Have Problems Working In	Jobs that have rigid, impersonal structures, or where the work is repetitive: the military, insurance, warehousing. FOURs don't work well with better-paid, more popular coworkers.
Where Business Wants Its FOURS	Onstage; creating in the lab or at the drafting table; modeling for Vogue.

ARE YOU A FOUR?

You want a career that expresses your feelings in a meaningful way. Why shouldn't work be an avenue for self-expression? You don't need to change the world, but you must have an emotional connection to what you do and to the people around you.

Ironically, that same drive for human contact makes you aware of what's missing at work. You can compete well, reaping the rewards of salary, status, and job advancement. But once the high drama of stretching for success has passed, it all seems like selling out for superficial prosperity.

The people you work with, however, may see the situation differently. They see you as a dynamic force on the upswing when there's something to prove, but then, just when success is in reach, you turn your attention elsewhere and sabotage their expectations.

To you, those same coworkers seem willing to settle for so little. Why continue working along a path that's already been traveled? Why not produce material that's never been seen before? Yes, success was worth striving for when it was distant and interesting, but it's the chase that's appealing.

Jorge, a well-respected art director known for his individualistic vision, shares the FOUR perspective. His design firm has been approached by the communications department of an expanding Fortune 500 company to produce an annual report "designed to drive our competition nuts." Early on, they decided they had to have Jorge's team, the city's premier design firm, do the report, and they begged and pleaded to have the corporation allocate them enough money.

The money is finally committed and preliminary negotiations have already been concluded. In this meeting to discuss the particulars, the small talk has gone well, and it is clear within seconds that the art director both understands that the company wants their annual report to mirror the look of their high-tech products and also has three or four ideas that can make the report look even better than they ever imagined.

"Great, so we're in total agreement," says the vice president of communications. "There is just one thing, Jorge. We don't want the report to look too slick. You know, we wouldn't want it to be overdesigned."

If you aren't watching carefully, you might not notice that Jorge's face goes from smiling to frozen mask and then back to smiling in the time it takes the vice president to say "overdesigned."

"I understand completely," Jorge says. "I think we are quite clear about where we stand."

Jorge gathers his papers.

To the group he says: "Thank you so much for thinking of our firm. I'll fax you a formal proposal in a couple of days."

To himself, he says: "There is no way on earth we are going to work for these clowns. 'Overdesigned...too slick.' If they offer this kind of interference, they can go hire another firm."

Without intending to, Jorge automatically bristles when his creativity is questioned. He is personally committed to elegance and innovation, and his firm's reputation is built on signature creations. Only an idiot would suppose that his designs could be modified for the conventional buyer. But if he's so convinced, why is he defensive?

HOW FOURS SORT INFORMATION

In the spiritual traditions that see type as an important facet of human development, FOURs are traditionally known as "monks of melancholy mind," not because they sigh and cry, but because their attention drifts to what's missing. Jorge is riveted by the single qualification that he receives, and that small part of the whole picture distracts him from the pleasure of accomplishment he deserves. After all, the communications department begged for enough money to hire him. Most people would be more than satisfied.

Spiritually, the melancholy-minded are prone to long for what they are missing, tantalized by the satisfaction that seems just out of reach. Yet Jorge doesn't see himself as envious. After all, he's at the top of his field, and other designers are likely to envy his success.

But if you saw the world through Jorge's lens of perception, you'd see an enormously magnified impression of the benefits that others enjoy. It seems as if they are satisfied, while in comparison he feels denied. This preoccupation with the missing ingredient for happiness undercuts his self-esteem, reduces pleasure, and makes him hypersensitive to criticism. But all of this is happening in his head, unbeknownst to the Fortune 500 company that wants to hire him.

Focused on the discrepancy between the full quota of encouragement he expected and the small qualification that he heard, Jorge's mental sorting system kicks in, and now he feels disinterested in the project and overly concerned about artistic censorship. Unlike Performer Threes, who believe that the world rewards a champion, or Epicure Sevens, who see a perpetually bright future, Jorge anticipates the possibility of loss precisely at the peak of success.

FOURS AT WORK

FOURS excel in work where creative expression counts, and this has always been true of Jorge. His urge to express himself in unique and unusual ways is rooted in feeling different from other people. He remembers loss and abandonment in childhood, being a bystander to the pleasures that others enjoyed. But standing out against that early background of sadness, he also remembers the pure relief of having this intense inner drama seen and understood by others.

So, like other FOURS, Jorge found a way to touch the hearts of others. Unlike Giver Twos, who adjust their persona to be pleasing, or Performer Threes, who grab people's attention with a bill-board of accomplishments, FOURs learn how to captivate the people who appreciate their creativity so that they will respond from the heart.

Jorge has certainly noticed that a great deal of time and energy has been expended to hire him. He wants the validation of being seen as unique and different from the competition, but because his emotions are invested in his product, he can't have some commercially minded v.p. tampering with his feelings.

If you're a FOUR, you'll feel called to emotionally intense lines of work. You want to participate at the junctures of life where people come close to real feelings, and you're painfully aware of the discrepancy between your own emotionality and the business mask you wear at work. If you're stuck in a routine position, you'll relate to the feeling of leading a double life, like this senior manager within one of the world's largest oil companies:

> *I thoroughly enjoy my work, but the unrelenting niceness of this white-picket-fence environment drives me crazy. It's not that I'm interested in some big spill-your-guts encounter session, but I do keep waiting for someone to shout, "Hey, read the papers! There's real pain in the world, and I'm suffering, too."*
>
> *I keep waiting for someone to get real—real ecstasy, real joy, a jolt of something really human.*
>
> *Why are they playing Muzak when I want opera?*

Of course, to be successful in his job, our senior manager has learned to perform in the Three-like style valued by corporate America. But unlike Performer Threes, who suspend their emotions to get the job done, FOURs are dedicated to work that provides a productive conduit for their feelings.

KEEP THIS IN MIND

FOURs on teams dislike being treated "the same as," so if you're on a team, try not to compare yourself to others. Find a domain that you can make beautiful so that your efforts are seen. The trick to good teamwork is in aligning yourself with the aesthetic or meaningful aspects of the operation. Hook your feelings to the beneficial outcome, and challenge yourself to find a unique approach to ordinary matters. You, alone among all the types, can remind the people in your workplace of a higher vision, or coach your team to elevate the ordinary.

> *Mood, elegance, passion, and panache—don't settle for less.*

Be aware that the team sees you as inconsistent when you cave in to moods or suffer over small oversights. The manager probably just forgot that today is your work anniversary and you're due for a raise. He didn't mean to insult you. The fact that your name was spelled wrong in the program probably has a lot more to do with the typist than it does with the way the company feels about you.

Try to separate your feelings about coworkers from their actual talent. You can work effectively as a team without being friends. Shoot for the best possible outcome, regardless of whose ideas are featured. When your ideas are questioned, you are not being rejected as a person.

Your spiritual path involves appreciating the ordinary—a real feat when you feel surrounded by mediocrity. Unlike Nines, who feel supported by the system, or Ones, who take pleasure in refining a system, FOURs are deadened by the ordinary.

But you can also benefit from the system. Your inner climate may be constantly changing, but clear guidelines and consistent, impartial feedback will balance your moods. Learn to observe and name your feelings—"This is sadness; I am feeling sad now"—not to make sadness go away or force happiness to come, but to separate yourself from your feelings rather than act them out.

FOURS typically get confused between productive creativity and just plain moodiness. Is your emotional lodestone accurate? Were you attracted to hiring a certain assistant because he was good or because you felt good on the day you interviewed him? Is the project going sour because you're in a bad mood? For sure, creativity expresses itself through imagery, intuition, and the feelings surrounding a project—but vision has to be balanced with the practicalities of details and deadlines.

Your emotional nature leads you to suppose that visionary ideas spring from the heart, but remember Jorge, the sought-after designer—he stands to lose the exposure that could boost his company's portfolio to the next level, and he has no idea that his emotional lens of perception inaccurately reflects events at the Fortune 500 company that wants to hire him. But Jorge could also observe himself, instead of acting out of habit. He would be right

SECURITY AND STRESS

Dynamics of Change for Point Four

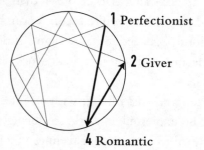

in refusing work that restricts his creative scope, but think how his talent could flower if he knew how his mind worked.

It's important to practice consistency. Be here now. Bring yourself back to the present task at hand. Notice when you start to long for things that are missing, and pay equal attention to what you already have. Take an inventory of your blessings, the ordinary daily treasures that you couldn't bear to lose. There's beauty in chopping wood and pleasure in carrying water if you're at home to enjoy it.

SECURITY RESPONSE AT POINT ONE

Your creative leanings inevitably trigger feelings, symbolic imagery, and a highly personal relationship to your work—all of which lends itself to chaotic follow-through. Generating concepts is relatively easy, but making those ideas practical requires organization, discrimination, and a clear course of action.

By focusing through a One-like lens, order emerges from chaos and practicality guides the process. Projects get finished and concepts are marketable when you adopt the editorial precision and right vs. wrong thinking characteristic of Perfectionists.

When you feel secure in your work, you see there's a right way and a wrong way to proceed, rather than relying on a constantly shifting inner world of impressions. A One-like task focus releases you from self-absorbed emotion and frees you to refine the product.

Paradoxically, FOURs often turn critical during periods of well-being. Now you're secure enough to pick at problems you previously ignored. Small irritants suddenly become intolerable; the details of the project don't work. How can a sensitive person bear it?

You're used to living with an intense inner drama that often can't be expressed at work, so during periods of calm and security, learn to express your feelings in a methodical manner so that others can understand your point of view. In security, you get into gear by pacing your work, balancing your interests, and finding emotional equanimity.

STRESS/RISK RESPONSE AT POINT TWO

Your usual FOUR-like defenses kick in at the first sign of stress. Feelings of grief and abandonment surface, and your emotions can drive you into a deep hole. Since you can't stay down indefinitely, this mood eventually leads you to seek out others, and you move to the Giver Two's perspective.

Here you deliberately challenge sadness by reaching out to others and revitalizing an interest in projects and teams. To the extent that reaching out is a maneuver to ditch depression, there is the possibility that you will overextend under stress, indiscriminately giving away time and energy. The best outcome for you is to make the alliances you need, pace your schedule, and enjoy the results of your outreach.

The low side of your stress response shows up as working too hard in a frantic attempt to stay emotionally engaged. There's too much going on, and none of it is efficient, with loose ends everywhere and dramatic last-minute saves.

But once you're out of the deep hole of sadness, eventually the new level of activity can settle into a productive schedule. Much of the chaos surrounding the FOUR work style has to do with inattention to practical bottom-line details of time, costs, and managing other people. Heart is great, and you lead with your heart, but you must learn that emotional neutrality won't derail your creative process.

How Others See fours

COMMUNICATION STYLE

FOURs radiate emotional intensity. If they're putting on a workshop, they want to produce a learning experience that's never been seen before, one that generates meaningful ideas instead of being "just another session." Even in giving a technical presentation, they can draw the audience beyond the ordinary into a realm where research data is just the springboard to dramatic heroism or a tragic story. Rather than simply stating the facts, they might reveal having to probe beneath the facts and figures to "the underlying significance" or the data's "crucial importance." They become a character woven into the story of relentlessly searching for—and finally finding—a missing ingredient, implying that the data is secondary to this human drama of persistence.

The audience gets both what FOURs think and how they feel about the material. It's like a mystery to be solved and the FOUR is deeply involved as the one solving it. The topic is simply a stage from which to evoke feelings. Why not make theater out of cutting-edge graphics or an intriguing interactive component? Why bother giving a mundane, predictable workshop that anybody could give? Unlike Threes, who demonstrate goals and results, FOURs pull on the heartstrings of an audience, speaking directly to those in the room who are open to an emotional encounter.

> *The content of a talk can be predictable, even boring, but a FOUR's intense demeanor creates an atmosphere of special disclosure.*

The effect on an audience can be mesmerizing. Romantics are famous for developing highly original presentation formats designed to draw attention, but their communication style oscillates between "This is distinctive!" and a strong hint of resentment: "Can't you grasp the distinctiveness of what I've done?" FOURs find ways of inserting themselves into the topic of discussion, because they want to be seen as a living soul behind the facade of abstract, disembodied information, so the message reads, "See me beneath the veneer of what I do—see *me*."

Romantics have a natural ability to position products as unique, special, and for the discriminating buyer. However, the same need to be special has them overreacting if they feel unappreciated. A presentation may come across as self-absorbed because they lead with their feelings. An audience's reaction is polarized between those who feel talked down to and others who feel uplifted. As people listen, they feel seduced and then rejected. They're attracted by the inviting format, and then feel dumped if they have questions or reservations.

FOURs also have to guard against self-sabotage. They typically rise to meet a challenging event or to promote a product they believe in and then blow an important—albeit simple—in-house talk "because it's been done before."

Nonverbal Communication
Romantics favor unique elegance in clothing and carriage, expressing the fact that they're different and slightly ahead of the current style. They may also convey a melancholy tone, all of which creates a dramatic initial impression. It's not specifically what gets said, but their tone indicates that something is missing, that they're not quite enthusiastic, not quite committed. "If only" comes up a lot. "If only the campaign were a bit more original." "If only we were known as the best, instead of merely the best known."

But feeling statements instantly get their attention. Eye contact is prolonged, and FOURs literally lean toward people who are passionate about their work. The topic itself might not interest the Romantic. What really matters is that someone cares deeply.

Listeners may feel pressured to match a FOUR's moods or feel somehow less sensitive, less interesting, less profound. It may be hard to give FOURs honest feedback. Some people give them high marks for emotional sincerity. Others may soften their feedback for fear of hurting a Romantic's feelings, and a few will simply withdraw from the nonverbal demand to be emotional.

COMMUNICATING WITH FOURS

- Romantics need a feeling connection as well as intellectual agreement. Provide personal support and warmth.
- Expect a FOUR's attention to come and go. Focus on results and task efficiency rather than constancy.
- Acknowledge the importance of their personal reactions and feelings, but help them come back to the facts and logic of the situation. Encourage them to mediate or set limits on their responses to others.
- FOURs can confuse evaluation with personal rejection. Support the person separately from the performance. Help them see the value of genuine criticism.
- Stand fast in the face of a FOUR's emotional reactions or upset. Simply hearing the FOUR out is usually the effective response. Don't react too much or shift your position. Have confidence that the crisis will pass.
- Be firm when FOURs seem willing to risk all for an innovative idea. Recognize their enthusiasm, but insist on examining the consequences and stick to procedure when appropriate.

MOTIVATION

FOURs are motivated by special attention from those in the field whom they respect. The best possible incentive is a personal communication from someone well known. They can work alone for long periods, producing a creative product that in their minds is energized by an association with a supportive mentor.

Romantics can bring good ideas to fruition without popular backing. It's the task itself that has merit, rather than the superficial recognition accorded to trendy products. The trick will be to stay motivated when those same ideas become mainstream and more commonly available. FOURs are motivated by mystique, by the unusual product, and will need to hold ground to receive deserved recognition when their ideas move into the marketplace.

For example, Romantics working in investment banking will be drawn to areas of the profession that bring out genuine feelings: funding a new company that is dedicated to a bold, creative vision will be inspiring. By comparison, the humdrum activities associated with helping another local municipality to build a high school feels maddening.

Their high-voltage originality and their insistence on doing things differently brings much-needed depth to decision making and encourages others to develop their own experimental ideas. However, motivated by the conviction that they have authentic emotional depth, FOURs are frequently disappointed by people who appear to have settled for a tinny, shallow existence.

When a FOUR is denied recognition for sensitivity and creative effort, the hunger for meaningful contact can lead to burnout. Then he feels like his is the only authentic voice among phonies, and when the work that was once infused with intensity becomes routine, then the rewards of work become reduced to a paycheck.

In burnout, a FOUR's attention becomes fixated on the shallowness of others. Caught in a cycle of wanting contact and feeling disconnected, FOURs swing between reaching out and aloof withdrawal. At their lowest, they are motivated by survival needs and the conviction that they have more value than those around them.

But such periods can also produce the right conditions for discovering work that really matters. That discovery allows Romantics to build reliable creative outlets, and once again they become energized.

To grow, FOURs must be aware when loss of meaning obscures the real value of work. The larger task is to return to where they have already been: those moments when emotional satisfaction made work worthwhile. A first step is to notice when melancholy first rises. When it does, FOURs should refocus by taking stock of the meaningful relationships they have already established and being grateful for them.

MOTIVATING FOURS

- FOURs seek meaning and authenticity in their work. Encourage them to find ways to accomplish their tasks that draw on creativity and insight.
- Value their unique contributions and style, while bringing attention to practical results. Reinforce genuine achievement while allowing room to express their individuality.
- Appreciate them for the aesthetic flair that they can bring to reports and presentations.
- Give FOURs special attention. Having a personal connection is very important for them to maintain involvement.
- Allow them to use an experiential approach to their work that incorporates interactions with others.
- FOURs combine emotional intuition with intellectual

analysis. Encourage their participation and feedback, drawing on both of these capacities.

TIME MANAGEMENT

FOURs live in mythic time, a place where grand-scale happenings are backlit in purple instead of being bound by time clocks, spreadsheets, or reports.

FOURs mark time. They wait for deeper themes to emerge in a business-as-usual meeting, for an original concept to appear out of nowhere, or for an idea whose time has finally come. Romantics know that destiny shows itself through timely coincidence, so they will ponder, "Why is this unique group seated at this particular meeting? Why this venture? Why now?"

It takes time to think about significant matters and then to reexamine them from different perspectives. To a FOUR, clock time is not as important as glimpsing the course of destiny behind conventional timetables.

All the types appear in every occupation, but they use time differently. For a FOUR manufacturer, time drags by during the tedious chore of determining exactly what a company has in its warehouse. Mentally the assignment's finished once the intensity of the decision to buy is over. Writing the report and justifying the numbers seem to take forever. On the other hand, this same FOUR typically moves triumphantly from deadline to deadline in an intense acquisition battle. He does not waver during the heightened scenes or emotional confrontation—such as a screaming match with a CEO who wants to use a more aggressive accounting position to make his numbers look better. But anticlimactic days sitting at the computer fiddling with the spreadsheet can feel defeating.

Procrastination for FOURs is tied to avoiding the ordinariness of a job. "What's the point of doing another routine acquisitions search? I've been here before. I deserve better than this."

> *Romantics need constantly to renew interest in their responsibilities, or they risk being washed out in the gritty stream of conventional time commitments. They often feel dragged down by matters that "simply aren't worth their time."*

This mind-set causes FOURs to fall prey to building emotional tension that culminates in theatrical procrastination with major on-the-job consequences. For example, a FOUR's feelings could keep him from completing a major piece of work that a client was counting on before the end of the fiscal quarter. Rather than feeling demeaned by daily drudgery, successful FOURs have found ingenious solutions for tackling the mundane. Romantics can be remarkably sophisticated in sensing the presence of deeper meaning, but that talent relies on being fully focused in the present.

HELPING FOURS MANAGE TIME

- FOURs have a very subjective sense of time. Help them remember clock time, schedules, and deadlines.
- Remind FOURs of the importance of structure and consistency. Set appointments and agree to consequences for lateness and absenteeism.
- FOURs can become impatient with mundane tasks. Help break a cycle of procrastination by finding creative solutions. Try saying: "If you do this for me, I'll do that for you."
- Take the time to reinforce the FOUR as a person, regardless of performance. Promote the project's special value in the eyes of others. Social recognition is very important.
- Expect high levels of involvement and a fast pace when goals seem distant and are romanticized, but a slowing down or disinterest near completion. Compensate by

providing special attention or recognition from important people.

NEGOTIATION

Romantics may come to the negotiating table like an actor in a play. They are often magnetic presenters with a graceful, even soulful style. None of this is calculated, it is simply their way of getting their message across.

You gain a FOUR's respect by treating them as individuals, separate from their role within the negotiation. They know they're special people who are playing a part to get a specific job done, so praise their abilities, even if you disagree with their argument.

This is where a face-saving solution really works, as FOURs need to maintain a unique public image. Even if you feel what they're asking for is way out of line, it will help to say, "I see why you're attracted to that position. I see the point you're trying to make."

Oddly, it's important to stay emotionally calm during any storms in the negotiation. FOURs will one-up you if you express hurt or anger. They've been hurt too and can get much more angry or joyful than you can, which shifts the discussion from the topic itself to how everybody feels about it.

> *Generosity and praise are great allies in adversarial settings.*

If someone demonstrates talent, it's not manipulative to say, "I see why you devote your skills and talents to this issue." Or to treat an opponent like a champion, jump the net and say, "Congratulations," regardless of who won the point. FOURs find it hard to collaborate or compromise until they receive personal recognition, but your validation opens the way to genuine give-and-take. The acknowledged FOUR can better hear your position, because you've noted their worth, moving negotiations smoothly past the roadblock of conflicting personalities.

TRAINING AND DEVELOPMENT

Trainers must remember that, more than any other type, FOURs are aware of the ambiance in the room. They are unusually sensitive to environment and setting. Romantics cringe at the usual barren training room or commercial hotel setting.

Still, what's hanging on the walls doesn't matter as much as what's happening inside them. For example, FOURs will be watching to see if the instructor is actually interacting with the class. FOURs want a trainer who listens to students, and they know the difference between genuine interest and phony catchwords about caring. More than any other type, they need to be drawn into a group and bonded with other participants.

FOURs are people with elite standards. They want a quality training, rather than an off-the-shelf package, and will travel, spending time, money, and energy to make sure they obtain a distinctive perspective. They will put out this kind of effort because they are inspired by originality and by people who dare to bring an innovative touch to the workplace.

They also want to know what graduates of the course are doing out in the field. Is there a personal connection between what is being taught and how graduates feel about their role in the workplace?

Trainers should treat participants as individuals, each with his own learning curve. In addition to measuring proficiency in the material being covered, they need to ask feeling questions ("How do you feel about...?") to discover each participant's reaction to the tasks at hand.

Two things to remember about FOURs: Don't cheer them on if they feel stuck, and don't insist that they push immediately toward a goal. Time constraints are real, but FOURs learn best when they hear, "Stay with your feelings for a while. Let's come back to this when you're ready."

And remember, FOURs hate being compared with other people. It feels demeaning to be the same as others, and devastating to be less.

THE CASE OF THE FIRED FOUR

It could not have been more unsettling. Out of the blue, it seems, family-owned Kramer and Co., a midwestern dairy concern with $18 million in sales, has been acquired by one of its national competitors.

Kramer's 125 employees are thunderstruck. Many of them have worked for the son of the founder for decades, and now, without an explanation beyond "Times are changing and we all have to keep up with the latest trends," they find themselves suddenly reporting to the "corporate vice president of finance— midwestern division" of a firm they used to battle with every day.

The Seven corporate v.p. is vaguely aware that the employees are unhappy, but that is not his primary concern. After all, he has been in this situation before. He knows his first task is to chop out the dead wood from the newly acquired firm. Then he will put in the financial and other reporting systems that will be in sync with those at corporate.

He's a whiz at these kinds of reorganizations. They're where he's made his mark. This is a relatively small company, well run, with no visible systems problems. He doesn't anticipate he'll be here longer than one month, six weeks at the most.

Many of the staff, including an accountant who's put in twelve years with the dairy company, received the news that they were going to be fired directly from the v.p. He tells the FOUR accountant she's being let go, not because her work isn't top-drawer, but because her skills are no longer needed in light of the merger. A data entry clerk will do the routine stuff at the dairy. The rest of her job will be handled at corporate. He closes their fifteen-minute conversation, a monologue really, by saying, "With your experience, obvious ability, and the recommendations we will be giving you, you'll have no trouble finding another position."

On receiving news of her dismissal, the FOUR feels stunned, devastated, and personally devalued. Although aware of the reasons for the pink slip, the blow to her self-esteem is still wounding.

Given the logical grounds for her dismissal, she has nowhere to go for relief, but her emotions are overpowering. She knows the takeover has affected others with redundant skills, so she hasn't been singled out. Still, her overwhelming reaction is: "How can they make me leave? I've built significant friendships here."

She feels flooded by her coworkers' confusion and reaches out to share their feelings. That wave of emotion causes her to remember the best moments of a job that no longer exists. Her fury rises. She didn't realize the strength of her feelings about her job until it was in jeopardy. She didn't realize the extent of her coworkers' pain.

Focused on the takeover drama, she rises to the occasion to become a spokesperson for the dismissed. Her basic message: "How could this situation have been handled in such a callous manner, without a ripple of warning? This is inhuman."

TYPICAL INTERACTIONS

Fueled by the shame of her dismissal, the Romantic FOUR rallies support for a confrontation. Well dressed and in control, she appears in the corporate v.p.'s temporary office, successfully tamping down her vindictive rage. With logical precision she requests a formal meeting in the name of those fired. The subtext, however, is equally clear: "How could you? You must acknowledge us. This is your fault."

The FOUR accountant's presence shocks the Seven corporate v.p., interrupting his racing thoughts about the reorganization. Her dismissal, like so many others he has conducted, seemed like a necessary step, without real emotional consequences. There are good, solid financial reasons for the layoffs. He didn't cast blame on the employees, and didn't he praise this very accountant's abilities?

The jarring reality of the accountant standing in his office makes him think: "Could this interrupt our reorganization schedule? I'm not responsible for her feelings. She's overreacting."

The Romantic mentally slows down the moment to savor fully the significance of the v.p.'s reaction: She is being heard, and the Seven v.p. is clearly uncomfortable. Aware that she cannot change his decision, the accountant seriously considers taking the case to court as a matter of principle.

"Don't you know the effect this is having?" she asks the v.p. The accountant wants him to recognize her human value.

The vice president, an unwilling authority figure, doesn't see the impact of his own position. Both he and the woman on the other side of his desk want closure, but for different reasons: She wants to leave feeling validated, and he wants a quick way out. Unwittingly, each has triggered a moment of truth for the other. The Romantic accountant is escalating her emotions, heading toward a punitive lawsuit, while the Epicure v.p. is trying to avoid pain.

THE TIDE TURNS

Because he is so focused on the pending reorganization, the Seven v.p. has been oblivious to the pain the takeover is causing employees at the dairy. The accountant has forced him to recognize the problem.

While the accountant knows she will not be able to sway the v.p.'s decision, she still feels victimized. His inattention justifies her outrage. She can handle the dismissal, but she won't be diminished. The Epicure now sees the blind spot in his unfolding plans; these dismissals could leave a turbulent wake, and he must send a reassuring message to the remaining employees.

"I'll ask corporate human resources to make outplacement services part of the severance package," he tells her. "I'll send a companywide memo to those left behind informing them of the first-class assistance we're providing to laid-off personnel."

RESOLUTION

When a FOUR's special contribution is lumped together with everyone else's, they feel shattered. Tending to dramatize emotional crisis, this FOUR sees her contribution to the company in terms of her unique emotional offerings to her colleagues and the significant friendships she has developed. Her memories are of people she will miss, rather than of her job performance.

Because she always searches to find the best in what's missing, her attention fixates on the desirability of the job as it disappears. The dismissal strikes at her FOUR-like feelings of deprivation, prompting her to contemplate legal action as a matter of principle.

The Seven's major shortcoming is that emotional displays play straight into his type's desire for pain avoidance. He does not want to think in terms of the personal pain brought on by the dismissals—after all, there was nothing personal in the actions he took—so he looks for a safe exit.

Yet, if the v.p. does not address her disappointment, the Romantic will turn an unpleasant situation volatile, and dramatically up the ante.

FOURs often feel like they're living in the closet at work because emotions are seen as inappropriate. Yet emotions are as much a part of our work lives as rational thinking. Now the Seven v.p. can place just a little attention on the FOUR's needs, allowing him the chance to "do the right thing." The result is that two people could walk away from a potentially lose-lose situation with a good chunk of something they each need.

Self-observation

When FOURs are in high drama, they can learn to pause, observe themselves, and ask: "What do I really need? What would give me satisfaction?"

A lawsuit wouldn't satisfy the accountant, because she would not win, there are no grounds for litigation. But she does need a hearing. She needs a place to air her feelings, to steady the pitch and roll of dramatic moods, so she can leave her job in peace.

Point Five: The Observer

Alias: **The Thinker, Philosopher, Sage, Witness, Analyst**

Motto	*Knowledge is power.*
Mental Model	*Reality can be grasped by pure reason.*
Lens of Perception	*How much time and energy will this take?*
Way of Sorting Information	*Discontinuous thinking.*
Blind Spot	*Unaware of existing abundance.*
Growth Edge	*Showing up to participate with people.*
Spiritual Path	*Developing emotional and body-based intelligence.*
Vice	*Avarice (withholding).*
Virtue	*Nonattachment, able to freely give and take.*
Inspired By	*Omniscience—the quality of all-knowing.*
Managerial Style	*Controls from a distance. Often paired with a more aggressive type, especially front-bench Performer Threes, or people person Twos. Models comprehensive analysis.*
Appearance to Others	*Content-focused. An emotional blank screen. Silently standing at the edge of the crowd.*
Typical Conflicts	*Lack of accessibility. FIVES can frustrate types who need emotional reinforcement like TWOS and FOURS.*
One-Minute Resolution	*FIVES can protect their time and energy by knowing exactly how long a meeting will last, who will attend, and whether you're expected to hang around afterward.*

The Signals FIVEs Send

Positive	*Scholarly, knowing and thoughtful. Dispassionate and calm in crisis.*
Negative	*FIVEs want privacy, making others feel rejected. They send signals of intellectual superiority and arrogance.*
Mixed	*FIVEs make you wonder if you're welcome, or whether you're intruding on their privacy.*
Security Response at Point Eight	*Here they are tough-minded and direct, speaking their minds instead of withholding.*
Stress/Risk Response at Point Seven	*Here they paradoxically reach out to others—looking friendly but inwardly frightened.*
Work Best In	*Jobs where there's time to think. Research and development, libraries, night shift at the computer lab.*
Have Problems Working In	*Jobs that require open competition or confrontation: the trading desk at a brokerage firm. Fast-paced interpersonal jobs, customer service desk at a department store. Jobs requiring emotional contact, day care provider, airline hostess, maitre d'.*
Where Business Wants Its FIVEs	*Jobs calling for continuous reanalysis: university professors, long-range planners, on the board of directors.*

ARE YOU A FIVE?

Observers believe that detached analysis brings order out of chaos. As a result, you like to work alone for long periods at a stretch, a habit that seems lonely, even secretive to more extroverted people. But from your detached point of view, a great many public activities seem pointless. Why waste valuable time and energy on small talk, when there's a world of information to make sense of?

However, most of the people you meet on a daily basis see the world differently, so you've adopted the survival strategy of withholding yourself. John is a perfect example of a FIVE who does just that.

John's office is quite a metaphor for the way his mind works. He's a very private person who heads a rapidly growing executive search firm located in one of the city's tallest buildings. From street level, the towering structure resembles an impregnable fortress, with darkened, hermetically sealed windows that can't be opened.

There are other barriers to sumount before you get to John: burly guards in the lobby, making sure you don't get to the elevators without a visitor's badge and telephone clearance from the office you intend to visit. John's search firm occupies the entire sixty-third floor; a receptionist buzzes you in after checking your badge on the video monitor. She walks you down the hall to his assistant, who double-checks to see that the boss is available, all of which guarantees the uninterrupted privacy he treasures.

John is isolated from the emotional baggage that burdens most corporate heads. In-house communications appear on his manager's E-mail, and recent hires may never have seen the boss in person, because he'd rather not walk down the hall to speak directly with managers. Easily depleted by other people's presence, he's famous for working late into the night when the building's empty, free from the draining hassles of supervision, competition, and office politics.

After wending your way past a wall of assistants, you might expect to find a shy recluse behind the door—and you're absolutely right. But John will bowl you over, by greeting you warmly in the pose of a skilled people person. This is a man who runs a TWO-like personality-oriented business—finding senior executives for some of the nation's largest companies. His success depends on customer satisfaction, so John has learned to rehearse his moves.

He's well prepared for the hour you'll spend together, and within that time frame exudes the confidential understanding you'd expect to see in someone dealing with sensitive personnel matters. But unbeknownst to you, John's aware of three presences at the meeting. You, John, and John's observer—the detached part of his mind that observes your interaction while it is taking place.

John is skilled at "hiding in a pose" that gets his message across. He's talking, but at the same time he's watching himself go through the motions of a well-strategized initial contact meeting. While interviewing you, his persona is outgoing, even aggressive on call, but as soon as your meeting ends he shuts the door, withdrawing back into himself as if behind hermetically sealed windows. Then he'll review what took place and decide how he feels about the encounter, because his feelings are suspended while he's in public.

HOW FIVES SORT INFORMATION

Observers are traditionally known as "monks of stingy mind," not because they hoard money, but because they keep their distance by withholding what is most precious to them—time, energy, autonomy, and privacy. But John probably doesn't see himself as greedy. After all, he likes to live frugally and prides himself on needing little personal attention. But he does feel nourished by his studies, and spends time and energy lavishly in researching the topics that interest him. He connects to the world through his mind and is devoted to private research and strategic information.

Greedy for useful data, his thought process resembles a file card catalogue, with a separate drawer for each topic. His files are stuffed with annotated trivia concerning his clients. He could write volumes about their corporate structures, major players, and deals, gleaned from media services, hearsay, and handwritten notes.

He also has a file for "home" and one for each of his friends. The friends may not know about each other, or about John's home life, because their compartments don't overlap much in his thinking. John's a discontinuous thinker. Like a man opening a single file drawer, he concentrates deeply on one topic at a time. When he's done with the topic, he drops it and moves on to think about something else. It's easy for John to honor his secrecy agreements with clients, not only because it's good business, but because his mind naturally segregates information into different compartments.

Like a miser hiding his valuables in different places—under the mattress, buried in the garden, or in the wall safe behind a picture—John amasses every bit of data he can find about every aspect of a new recruiting assignment. If you looked through his lens of perception, you'd see clusters of data impinging on his client's decision, and it's John's job to detect the key patterns that emerge from all those clusters. His corporate strategy depends on the quality of his data, so from John's perspective, knowledge is power.

Unlike Sixes, who troubleshoot by anticipating worst-case sceanarios, and Sevens, who plan for positive possibilities, John the FIVE accumulates information, seeking the patterns that will predict success for his client.

FIVES AT WORK

FIVES excel at abstract analysis, and this has always been true of John. His devotion to private study originated in childhood, when he remembers trying to escape the intrusive emotional demands placed upon him. But his need for solitude lies deeper than wanting to shut the door to his room or bury himself in books. He also learned to detach from his feelings, preferring the clarity of analysis to the chaos of sticky, unpredictable emotions.

If you're a FIVE, you'll relate to John's avid interest in information and to feeling drained by other people's needs. Why spend time on other people's projects? Why waste yourself in emotionality? Why not just drop it?

Many FIVEs feel challenged by an organizational culture that runs on high octane emotional drama and confrontation, like this CEO of a giant San Francisco entertainment syndicate who felt like a fish out of water in the Seven-like culture of the music industry:

> *It's like everyone here wants to be an artist, but my job is fiduciary. I'm paid to come up with a budget and hold the managers to it. I'm hired to think ahead, not to hold hands, not to hang out and play, and for sure not to finance everybody's pet musical scheme. This business is about making money. It is not about flamboyant artistic ego.*

The Enneagram gave the CEO a model for understanding the extroverted and emotional people around him. He saw himself as being an underappreciated FIVE, intent on bringing fiscal order out of chaos. But his managerial team had a different perception. Where the CEO saw delegation, they saw passing the buck. This FIVE went on vacation immediately after posting the new budget, thereby avoiding an uproar of questions and arguments—a typical move for an Observer.

If you're a FIVE on a team, you may find yourself wanting to escape the nitty-gritty of factions, favoritism, and personality clashes. Instead of running away, try speaking up first, rather than wait to see what everybody else thinks. Volunteer your thoughts, and don't censor what you have to say. It's far too easy to sit back and observe, expecting others to ask only the narrow questions pertaining to your role. Try to generalize what you know to other aspects of the project. It's important that coworkers be aware of what you think and how you go about solving problems so they can anticipate and appreciate your reasoning.

KEEP THIS IN MIND

Your spiritual path has to do with reconnecting to your feelings and pleasure in being with people. Analysis has its place, but there are other sources of information. You have a tendency to think about your feelings instead of experiencing them. Unlike Fours, who follow their feelings, or Twos, who move toward people in a pleasing way, you depend primarily on powers of logic and foresight.

Far from being irrational, your feelings about people can be a valid source of information. I remember one of my FIVE clients, a highly detached real estate broker, who had the good spiritual fortune to lose money in a housing market collapse. He called to consult in a state of shock, not about financial losses, which after all were largely covered by insurance, but by an unexpected outpouring of concern from colleagues. As a FIVE, he expected to be ridiculed for incompetence and financially beached. Yet many had offered condolences, and he'd received an offer to back him in another venture.

My client discovered a missing source of information. Colleagues had written letters citing his patience, kindness, and steadfast effort, but those qualities had never entered his thinking. FIVE-like, he was simply trying to be a good analyst, but others saw in him attributes essential to doing business, of which he was unaware.

A FINAL THOUGHT

A low emotional profile encourages people to make assumptions about Observer FIVEs. Their blank effect can easily be misinterpreted. Without feedback, it's easy for others to think: "She seemed to like what I suggested, as far as I can tell." Or "He seems disinterested; maybe we should forget about the whole deal."

Unfortunately, projections increase a FIVE's sense of alienation. If people are going to misread your intentions, why should you fill them in?

FIVEs can seem uncaring. Consider how others feel when a blank screen suddenly announces a decision, apparently made without input from the people affected. To avoid confrontation, you came to a decision privately and then make a simple announcement. There. It's done. No further explanation.

Those on the receiving end are bound to see callous intent, whereas you were hoping to minimize conflict.

Practice making small disclosures, instead of censoring what you have to say.

Observer FIVEs need to learn to speak on the spot. Trust the process and realize that you don't have to be fully prepared. Any effort to make yourself visible and known to others offsets the deadly mistake of withholding yourself.

Remember John, our successful executive recruiter who positioned himself behind a wall of secretaries? He protects his energy by isolating himself, but his coworkers are bound to find his distance unsettling.

SECURITY RESPONSE AT POINT EIGHT

Secure FIVEs are highly valued in the workplace because they speak their mind. By combining the detached clarity of an

SECURITY AND STRESS

Dynamics of Change for Point Five

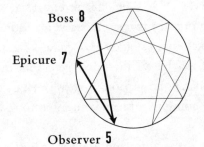

Boss **8**

Epicure **7**

Observer **5**

Observer with the direct, tough-minded follow-through of a Boss Eight, you can bring good ideas to fruition, much to the relief of your coworkers, who don't have to guess what you're thinking. Finally you have become a definite presence, a figure to rally around, instead of a bystander.

Once secure in your information, you formulate a crystal-clear internal picture of the job to be done. It's an effective strategy to the extent that you can communicate the image in your mind, so that others can carry the vision forward. Typically FIVES complain about lack of energy during follow-through, but with enough Eight-like momentum they'll find the energy needed for completion.

In acting out the low side of your security position, you may be perceived as a petty tyrant. You get everyone on the same page, give instructions, and then leave. In your eyes, it's not your job to supervise, so you get angry at having to spend valuable time encouraging or supporting other people. You observe from a distance until a crisis emerges. Then you'll reenter to execute a brilliant, high-powered save, and quickly retreat again to avoid emotional stickiness. Staff can rely on their FIVES for analysis and clear direction, but typically learn to handle the inevitable glitches on their own.

STRESS/RISK RESPONSE AT POINT SEVEN

FIVES may find corporate softball leagues and departmental retreats to be the stuff of nightmares, yet they handle the stress of decision making well, and are sought out as a cool, detached thinker that more emotional people can count on.

At the first signs of stress, you scramble to get away and figure things out. Like all Observers, rather than be overwhelmed by input, you'll want to turn off the phones and isolate; unfortunately, a retreat often coincides precisely with the time your presence is needed. Questions of deteriorating morale and your part in a group dynamic may not register on your screen, but your withdrawal from the situation can add to the problem.

HOW OTHERS SEE FIVES

COMMUNICATION STYLE

FIVES have a communication style that can be best described as "extremely close to the vest." Almost everything that goes on in their minds is kept to themselves. They're cerebral, objective, unemotional, and private to a fault. It's not uncommon that people who work with them for years may not know if they have kids, or even how long it takes them to get to work. Similarly, their neighbors may not know where they work.

Given all this, it is not surprising that FIVES want as much structure as possible when it comes to communications. They want a specific agenda and a time frame for each appointment. Colleagues have learned to say: "The meeting on our staffing needs for next year will take an hour." And if they're clever, they have also learned to say it well in advance of the meeting. They know that the FIVE will participate at the meeting if there are no surprises and no chitchat. Spontaneous communications are draining for FIVEs, and small talk can be a form of torture.

Observers like to concentrate on one thing at a time, and tend to be world-class experts in tiny fields of knowledge. They are famous for obscure intellectual pursuits. A FIVE stock analyst, for example, may know everything about now defunct stock exchanges, or how the value of the British pound has changed over the years.

They respond exactly to the question asked, avoiding generalities and fuzzy thinking. People are used to hearing FIVES say, "Please be specific" or "I am not sure what you are asking me. Can you try it again?" Their communication model produces chunks of information that tend to be treated as separate unrelated units of data. To FIVEs, big-picture thinking means discovering a framework that unites the different information nuggets.

The Internet is a classic illustration of a FIVE's communication loop. On the Net, pure information can be silently exchanged between a few avid minds who have no inclination for a face-to-face meeting. In conversation, their focus is factual rather than persuasive. Facts are safe, neutral, and without hidden expectations, whereas emotional attention can feel coercive, triggering inner questions such as "How much time and energy will this take?" or "What more will be expected of me?"

> *The more you press FIVEs for personal attention, the more they will want to withdraw.*

Preoccupied with making sure the factual context is correct, FIVEs may be oblivious to how their message is received. They communicate facts without frills, often in memo form or in tiny handwritten messages. Both good news and bad news are neatly and unemotionally notated. Their memos are neutral in tone, free of personal intentions, purposes, and reactions.

Even loaded issues, like hiring and firing decisions, made by FIVES are often transmitted on paper, creating an impression of cold disinterest. The impact of a faceless interaction may not be apparent to FIVES, so their communication skills can be helped by pairing them with types who prefer to work interactively.

People tend to see a FIVE's withholding stance as negative. It comes across as "I don't care about what you are saying or doing." On the contrary, FIVES see their distance as showing a deep respect for personal boundaries and the confidentiality of sensitive material.

Emotional distancing makes FIVES seem like intellectual observers rather than active participants in a conversation. They are often impassive when they withdraw inside themselves, giving others the impression that they are being watched through a one-way mirror. In conversations with a FIVE, there may be long periods of silence, moving some to fill in the emptiness with their own impromptu monologues.

> *Part of the reason for keeping their distance is a fear that visibility makes them a target. It is unusually difficult for most FIVES to bring out their own work, but when they do, the presentation will be well organized, well documented, and probably so well rehearsed that they can mentally detach and watch themselves present the material.*

Detachment means separating thought from the ordinary feedback of feelings and sensations. So within a practiced role, FIVES can come across as witty, knowledgeable, or whatever else the presentation requires. Yet, real communication begins when FIVES feel free to share their thought processes and ideas, not merely their conclusions.

Nonverbal Communication

FIVEs can sit without moving for a very long time, providing little in the way of body language or facial cues to reveal their inner state. Their attention is absorbed in thought. They present a low-key profile that is difficult to read. In fact, they can withdraw so much into themselves that they seem to disappear.

This blank-screen impassivity invites projection. It's easy for people to project their own beliefs onto that blank screen. Don't expect any strong nonverbal cues from a FIVE. A positive glance speaks volumes. So does a meaningful shrug.

> *FIVEs find ways to express their warmth through small, well-chosen tokens.*

Positioning is a strong positive nonverbal sign. FIVEs place themselves where they can be drawn out, and they won't appear unless they're interested. Simple social gestures, like sitting in a specific chair, going to the coffee room when a certain person is there, or sending an E-mail message, are all strong come-hither signals from the Observer perspective.

Pairing off in an activity of mutual interest is a nonverbal request for contact. It's much easier to communicate when there's a shared activity to buffer the personal contact that FIVEs try to avoid. Important business may be transacted while walking the golf links between shots, because the game deflects attention from the FIVE himself.

COMMUNICATING WITH FIVES

- FIVEs are extremely sensitive to intrusion. Respect their boundaries. Give them advance notice of a visit rather than spontaneously dropping in. Don't pry for personal information.
- FIVEs are uncomfortable being put on the spot for their

response. Give them time to reflect and prepare what they have to say. Avoid surprises.

- Identify a mutual intellectual interest to engage them in conversation. They are more comfortable with ideas. Don't push for feelings.

- Expect a period of withdrawal after important interactions. Don't interpret this as personal animosity or disinterest. Structure regular debriefing sessions.

- Make agreements on who will initiate meeting times, phone calls, etc., and plan a schedule. Otherwise you will end up being the active agent.

- Don't make assumptions about what a FIVE thinks or feels. Their presentation of a blank screen invites projections. Get a reality check by asking them for information, with the option of getting back to you later.

- FIVEs tend to be very uncomfortable with conflict or emotional intensity. Keep these situations short and create a structure that cushions their impact.

MOTIVATION

FIVEs acquire information and hoard useful data, motivated by the belief that reality can be known, shaped, and predicted by a powerful mind. Since knowledge is true wealth, avarice motivates them to protect their intellectual riches. FIVEs often circulate materials only within a limited circle of colleagues, who in turn spend their time tracking down experts in special content areas, locating obscure references, and refining conceptual ideas. Because FIVEs rely on the protective value of precise predictions, those moments when a difficult problem yields to careful analysis are a great source of satisfaction.

Typically detached from feelings, Observers are motivated to think things through, rather than rely on sensory or emotional input. When their privacy needs are overwhelmed by on-the-job demands for interactive commitment, when there's no time to think and no place to be alone, when emotions break through intellectual barriers, FIVES are strongly motivated to withdraw.

For FIVES, burnout means being emotionally overwhelmed and then their attention fixates on controlling private time and space. Interactions are kept to a bare minimum. To the outside world, a truly detached FIVE appears to be an isolated survivor who can stay apart forever. At their lowest points, they are caught between the distress of showing up to earn a living and having to survive. Then they are motivated by pure necessity and a sense of superiority over people who seem driven by emotion.

> *A first step for FIVES in coping with potential burnout is to notice when the tendency to withdraw takes over. Instead of acting on the need to get away, they can stand fast, by acknowledging their reactions and allowing their feelings to surface.*

Like seasoned actors, Observers can go through the appropriate motions on cue, wearing an engaging social mask, while being inwardly detached. But eventually the safety of privacy shifts to loneliness and intellectual deprivation. We all need company to stimulate our thinking, and even a highly independent FIVE will finally want to reach out.

But loneliness can also awaken a FIVE's intrinsic motivations— the attraction to knowledge, to new information, and to the powers of the mind. Their growth edge lies in engaging emotions instead of retreating to think, in understanding that full comprehension requires a union of body, heart, and mind.

MOTIVATING FIVES

- FIVES want to be valued for their intellectual contributions. Make specific times for them to present their vision, concepts, analysis, and systems. They like to take the role of expert.

* Allow FIVES to start out in an observer role. Don't expect them to jump in and participate right away.
* Provide FIVES with the opportunity to develop expertise and skill in their field of choice. When their interest is engaged, they are highly motivated learners of new material.
* FIVES like to comment on other people's work as well as the overall system. Solicit their feedback. They are good at evaluations but may find it hard to go first or take the lead in presentations or meetings.
* Give FIVES room to work on their own. A flexible schedule and a private workstation can make great incentives.
* Help them to be aware of the impact of their withdrawal on other people. Teaming them with someone who has relational skills may make participation easier.

TIME MANAGEMENT

FIVES live on private time. Time alone to disengage, reflect, and gather their thoughts is vital. For them, public time is teeming with distractions that drain their vitality. Plus, it's annoying to be on someone else's time.

FIVES dislike having to be socially "on," especially when the conversation's a waste of time. Controlling their own time is a key ingredient for the independent lifestyle they crave.

A FIVE's typical day is organized as a series of compartmentalized events, each activity being an entity unto itself. An Observer goes public for the amount of time required by each category, then disengages when it's over, and goes public again as the next event requires.

Time is handled like currency. It's hoarded and spent and

carefully traded for commodities of equal value. When asked to go somewhere, the FIVE's first thought is "I don't have enough time. I won't be able to recoup my time." Like a shrewd banker, FIVES treat time as a business transaction: "Will there be a return on my time investment? If I go, what will I get for my time?"

A FIVE researcher, for example, will consider time well spent in intellectual pursuits. She likes digging through the library stacks, researching contradictory sources, and the sleuthing that goes into unearthing the necessary information.

But in writing that report, the Observer researcher can procrastinate in the face of a deadline. Since knowledge is power, she hesitates to give it up. That can be a problem. As can this: Sometimes FIVES don't distinguish between mental time and external follow-through—that is, their mental abstractions are so economical and definitive that they can seem deceptively easy to actualize. FIVES can become so absorbed in thought that time stands still. Then, at the last minute, they produce a small, exquisite synopsis, given how little time is left. Often, FIVES are the last to speak, recapitulating others' remarks without revealing their own thoughts.

> *FIVEs wrestle with deciding the optimum time to come forward, to give or withhold, to speak or remain silent. They can be genuinely surprised when colleagues tell them that they seem to be withholding.*

HELPING FIVES MANAGE TIME

- Remember that FIVES need their private time—it's like oxygen to them. They can become depleted from extended periods of contact such as meetings and presentations. Allow them downtime between commitments.
- FIVES tend to analyze after the fact, rather than on their feet. They need time to think things over. It will speed

decision making if facts, figures, and memos for a meeting are circulated beforehand.

- FIVEs tend to get on a mental track and pursue it to great length. They find it hard to switch tracks or entertain several time frames at once. It helps to break down a project into separate units that can be completed independently of each other.

- FIVEs can equate thinking with doing. Structure time to check in and discuss the work in progress, offering suggestions and counterarguments. Help FIVEs stay focused on the end result.

- FIVEs may spend a lot of time in the "Search and Discovery" phase, which can leave team members stranded or going in different directions. Ask FIVEs to report out at regular intervals, perhaps getting it down on paper.

- FIVEs typically procrastinate as they gather data and search for patterns in a sea of information. Set clear time limits on research and explicit boundaries on what you expect the FIVE to produce.

NEGOTIATION

FIVEs gravitate to the classic Japanese negotiating style, so impassive and silent that you often don't know where you stand. They give few emotional signals, showing little apparent openness to discussion. To the casual observer, they don't even seem interested.

The reason you're not getting much information is that the Observer strategy relies on gathering information and waiting you out, forcing an opponent to go first. Protecting a position by apparent lack of interest in the outcome, FIVEs want to learn more about you than you know about them. It lubricates the process if you disclose first, allowing Observers to react rather than initiate. If you play it equally close to the vest, you'll wind up having two straight-faced poker players who won't put their cards on the table. If you force their involvement, you may get a statement of demands that sound nonnegotiable, or a bare minimum of information. It seems you either have to give exactly what they want or they walk away.

The FIVE style of controlling the pace and withholding information can be irritating to people who depend on interactive feedback. But from their side of the table, FIVEs are quite aware of their impact and your reactivity will be seen as losing control of yourself.

A FIVE's actual position is revealed in small bits, distracting attention from the big picture, where all the bits of information are connected. Observers control the stage by dealing with each point on the agenda separately, slowing progress and, in the process, draining the energy from an interaction.

You will best promote genuine negotiation with FIVEs if you are formally prepared and emotionally restrained. Observers don't usually respond to coercion or threats, but they do respond to an orderly presentation of each specific item being contested. It speeds things up to treat the elements of the negotiation almost as separate line items, not focusing on the big picture. FIVEs prefer to dwell on smaller matters, not because they're unaware of the larger issue, but they like to observe how you deal with little stuff, to better predict your strategy in larger matters.

TRAINING AND DEVELOPMENT

FIVEs are content-oriented. They want the target goal stated up front with a linear progression of steps to the goal spelled out. They are likely to be building up a mental image of the training components and will want to faithfully replicate those mental pictures in their job. FIVEs are cognitive learners who have to understand the material before they can participate freely. They want to know what's expected ahead of time, and have time to prepare and to review after an exercise is completed. They dislike learning on their feet or being asked to express themselves spontaneously, especially in regard to their feelings. FIVEs typically censor what they say, and feel inhibited during experiential exercises. A call for spontaneous or off-the-cuff interactions are likely to inhibit rather than enhance their learning.

Trainers should not withhold information, especially about competing theories or products. FIVEs want to know each analyst's point of view, and every product's value, not just one opinion. They will privately read other authors to make their own analysis rather than readily adopt an instructor's position. FIVE trainees appreciate trainers who acknowledge the full spectrum of published materials, sparing them from time-consuming private research.

To gain a FIVE's respect, trainers must model intellectual mastery of the material. Interpersonal connection is less important than for other types such as the emotional Twos and Fours. However, FIVEs must be protected from public exposure of any incompetence. They want to know exactly what they will be tested on, how long each answer should be, and exactly how they will be graded. They don't want to be assessed on interpersonal skills or popularity. To avoid violating an Observer's privacy needs, don't post public grades or ask for peer review.

FIVEs learn best if trainers begin with a narrow, specific topic, then move to a general statement. They feel trapped by learning that starts with a broad perspective. A "general question" is hard for them to handle because FIVEs organize information in separate compartments and don't know which file drawer to open in response. For example, "How would you build a specific type of bridge across a specific river in China?" is a better engineering question than "Tell me about suspension bridge design."

THE CASE OF THE FIVE TRAINEE AND HIS EIGHT MENTOR

The company hires graduates straight out of college and places them in a six-month program. Mentors in the program train them in product knowledge and sales techniques.

During the training period, the new hires receive a relatively low salary and their mentors receive a small commission on the sales that trainees produce. At the end of six months it is the mentor's decision whether to let go or to hire.

This trainee, an Observer FIVE, is right on the cusp. He knows the product line and represents it well, but the mentor, a Boss Eight, feels he has to spend too much time backing him up.

The mentor's inclination is to let the trainee go. He's tried hard. Self-assured in his authority and exuding a can-do flair, he's tried to draw out the retiring young FIVE. There's no doubt that this tall and lanky kid is bright, but is there a salesman in there?

It always surprises the Eight when the kid stands up, because suddenly he's six feet tall. He appears to be much smaller sitting at his telephone station.

The trainee's low-key sales pitch is filled with silences on his end of the phone, with little attempt to capture and pin a client down. The mentor is frustrated. He's been in the business a long time. Why can't the kid simply follow his example? Cold calls and follow-up need a special touch to be effective. He's survived well and is happy to pass on what he knows, yet the kid doesn't ask questions, doesn't interact, and doesn't seem enthusiastic.

The Eight mentor encourages trainees to share their client's interests. "Everybody loves to talk about whatever interests them," he explains, "be it themselves, or politics, or the Green Bay Packers." Clients respond to the enthusiasm that a salesperson brings to the product, but this kid won't chat, won't engage.

Maybe the kid's being insubordinate, the Eight thinks. Still, there have been other weak candidates over the years, and the mentor pulled most of them through. Determination is key, he believes. A plucky kid with determination would do fine, but this trainee really doesn't seem to be trying.

"The kid doesn't want to take control," the mentor thinks. "He's either a loser or doesn't have the guts for this."

The mentor has targeted what he sees as the problem, but he's missed the mark entirely, falsely attributing his own outlook to the quiet, sober Observer. Motivated by good intentions, the mentor sends the message: "Do as I say, and you'll be OK"—but that is the wrong way to go with a FIVE.

TYPICAL INTERACTIONS

The FIVE trainee comes at any job from a different perspective. He correctly hears the unspoken communication from the Eight: "Do as I say and you'll get the job." This expectation of unqualified obedience affects all his interactions with his mentor, making the FIVE withdraw as far as possible.

He doesn't want to sell the way the mentor does—it makes him extremely uncomfortable to pretend to be someone he's not—so he tries to wait it out, hoping to neutralize the Eight's energy with an unresponsive vacuum. Strongly aware of the invitation to engage, he detaches, pretending that what the mentor has to offer is unimportant. "I'll refine my technique later, when I'm on my own," he tells himself. He adamantly refuses to be controlled by the mentor's criteria for selling, and he feels drained by the pressure to interact. As a result, he finds himself withdrawing further and further into himself.

Time passes in silence while the trainee muses: "I hit every point in the sales manual when I make a pitch. I memorized everything—why isn't this good enough? What do they want from me?"

Underestimating the impact of his own low profile, the FIVE

thinks: "I'm glad I don't pressure customers. I can't stand the way my boss, John, pushes people around." The FIVE's aversion to his mentor's forceful style is tied to denial of these characteristics in himself.

Instead of getting mad at the mentor, the Observer's real task is to work with his own need to withdraw. Expectations from a powerful authority figure trigger anger, and, FIVE-like, he disappears further into himself rather than deal with his feelings.

> *Without much insight or self-awareness, an authority dance begins. The Eight presses forward, and the FIVE falls back. The Eight lets go, and the FIVE reengages. Each is entrenched in his automatic habit, and so far it's a no-win.*

The mentor interprets the trainee's lack of social initiative as either laziness or cowardice. He tries to ignite a competitive spark. Over and over he asks himself: "How do I deal with this kid? How do I get something going?"

At the point of the hire-or-fire decision process, each believes his own version of events. The Eight mentor sees a trainee who requires constant prodding to meet a quota, while the Observer FIVE thinks: "Customers don't want to be treated the way he wants me to sell."

THE TIDE TURNS

On hearing he didn't make the cut, the trainee feels a mix of disappointment and relief: disappointment in realizing that his familiar pattern of withdrawal influenced the decision and relief at having escaped working in a job that went against his style. Whether he knows it or not, seeing his own participation in the outcome is an important shift in self-awareness. Reeling from the impact of the mentor's excessive energy, he needs to acknowledge the equally important undertow of his own disengagement.

Though at the time retreat seemed like a sensible course of action, at some level the Observer knows he drained the energy from a job opportunity.

> *FIVEs withhold themselves from others to avoid being coerced. But this strategy often means they wind up feeling isolated.*

The mentor misinterprets the Observer's emotional detachment as rebelliously opposing his own forceful salesmanship. Feeling undermined and out of control, he chooses to blame and fire, rather than to find out why someone who won't fight makes him feel so vulnerable. An Eight's lens of perception is focused on control through confrontation, creating a blind spot for other forms of persuasion.

If the Eight had encouraged the FIVE to question freely, given him the chance to develop his own sales style, and allowed him to make mistakes without serious consequences, then the trainee would have been less stingy with his time, energy, and level of cooperation.

RESOLUTION

The Observer withholds under pressure, but believes he can be a forthright salesperson if he is allowed to do it his way and be in control of his own schedule. He comes to work each day but is so emotionally distant that the frustrated Eight doubts that "anyone is at home."

Determined to ward off intrusions, the trainee cannot see the value of different work rhythms. He will not extend himself to please others and this isolates himself from the mentor's good intentions.

Things could have turned out differently for both of them. When the FIVE realized he was pulling back from his trainer's advances, he should have held his position and perhaps used his intellect to suggest a compromise: "I see your way, but I think I personally might be more effective if I could use my own approach. Can you explain why your approach works for you? Maybe I can adapt it to fit my style. Can I try it my own way once or twice to see how it goes?"

Self-observation
FIVES need to notice when their desire to pull back becomes urgent. Rather than standing back and observing, it helps to engage in small, unobtrusive actions. Opening a new file, checking the schedule, sitting down at the computer instead of leaving the room—all of these things can ensure that FIVES stay engaged.

When the desire to get away is deflected, a good way for the trainee to stay on track would be to ask the question "Where am I?" Taking stock of whether he is connected to his feelings, or detached, he is in a position to return to what he feels, rather than to intellectualize his emotions.

Point Six: The Loyal Skeptic

Alias: **Devil's Advocate, Guardian, the Trooper**

Motto	*Question authority.*
Mental Model	*The world is a dangerous place; think of what might happen!*
Lens of Perception	*Contradictory evidence.*
Way of Sorting Information	*Inner questioning: "What if?" "Is this true?" "What about the other side?"*
Blind Spot	*Overestimating authority's power.*
Growth Edge	*Learning to trust self and others.*
Spiritual Path	*Developing inner certainty.*
Vice	*Fear.*
Virtue	*Courage.*
Inspired by	*Faith.*
Managerial Style	*Troubleshooting and overcoming obstacles. Concerned about finding certainty and eliminating doubt. Models fortitude under fire. Superb in a turnaround, but may become overcautious when it's easy.*
Appearance to Others	*Responsible, concerned, focused on hazards and risk. Flight or fight: either voices fears or aggressively muscles up, "I'm strong, I'm not afraid."*
Typical Conflicts	*A SIX's constant questioning can act like a wet blanket during times of expansion. SIXes can frustrate positive types such as Sevens, who imagine best-case scenarios, and Threes, who promote a winning image.*

One-Minute Resolution	*Ask for the ground rules. Make sure to soften hard questions and balance them with positive options.*

The Signals SIXes Send

Positive	*Loyal to those who can be trusted. Keeping faith with supporters. Grateful to allies. Protective of the team.*
Negative	*Put people under the gun. Others feel cross-examined: their motives are questioned, their intentions are made to feel dubious.*
Mixed	*Unexpressed doubts send an inconsistent signal. When a SIX flips into doubt, suddenly everything changes.*
Security Response at Point Nine	*Here SIXes are able to accept praise, believe in positive outcomes, and shift agendas without question.*
Stress/Risk Response at Point Three	*Here SIXes focus on the job to be done, but are inwardly frozen and afraid.*
Work Best In	*Environments where there are clear lines of authority and defined problems. Jobs where honesty and asking hard questions are valued: university classrooms, auditing, investigative work.*
Have Problems Working In	*Environments that have ambiguous guidelines, an insider track, and lots of behind-the-scenes wheeling and dealing.*
Where Business Wants Its SIXes	*Prosecuting attorneys; chief financial officers; heading planning departments and compliance officers.*

ARE YOU A SIX?

Loyal Skeptics ask a lot of questions. It's more than the usual pattern of inquisitive problem solving, where ideas are proposed and analyzed. For you, questioning is more like constantly evaluating what you've been told, rather than accepting what's been said at face value.

From your point of view, a great deal of contradictory evidence goes unnoticed. How can people fall for slick propaganda? For pumped-up ads? For media hype? You are not easily manipulated because you're willing to ask hard questions and probe beneath surface appearances.

While many of the people you work with don't seem at all doubtful, you still anticipate being questioned. That concern causes you to prepare thoroughly so you'll be able to handle any inquiry.

Betsy, a computer software salesperson, is representative.

Imagine yourself as the proverbial fly on the wall and right now you are in Betsy's office on the day before the biggest presentation of her career. Tomorrow Betsy will be pitching a potential client who, with one simple "I'll take it," has the potential to double what she earned all of last year.

She's very anxious, although she's done dozens of presentations, but Betsy doesn't start by rehearsing her moves, remembering key phrases, or recalling past successes. Preparing in her own way, Betsy begins to pace in her office, becoming quickly absorbed in imagining how her pitch could be stopped by the client's objections.

> *Betsy is not really aware of the positive impression she actually makes. And although she knows that the possibilities for a sale are good, most of the encouraging signs slide off her screen.*

She's vaguely aware that her colleagues would be using this time to go out and buy a new suit, or to double-check that their shoes are shined and all their collateral material is in place. But that is not the primary way that Betsy sells. What's she's wearing or how professionally she spins her flip charts is secondary. Unlike a Three, she is not going to sell through powers of persuasion. And she won't, like a Two, present herself as someone who is in search of a new best friend. That's not her style.

Betsy concentrates her presentation on the things that a customer might worry about: Is this the best package on the market? Is this the best price? What happens if something goes wrong? As we watch her work silently at her desk, Betsy is making sure that she has anticipated every one of those questions and a host of others.

As she continues to cross-examine herself, Betsy's confidence builds. Far from being discouraged, when she finds a potential loophole in her reasoning, Betsy gets interested in finding new ways to counter those potential objections.

Fueled by her own convictions, she'll spend very little time in preliminaries tomorrow, wanting to get to the heart of the matter as quickly as possible. In moving so swiftly to content, she may, indeed, miss openings where adroit persuasion or a pleasing facade could help position the software package she's selling. But by the end of Betsy's presentation, the client will know everything there is to know about the software's performance. The emotional connection to the product may not be there, but he can feel good about making a sound decision to go with Betsy's advice.

How sixes Sort Information

In the spiritual traditions that see type as important in human development, sixes are called "monks of doubting mind," not because they act in negative ways, but because they constantly reevaluate their beliefs. If you are a SIX, safety lies in seeing through appearances, in delving beneath the surface argument, in finding the hidden agenda cloaked in superficial answers. Cautious about the intentions of others, you figure things out to make sure you are prepared.

But Betsy probably doesn't see herself as doubtful or cautious. She might describe her approach as savvy problem solving, getting the kinks out of her presentation, so she's prepared to handle any of the customer's questions. She examines everything—including the claims made by the different manufacturers of the software she is selling—to make sure she's ready.

In her need for certainty, Betsy asks herself: "Does the competition have a legitimate edge?" It's a good question, but Betsy may then weaken her own case by making the competitor's advantage the centerpiece of her thinking.

If you looked through Betsy's lens of perception, you'd see the competition's claims etched in bold. She has to defend her product against those claims, because she is convinced that customers will be concerned. Trying to ward off harm, her attention shifts from enthusiastically promoting the merits of her own software package to thinking about how the competition would attack her product.

Betsy automatically challenges her own case. That approach is her way of building certainty in her position. Once convinced, she'll move into high gear and perform beautifully, but this takes time. Of all the types in the Enneagram, SIXes are the hardest to convince about anything.

SIXES AT WORK

Betsy is a troubleshooter, and this has always been her strength. As a child, she remembers, she was always trying to figure out what her parents and teachers were thinking, and how she would have to behave as a result. She had to be wary, because they did not always use their power wisely, so she learned to be on the look-out for inconsistency and has never lost that skill.

> *No matter how pleasantly other people behave or how welcoming they seem to be, SIXes find that it just makes sense to doubt others' intentions.*

If you're a SIX, you'll relate to Betsy's need to know the worst before committing herself. Why be taken in by compliments? Why not presume that people are self-interested? Isn't it sensible to investigate further to get the full story?

Because they question appearances, many Loyal Skeptics have difficulty in an organizational culture that emphasizes persuasion, like this university student who took a temporary telemarketing job and felt at war with the fast-sell expectations of the Three-culture marketing industry.

> *What I can't believe is that my boss thinks we're offering a service when this is the biggest snow job I've ever seen. All I see is operators ducking customers' questions and weaving success stories that probably never happened. And my boss keeps talking about a valuable social contribution. He's got this system for enrolling people in educational programs by telling them they can get the job they've always dreamed about. To me, he's just playing on people's gullibility and expects us operators to do the same.*

The young telemarketer, a SIX, is skeptical of his supervisor's intentions. He automatically searches for verification of his belief that certain types of people are naturally unscrupulous. He thinks the company is taking advantage of people by selling to their hopes and dreams. But his boss takes a different position, encouraging the crew to be pleasant and teaching them how to listen to their customers' needs and how to present an interesting and satisfying solution.

Their perceptions of the job couldn't have been more different. What the boss saw as convincing salesmanship, the young SIX saw as lying. That, coupled with the fact that as a Loyal Skeptic SIX, he felt uncomfortable focusing solely on the positive points of the program, made him extremely unhappy making cold calls.

KEEP THIS IN MIND

If you're a SIX working on a team, you may become too preoccupied with interpersonal dynamics. Remember to focus on your task, rather than wonder about what everyone is thinking. Get a reality check from a teammate you trust and check out your concerns. Once you are reassured, most of your doubts vanish, and just voicing your observations will help clear the air.

> *You have a tendency toward fight or flight—either challenging the status quo to see where everyone stands, or avoiding confrontation by being warm and dutiful.*

Although the time and attention paid to interaction is highly productive from the standpoint of anticipating how team players think, react, and make their decisions, things will move a lot faster if you find compassionate, effective ways to answer the questions that drive you. Institute a roundtable where the team gets to unload its concerns and air doubts. Find out what people are really intending, rather than assuming the worst.

Remember, faith is the traditional remedy for doubt, so your spiritual path is directed toward trusting yourself and others. Trust doesn't mean sacrificing good analysis, or employing the blind faith that leads people to ignore contradictory evidence.

Every business faces hazards, but don't let the objective risk fill your whole field of perception. In the spiritual sense, faith means keeping your mind steady on the task, without falling into doubt.

A FINAL THOUGHT

Your questioning mind can either produce constructive solutions or generate an atmosphere of mistrust. Of course it's important to review established ideas in the light of new evidence, but learn to balance doubt with belief. What have you not looked at that's encouraging? What's the upside? The best possible scenario?

Most important of all—learn to keep going. The devastating thing about doubt is that when it's plausible—although not necessarily right—you stop moving.

Practice acting "as if": as if things will turn out well, or as if you fully believed. Once a decision is made, it's important to support the best-case scenario without hesitation.

Remember Betsy, our gutsy software salesperson? She's a prime candidate for misinterpreting an important client's genuine interest in her software package. Adept in the defensive art of

SECURITY AND STRESS

Dynamics of Change for Point Six

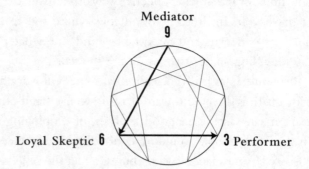

anticipating tough questions, she's less focused on staunchly promoting the real merits of her product.

Instead, if she went into the presentation confident of her client's genuine interest, she could relax her usual focus on potential problems and turn her analytic abilities to the client's real questions.

SECURITY RESPONSE AT POINT NINE

For hypervigilant sixes, relaxation frequently feels like losing your edge. You wonder if you're going soft, losing a certain precision of mind, losing your smarts. Maybe you'll meander or forget something important or forget to watch your back. In times of security, you have less adrenaline, less push, and sometimes less initiative. You look peaceful on the outside, and you're less braced for action, so internally it can feel like nothing's happening.

But the feedback you get during these times is invariably positive. People like you when you're slowed down and feeling amiable. You start hearing, "You're really nice to be around" and "You seem to be warming up to me." All this is good news to someone whose narrow beam of attention is normally focused on problem areas.

In this secure state, you naturally adjust to other people's pacing, miraculously trusting that the job will get done. You may have known intellectually that your coworkers are capable, but now you can actually see how different types of people get their work done.

When you are secure, your attention naturally shifts to seeing best-case outcomes, and you are not afraid to move ahead.

STRESS/RISK RESPONSE AT POINT THREE

The first signs of stress show you looking worried and doubtful. It's too hard to move forward. Everything looks difficult, and the words "I can't" come to the fore: "I can't do whatever I'm supposed to be doing. And even if I could, I can't tell if it's the right choice."

This "analysis paralysis" is usually broken by a deadline or by a coworker who has the sense to walk you through the first step of what needs to be done. Once your doubt drops, action takes over and you're in motion, feeling incredibly glad to be headed toward a reasonable goal.

The shift into Three can be either energizing or terrifying because the same neurological pattern supports both excitement and fear. It just depends on where your attention goes. You can either run on high octane, or else you'll be running scared.

When the energy comes up, you should focus on the task at hand so the energy release is constructive. Then it feels like there are worlds to conquer and challenges to meet. However, if you channel that adrenaline rush into worst-case-scenario thinking, real stress will hit. Then you're acting in the face of danger, moving toward sure death at high speed. The instinctive tendency is to tense up, fight the energy, and lose concentration. The solution, however, lies in learning to relax at high speed. The energy's there and will turn toward excitement if you stay focused on the task. The trick is to relax, collect yourself, and allow the energy to circulate through your system.

How Others See sixes

COMMUNICATION STYLE

sixes are cautionary. Others hear a lot of, "Yes, buts..." "Yes, but that raises another question." "Yes, but there's another point of view."

At first they voice great interest in a project, but that enthusiasm is typically followed by doubt, and doubt produces hesitation. The upshot is that SIXes can give an initial supportive yes, which ends up becoming conditional and qualified.

However, colleagues know that a questioning mind makes a good analyst. SIXes are therefore highly valued as troubleshooters, precisely because they are willing to raise hard questions in their search for absolute certainty.

What is clear to everyone is that SIXes are a hard sell. They're skeptical. They see all the potential loopholes. That's great when they're the person in charge of making sure everything is nailed down. But chronic questioning can lead to inaction if you get stuck spending too much time digging further.

Oddly, procrastination can seem active to SIXes—"I'm thinking; I haven't figured it out yet—but I'm working on it." If this uncertainty is communicated to others by describing in detail what could go wrong, a six's inner tension broadcasts to coworkers.

Loyal Skeptics tend to focus on the loopholes in an argument, rather than concentrating on points of agreement. Primed to expect opposition, they come equipped with an internal scanning device that sweeps the horizon looking for inefficiency, inconsistencies, and hidden agendas.

To convince themselves and to alert others, SIXes voice their doubts. Their intention is to reduce risk, but unless they pay equal attention to best-case outcomes, their genuine analytic abilities may be discounted as negative thinking.

SIXes also question their own material. When talking about their work, what comes across is a sense of almost ruthless objectivity and honest appraisal, shot through the prism of their own investigative logic. Doubt may also produce a self-contradictory pattern of speech, as if the SIX speaker wants to put the message out and then take it back, raising an unspoken alarm in others. For example, "I'm very impressed with our new product, but I don't think I'm explaining it very well," or "I think you'll be glad you bought our product, even though I'm its worst critic."

> *A SIX's analysis is often astute, but cautionary warnings can become a real wet blanket, especially during periods of corporate expansion and rising optimism.*

When they feel unsafe, SIXes adopt a resigned, hunkering-down tone that says: "I'll say this anyway, but I doubt that you'll believe me."

But once assured of safety, the tone changes to one of warmth and camaraderie. SIXes are a real rallying point when the future looks bleak. Their talent for troubleshooting works wonders in a turnaround situation, and they are oddly freed from doubt in an underdog cause, where they know exactly what they're up against.

Public speaking is a challenge for SIXes because, from their perspective, success and visibility invite animosity. It takes courage for Loyal Skeptics to keep their attention focused on the material at hand and away from the audience, which is perceived as potentially critical or disinterested.

> *Loyal Skeptics are classic stage-fright candidates. They learn to look for friendly faces and get a reality check by asking, "Do you understand what I'm saying?" several times during a talk. They can be magnetic speakers for a cause that they believe in, but it's rare for them to produce a neat package of ideas or work the audience.*

SIXes go for content and not the seductive feeling that comes from connecting with an audience. In fact, Loyal Skeptics may not be much interested in the audience. They must have an inner conviction about the product, idea, or service they're talking about before they'll put themselves on the line for it.

As you listen to a SIX make a presentation, you can see his doubts fade as he becomes progressively more convinced of his material. Slow at the start, SIXes can initially come across as unfocused: "I'll try to cover my own doubts by raising all the theoretical possibilities and technical details." The audience senses anxiety as the SIX scans the crowd for a friendly face to interact with.

But by the end of the presentation, the SIX is so internally focused on the purity of his ideas and the logic of his argument that he is lost within what the audience sees as a brilliant presentation. The applause is a surprise that breaks the SIX's mental contact with the material, a cue to return to the room.

Even with repeated practice, it may not become easier for the SIX to speak in public. No matter how many times he has done it, and no matter how thunderous the applause the last time out, being asked—or told—to speak before an audience may feel like facing enemy lines all over again.

Nonverbal Communication

SIXes typically seem "wired" and tense in the spotlight, much like a rabbit frozen in the headlights. Even experienced presenters have occasional bouts of amnesia about their past performances. "Have I really done this before?" "What if I'm challenged and blank out?"

Like a radar scanner, a SIX's vigilant eyes seek out the possible opponent. This vigilance sometimes comes across as social awkwardness and standoffishness, or as a nonverbal strategy of seeking safety.

If that sounds inconsistent, it is. SIXes send mixed messages with their bodies as well as their minds. Constant inner questioning creates yes/no, hot/cold facial expressions and posture. As a result, others aren't sure whether a Loyal Skeptic likes them or not. Communication about objective data or a business commitment can be far more consistent than a personal interaction. In fact, the objective focus of a document or a report may noticeably relax a SIX's tension.

COMMUNICATING WITH SIXES

- SIXes need reassurance before moving into action. Maintain the positive vision while acknowledging problems or dangers. Be truthful, as in: "This part will be easy, but the danger lies there."
- Support SIXes in taking one step at a time. They tend to worry about hypothetical consequences in the future. Help them set limits on their worry, not by painting a rosy picture, but by saying, "We'll deal with that problem if and when it arises."
- Don't change the rules or the plan arbitrarily. Give plenty of advance notice with your reasons. Allow SIXes some time to readjust and expect some complaining or resistance before they are willing to move on.
- SIXes can become fearful or suspicious of others when they don't understand what's going on. Support them in doing reality checks, asking for more information, talking it over with people.
- Don't impose too many social expectations, but do encourage SIXes to understand the importance of rapport and personal contact. Warmth and friendliness support good teamwork.
- SIXes may give too much power to their boss or other authority figures and then either become rebellious or overly compliant. Help them stay in the middle ground

and support them in keeping their own sense of personal authority.

MOTIVATION

SIXes come in two distinct varieties—those who shy away from danger, and those who aggressively confront their fears as an exercise in self-mastery. The aggressive style finds answers by directly challenging authority, as an Eight or a One might do, whereas the shy variety withdraws to strategize, a behavior typical of Fives. Both shy and aggressive, SIXes are motivated by the same question, "Whom can you trust?"

Seeking an unshakable base of certainty, Loyal Skeptics gravitate to protective authorities. That makes sense, but it produces a classic double bind: Aligning with an authority figure buys temporary safety, but the resulting loss of personal power increases doubt.

Apprehension swings the SIX like a pendulum between submission to authority and rebellion from it, sending a yes-no message to colleagues. Their probing for certainty and ongoing questioning is simply to find out if this is a workplace where appearances can be trusted, where authority is consistent and there are no hidden agendas.

A Loyal Skeptic's radar is finely tuned to changes in the power structure. For example, in the restaurant business, a general manager will be invested with undue authority by a SIX shift supervisor, who consistently undervalues her own importance in the system. Without any evidence, she will question her job security, especially if there is even a hint of a management shakeup.

SIXes are loyal to a cause that promises safety. They will enthusiastically endorse an employee union or, with equal vigor, will support management against the union, depending on where their own security lies.

Aligning themselves with underdog causes, SIXes are often drawn to work that expresses loyalty to the disadvantaged. SIXes working in our schools identify with and champion special-needs children whose services are being cut. They are also likely to support the school's maintenance staff in a go-slow action for better work conditions. But their all-consuming loyalty can pave the way for burnout when "the authority" seems intractably punitive to the people around them.

In burnout, massive doubt sets in, and their attention becomes fixated on finding "a reason why" people do what they do. For example, SIXes wonder: Is it lack of education or social conditioning or simply blind self-interest? Loyal Skeptics suffer because they feel incapable of eliminating the tide of abuse; they both want to flee and need to stand and fight.

At their most stressed, SIXes are motivated by habitual questioning aimed at uncovering the intentions of people in power. Loyal Skeptics need to know what they're up against, even if they can't do anything with that information.

But burnout can also produce the right conditions to rediscover intrinsic motivations, which for Loyal Skeptics is finding the faith to take action.

SIXes have a choice when they have the courage to back their own beliefs and do not doubt their strength. Their goal is to find an inner place of courage, from which they can speak without fear of consequences.

A first step is to question the state of mind that continuously poses questions. It is helpful to name this phenomenon: "This is doubt. This is a habit. What I think is happening may not be entirely accurate."

SIXes would do well to voice the doubts out loud—and question *them*: "Has this actually happened? Is it likely to happen now?" The best help is getting a reality check, an objective clarification from a reliable source.

MOTIVATING SIXES

- A good role model is the best motivator for SIXes. Unpretentious, consistent leadership helps to relax their doubting mind. Try to embody what you teach or say and you will earn their loyalty.
- SIXes are interested in the content of the matter and have a natural tendency to analyze. Give them time to thoroughly understand the issues or the plan before moving into action. Value their intellect and perceptiveness.
- To gain the trust of SIXes, state your own bias at the beginning. Present alternatives and the limitations of your position. SIXes want to know the downside or potential problems. Play the Devil's Advocate to your own material.
- Stay friendly under questioning. SIXes will ask hard questions that may appear to be unsupportive, but this will enable them to come on board. Value their ability as troubleshooters.
- Support SIXes by establishing a predictable work environment with clear lines of authority and policy, whether operating in a hierarchical or a team-based approach.
- Help SIXes structure a "safe" working environment where they can speak their minds without fear of being attacked. Allow opposing opinions to be heard.
- Recognize the loyalty and commitment of sixes who keep going despite their doubts.

TIME MANAGEMENT

SIXes keep track of time. The world is a hazardous place, so they spend time building a secure bunker. Today's efforts are focused on future safety for "when hard times come" or "when time runs out."

Time is also an objective factor to be either challenged—"Who said it was time to do this?"—or obeyed—"Of course, I'll be on time." Deadlines can feel coercive when there's not enough time for a thorough analysis or to anticipate tough questions. But SIXes lavish time on people to whom they feel loyal. They typically find it easy to stay on track in the service of a worthwhile cause, because the success is shared by others.

Paradoxically, Loyal Skeptics sometimes have problems acting on their own behalf. When winning is easy, SIXes may start to rethink their position, stop, and then rethink again before being willing to act. From their perspective, success and the higher visibility it brings produce only envy and animosity on the part of others. As a result, "what if?" thinking, which is consummately time-consuming, takes over.

For example, a Loyal Skeptic architect can organize around deadlines like a warrior entering battle. Driven by the possibility of angry clients, and impatient builders, he focuses on getting the job done on time as a matter of survival.

Mobilizing against the odds is energizing because in a turnaround there's no time to think. Loyal Skeptics do not procrastinate and are often at their brilliant best when facing objective crises. There's an adrenaline rush while working in the trenches, and heroics cut through procrastination and doubt.

HELPING SIXES MANAGE TIME

- Concerns peak at two points in the project: at the start of the action and just before completion. Provide reassurance when necessary and bring attention to possible slowdown as the project or presentation nears completion.
- Support SIXes in getting their questions and doubts out of their heads and on the table. Admitting your own errors can save enormous amounts of time.

- SIXes have trouble with ambiguity. Help them establish clarity when possible. Ask them to participate in setting guidelines for reporting, accountability, and grievances.
- Build in enough time for SIXes' pattern of starting and stopping. Once trust is established, they will take responsibility for seeing things through.
- SIXes tend to come through for the cause in the crunch, and yet may procrastinate when the project is for their own benefit or when the pressure is off. Help them to stay on track throughout by engaging their loyalty and responsibility.
- Support SIXes in scheduling time away from their duties. They tend to forget about having fun, or the recognition and help that is available from others.

NEGOTIATION

A SIX's survival strategy depends on preparation and foresight. Blessed and cursed by a vivid imagination, they have a tendency to magnify potential points of disagreement to catastrophic proportions. They pay less attention to best-case outcomes, and this bias accounts for the enormous reluctance they feel in coming to the negotiating table.

Because Loyal Skeptics overestimate the power, daring, and hostile intentions of the opposition, they tend to be inflexible in a negotiation. They do not want to deviate from their position for fear of being disadvantaged, making it difficult to see gestures of reconciliation. Rather than take a risk, they typically entrench in a characteristic fight-or-flight response. To the outside, flight looks like evasive action, usually in the form of requests for postponements, delays, or the SIX going incommunicado. Fight, on the other hand, looks like the no-nonsense confrontation of an Eight—a go-for-the-throat maneuver focused on uncovering mismanagement, inaccurate information, and abuse of the system.

Putting a human face on the negotiation and acting civilly toward a Loyal Skeptic will save an enormous amount of time and energy. While threats will only confirm a SIX's mistrust and increase his inflexibility, a friendly gesture can be disarming. If possible, introduce "survivors" of previously successful negotiations and enroll trustworthy intermediaries. Your position will seem far more reasonable if it's promoted by someone a SIX trusts.

Remember, SIXes monitor any discrepancy between what people say and what they do. They assume others will hide their real intentions, so be as forthright as possible. The best tactic is to ally yourself with someone the Loyal Skeptic already respects, place your cards on the table, and stick to your word.

TRAINING AND DEVELOPMENT

SIXes want to know what they're getting into. They need to be fully informed about the class materials, about forms of evaluation and especially about the other people in the room. Typically, they prefer a long orientation period where they can listen without having to participate. This allows them time to check out the other trainees and the leader's style of delivery. Like FIVEs, who often retreat to the periphery of the group to observe, SIXes typically withdraw their presence until they feel it's safe to come out.

The initial impression a trainer makes is crucial, because SIXes very quickly decide whether or not to trust someone in authority. Believing they can see through image and a convincing facade, they tend to view group bonding and a trainer's energetic endorsement of the program as faked. It really pays off when trainers can be somewhat self-revealing rather than playing a professional role. A simple statement like "I hate this part of the program, because..." can make the trainer seem far more human. Anyone in authority looks unusually opinionated and dogmatic to SIXes.

To establish trust, trainers should mention their own background, sources, theoretical orientation, and school of thought. All of this lets the Loyal Skeptic know what he's getting into.

Above all, trainers must handle probing questions in a direct manner. SIXes (along with Boss Eights and Perfectionist Ones) will be checking to see how an authority reacts under pressure. SIXes, especially, are looking for consistency between words and action.

THE CASE OF THE SIX TECHNICAL SPECIALIST

This is the technician's first review since he started on the job six months ago.

His Two supervisor is not looking forward to the appraisal. She likes the young man. She hired the technician and spent time teaching him the ropes. Then, to give him space, she backed off. In recent weeks she's received several memos complaining that while the specs summaries he's provided, which outline the new software package, are accurate, they've often been late and not specific enough about the most important changes. How will he react to the negative feedback? He has to acknowledge there's a problem. Then she can devise ways to overcome it.

TYPICAL INTERACTIONS

The Two supervisor thinks: "If only I didn't like him. He seemed so promising when I hired him—fresh-faced and bright, with good personal recommendations." She felt he'd be a real addition, and he cooperated during training when she put him through his paces.

They really like each other, but now she finds herself confronted with a pile of complaints stuck in her file drawer. What happened? She believed in him. It pricks her pride to know that he's making her look bad in front of the whole office. This deflated feeling upsets her Two-like need for approval.

Thinking about the SIX technician brings back the feeling of insecure edginess that he seems to carry with him. His tendency to say "yes, but" to everything and his habit of starting on a project and then suddenly rethinking it are unsettling.

The news is bad. How can she best deliver it so he won't panic? Firmly? Confidentially? What's the right note? The Giver supervisor wants to assume a positive tone. Which of her different professional selves will turn the tide in his favor, make him feel better about himself?

While she's figuring this out, she'll hide her own discomfort because it makes her feel better to think that he needs her.

But as soon as the technician walks into the office, she remembers what a nice kid he is, and her warm reaction undermines her resolve about the memos. She's caught between showing him the unflattering notes and still making this situation OK for him.

As the technician enters the room he sees a picture that makes him uneasy. There's a closed file with his name on it sitting on the supervisor's desk, and her smile seems forced.

He registers the double message, and from the outset of the meeting, his SIX-ish antiauthoritarian reactions begin to surface as he starts to weigh the evidence: "She's being nice, but that's part of her job. Is she on my side or not? Am I being manipulated? She probably doesn't know how many late nights it cost me to get those specs finished." He hates being evaluated.

Last night the technician had tried to relax by going to a movie, but the upcoming evaluation was on his mind all through the film. In training, she was so obligingly supportive that he was never certain which projects had priority and which were less important. He kept worrying as he stared at the screen.

The technician procrastinates when he feels uncertain. Now he wishes he'd been more forthcoming with his questions about priorities. "She could find a reason to fire me, and I'd have no way of challenging her evaluation," he thinks as he stands before her desk.

Unwittingly, the Loyal Skeptic's attention moves from his uncertainty about the specs to worst-case scenarios. Where will he go if he loses this job? Will he still be able to get into graduate school? What will his family say? He tries reading her face to discover what he's up against. "What is she waiting for? Why won't she be up front?"

An interplay of personalities emerges without a word being said. The Giver thinks: "I can help him once he'll admit that he has a problem meeting deadlines. How am I going to show him these memos? Will it be crushing?"

Her pleasant facade seems to confirm his rising suspicions as the meeting begins. They both mark time with small talk, and both are aware of the manila folder on the desk. The supervisor hasn't opened it yet; both are unwilling to begin discussing the real issues. The more the supervisor talks around the issue, the more the technician withdraws into his dark imagination. Each is seeing the world solely from his or her perspective. The Loyal Skeptic thinks he's about to be fired and wishes she'd get it over with, while the Giver is struggling to gain his confidence and devise a credible safety net.

Biting the bullet, the supervisor finally opens the file and reads him the first memo. The SIX technician's paranoia peaks when he hears the complaint that his specs summaries have been late and not focused on important changes: "Who wrote that? Do I have an enemy?" he immediately asks himself. "How many other memos are there? How many other people don't like me?" Catastrophic thinking takes over: Why go through this charade of a performance appraisal? The supervisor's already made her decision; this is actually a dismissal. He thinks of how he worried all through that movie and he tells himself his intuition was right.

The frozen look on his face at hearing the negative feedback confirms the supervisor's apprehension. The Two feels exposed, she looks foolish, and she knows she has mishandled the evaluation. Word will spread to the rest of the office. She can't stand being humiliated. If only the memos had been flattering, then the technician would still like her.

THE TIDE TURNS

As evaluators, Giver Twos want to look good to all parties concerned. If people are alienated, what's the point of a job well done? Yet, to her astonishment, the supervisor sees the technician's face start to unfreeze as his first shocked response to the bad news starts to wear off. Simultaneously, her insecurity starts to lift. In light of the technician's new reaction, she feels more solid sitting in the chair. Instead of looking like a hostile stranger, he's just the naive kid she hired six months before.

With relief she realizes that by biting the bullet, by giving him the unflattering news, she was of genuine help. The hard reality of the report has helped the technician come to grips with his fears.

From his side of the desk, the technician feels his customary relief when he knows exactly what he's up against. Suddenly the supervisor looks less menacing, more honest, and less powerful.

He would still love to know who wrote that memo she read, and the identities of the other memo writers, so that he could go and argue with them, but the worst thing was not knowing what he was up against, and he is willing to respect the confidential nature of the information. He can also see that the supervisor still likes him, and this gives him the courage to ask her, "So what should I do?"

RESOLUTION

The problematic memos were humiliating for the Giver, because *she* had hired the SIX technician: *she* had believed in him. Her pride was wounded when she thought he was making her look bad—an interpretation rising from her need to be indispensable.

In addition, she worried that because she was the bearer of bad news, the technician might no longer like her. Yes, she is his supervisor, but still she has an extremely strong desire to be liked.

Eager for approval, Givers adapt to meet the needs of others. She believed she had gained his confidence by being supportive during his training. Two-like, she disguises her own insecurity in the costume of compassion.

All this unease brought the Loyal Skeptic's mental radar to full alert; he thought the supervisor was trying to manipulate him through pretending to like him, that she was withholding information, that she was about to fire him.

Once the technician knows what he's dealing with, he can take steps to rectify the situation. The supervisor still likes him, she was not being deceitful, and it's safe to ask for help. The tide turns when the question marks are erased. Once the supervisor shows her cards, she no longer appears cagey and untrustworthy, so the technician feels better. The Two supervisor almost undermined herself by stalling, instead of remembering that a SIX needs full disclosure up front. Her own need to be liked is secondary in this situation.

Self-observation

SIXes need to be aware when anxiety first appears. The Loyal Skeptic technician needs to ask: "What would motivate someone to manipulate me?" Much of his apprehension would vanish with a simple reality check. He needs to solicit the supervisor's actual opinion before his imagination escalates into worst-case-scenario thinking.

Point Seven: The Epicure

Alias: **Gourmet, Planner, Optimist, The Entertainer**

Motto	*Everything will change by tomorrow.*
Mental Model	*The world is full of opportunities and options.*
Lens of Perception	*Best-case possibilities.*
Way of Sorting Information	*Synthesizing positive plans.*
Blind Spot	*Actual limitations.*
Growth Edge	*Learning commitment to a single course of action.*
Spiritual Path	*Concentration, moderation, and commitment.*
Vice	*Gluttony—for ideas and experiences.*
Virtue	*Sobriety—sticking to one thing at a time.*
Inspired By	*Becoming a master of one field, rather than knowing about many.*
Managerial Style	*Devise the plan and delegate.* SEVENs *are idea people who are weak on follow-through. Strong on networking, outreach, and positive big-picture planning.*
Appearance to Others	*Buoyant, optimistic, and highly entertaining —or slippery and irresponsible.*
Typical Conflicts	*Exaggerated promises and claims, resulting in imprudent follow-through.*
One-Minute Resolution	*Remember to finish your current project before brainstorming others.*

The Signals SEVENs Send

Positive	*Making the ordinary seem extravagant and bountiful. Playful and positive, imaginative and inventive.*
Negative	*Preoccupation with own pleasure and interests make SEVENs seem uncaring or unreliable.*
Mixed	*Fluid, erratic follow-through sends the message that SEVENs are in transition. This job may be only one of many in the grand plan of the future.*
Security Response at Point Five	*Here SEVENs withdraw into solitude for rest and recuperation. Undistracted by outer stimulation, there's time to turn inward.*
Stress/Risk Response at Point One	*Here SEVENs resent having to sacrifice their options. Judgments and anger about limitations are aired.*
Work Best In	*Jobs where there's a spirit of adventure and bold new worlds to conquer; fast-paced settings with rapidly changing information. SEVENs are theoreticians, futurists, and multitask people.*
Have Problems Working In	*Jobs with predictable futures that can't be finessed to make them more interesting, or repetitive work isolated from stimulation: laboratory technician, CEO of a bureaucracy, bank teller, assembly-line worker, tailor.*
Where Business Wants Its SEVENs	*The brainstorming and planning stage of any interesting project; discovering points of similarity between different fields of interest; university interdisciplinary studies tracks; jobs requiring networking and promoting complex ideas, such as politics, lobbying, media production manager, public relations outreach; fun fields of work for the vibrantly healthy and eternally young; ace reporter, sports equipment sales, health food and fitness centers.*

You want a career that will be a cornucopia of options. Life is filled with opportunities, and all it takes to exploit them is vision and a little creative problem solving.

This buoyant belief is greatly enhanced by the way your mind works. You have several ideas and positive plans that all seem intertwined in your thinking. If plan A looks shaky, go to B as the backup. If B isn't funded, you always have C. If C gets routine and you can't revive B, fall back to A, which could lead to D. In your mind, plans A through D are intrinsically related, so if any one of them hits, you'll pull in all the others. Why limit your options?

However, the people you work with may see these plans as entirely different from each other. Those same coworkers also go about things in a routine way, while it drives you crazy when you can't find an adventurous outlet for your talents. Bob, for example, expresses his desire for new experiences during a planning session.

"My God, what could be better?" Bob all but gushes the moment the chairman leaves the room. But the reaction of the three people surrounding him is one of absolute disbelief.

The chairman just gave the four-member team the charge of "putting on the best damn convention in the history of this corporation," and the first thought crossing the minds of Bob's three colleagues is how quickly they can find other jobs once they're fired.

Everyone except Bob is imagining the incredible pressures of fielding a three-day convention—planes could be late, whatever exotic locale they pick could have weather problems, no single menu would appeal to everyone...the horrific list of tasks is endless as far as they're concerned.

Bob, on the other hand, can see only opportunities. There'll be convention sites to visit, a chance to indulge "what if" fantasies, and countless ingenious ways to pull off the meeting.

As he tells his coworkers: "We could make it a theme convention, maybe based on location. And then for entertainment, we could get..."

Where others see limitations, Bob sees positive options. That's a trait of SEVENs at their finest. However, structuring the convention will mean hundreds of phone calls and checking thousands of items off lists. In those situations, Bob will have to pay extra attention because details are not his strong suit.

It's going to be hard to restrain his enthusiasm, because he's hugely excited by the mandate. His immediate response is to reprioritize other business in favor of this new opportunity, pulling whatever resources he'll need from wherever he can find them.

Bob's vaguely aware that his colleagues don't share his enthusiasm, but he already sees how every department will benefit by simply reframing their projects in convention-speak. Marketing, for example, should adopt the theme "Marketing in the Twenty-first-Century" for all the current projects on its calendar.

In Bob's mind, the marketing department now plays a key research role for the upcoming conference. He envisions the head manager, well prepped about global marketing theory, delivering a keynote address on the positive impact of twenty-first-century systems in Bob's corporation.

Powered by his own enthusiasm, he is likely to make headway enrolling others, but all this excitement is happening in his head, unbeknownst to the chairman or the marketing manager. Bob's future lights up when he thinks of heading the whole corporation down a promising road to the twenty-first century. But his gluttony for positive ideas blinds him to the real limitations of time, resources, and the cooperation he needs from others.

How sevens Sort Information

In the spiritual traditions that use type as a factor in human development, Epicures are traditionally known as "monks of gluttonous mind" because they voraciously devour experience. Bob's worldview is about having it all—a bright future in which all his desires come to fruition. But Bob probably doesn't see himself as a glutton. If you looked through his lens of perception, you'd see a vista full of ideas, all networked together in a grand plan for the future. What a great way to do business!

Unlike Sixes, who prepare themselves by imagining worst-case scenarios, Bob sees the best. He's a dedicated networker within the corporation, because he needs allies who share his vision and have the resources to implement the ideas that tantalize him.

His SEVEN way of sorting information actually resembles the network of the human nervous system that you see in anatomy books. The convention proposal triggered a chain of mental associations that pulsed through the synapses of Bob's interconnected plans. The convention has now become a major neuron in Bob's vision of the future. "This is really a big deal," he thinks. "Big enough to require its own director. The chairman probably realizes this already. And surely the head manager at marketing will be receptive, because after all he's doing research for marketing in the twenty-first century."

The possibilities are endless, and some of those possibilities could help Bob a lot. For months he's been trying to dump some tedious on-line responsibilities, and he's dreamed about a flexible schedule. He hates reporting to his direct supervisor, and is aware that he needs more money. But right now Bob's vastly excited by the prospect of directing the convention, and will hurry to put his thoughts in a memo to the chairman.

SEVENS AT WORK

Epicures excel at envisioning the future, and this has always been true for Bob. His brainstorming abilities originated in childhood; he remembers being a bright, sunny boy who lifted the spirits of the people around him. But his dedication to a positive future is far more mature than simple wish fulfillment. Bob also learned to capitalize on the opportunities that came his way, moving him toward success and therefore away from pain.

If you're a SEVEN, you'll understand Bob's focus on synthesizing the best aspects of different ideas. Every system has worthwhile information, so why not draw from them all? Bob keeps several systems afloat at the same time, finding points of similarity between them. His lens magnifies areas of agreement while obscuring very real differences. Bob can brilliantly weave different kinds of data into a coherent pattern, but his way of paying attention tends to let details slip through the cracks.

SEVENS often feel confined in organizational cultures that run on bureaucracy. Those who do commit to a routine job typically find ingenious ways to keep the spirit of adventure alive—like this twenty-year veteran of the insurance industry. He spoke on a SEVEN panel at an Enneagram class in the basement of a church in Chicago and briefly thought he was mistyped, as he spoke of a thirty-eight-year marriage as well as his long career selling insurance.

> When I first learned about the Enneagram, I found out that SEVENS have trouble with commitment. So how could I be one of them? But the description fit: optimistic, easily bored, and interested in just about everything. Now when I look at it, my whole sales concept comes from being a SEVEN. I sell more insurance than anyone in the office, but I'm hardly in the office. I'm out with my wife, enjoying my hobbies.

It would help if you understand that I've been married a long time, but to many different women. She hasn't been the same person year after year. For a while we were young and changing, but then I started seeing all the different people my wife was, and it's kept me fascinated.

It's the same with my job. I'm outgoing, I like to meet people, but it's not about backslapping. My biggest commission happened on a ropes course up in Aspen. An HMO was doing a team-building session, and I got along with the managers. That led me to a whole skiers' network, people who like to take chances but worry about accidents. That got me here to this [Enneagram] class. A skier client said he was a Six, and that's why he worried about his family if he got hurt.

So now I'm reading Enneagram books, and I'm also sort of networking, because I'm up here onstage and now you Enneagram people all know my business, but to me selling isn't work. It's a pastime.

The insurance broker had found a way to stay interested, based on his considerable charm. But the next man on the SEVEN panel had a different take on commitment:

I went down the MBA track when I saw the options that those guys had, and now I'm living the American-dream lifestyle for someone of my generation—great cars, the good designer clothes, flying all around the country on business. Spontaneity is crucial. I have to feel that I can pick up and leave at a moment's notice. All this is great, but I've recently been offered a nearly irresistible half-time job in Boston. It's also a five-year contract, and I just can't commit to it.

It turned out the MBA had accumulated 600,000 frequent-flyer miles. Because of those miles he could travel anywhere at a moment's notice, but he never went. He had options but never committed to any one place, preferring the imaginative world of possibilities where nothing is fixed and no one is accountable. He'd had lots of virtual vacations, but missed the deeper pleasure that commitment brings.

KEEP THIS IN MIND

SEVENs on teams are famous for leading the charge during the planning stage of a project and then wanting to bail when the plan is implemented. Like Fives, who withdraw to protect their privacy, or Sixes, who stall because they get performance anxiety, as a SEVEN, you procrastinate because committing to a single project brings up the extreme discomfort of feeling your freedom vanish.

What the team sees is an upbeat, attractive player who suddenly makes excuses. Why didn't the SEVEN show? No real reason except that the whole thing got boring. *Boring* is a key word. You should question yourself when you think the job is getting boring. "Why bored? Why now?" Is it because the long haul requires too much commitment?

In your spiritual path, gluttony is more than stuffing the schedule. It's a state of mind where good ideas are so real and complete in themselves that the tedious steps in between seem almost incidental. It takes discipline to concentrate on one thing at a time in a sober, measured effort to make ideas viable. Most long-term gain requires short-term pain. So look over your shoulder. Your fascination with many things may prevent commitment to any one of them.

A FINAL THOUGHT

Why would anyone want to face sadness or disappointment or failure? It just doesn't seem productive to question a positive self-image. Fascinated by stimulating work, you, along with Performer Threes, are the Enneagram optimists.

Remember Bob, the planner of conventions? Buoyed by a sense of personal worth, he's following the flow of opportunity, leading to resources and people who appreciate his vision. Being open to new possibilities seems natural, but the flaw in his reasoning is the expectation of bounty. Sacrifice and limitation are simply not of interest.

Before Bob's excitement gets the best of him, he needs to slow down and map out which of his expectations are realistic and which are simply the products of his optimistic imagination. He needs to wait for feedback from the chairman before he orders his new letterhead. He should also talk with the three other members of his team and really listen to their reservations and questions. SEVENs need reality checks along the way to keep them grounded. It is true this opportunity may lead to other personal benefits for Bob, but he needs to begin the project with more realistic expectations so he can avoid later disappointments and keep the team working for a common goal. SEVENs have a bagful of tricks to avoid dealing with negativity, confronting a difficult, messy problem, or being rejected. One trick is to put the issue on the back burner: "We'll deal with that as soon as this project is over." Another is to distract everyone's attention to a more fascinating and hopeful part of the project. A third is to reframe a problem into an opportunity or a rejection into an interesting experience.

SECURITY RESPONSE AT POINT FIVE

Secure life situations may stimulate a crisis of choice for multi-option SEVENs. Now it's time to carry a single idea forward, rather than move to the next plan on the list. But even a spectacular choice feels limiting in comparison to a cornucopia of options.

SECURITY AND STRESS

Dynamics of Change for Point Seven

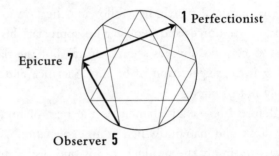

Only one? Just one option? Why sacrifice all the other interesting possibilities? Why settle for so little?

Moving from the stimulation of SEVEN to the solitude of Five signals a search for privacy—a quiet place in which to withdraw from a packed schedule. A solo vacation, or a retreat into the peace of nature, helps turn off the swarm of mental plans, redirecting your attention to priorities. The silence of Five helps you choose between options, eliminate distracting stimulation, and commit yourself to a sober course of action.

The downside of the security response causes SEVENs to withdraw from participation. Suddenly the charismatic visionary vanishes from the office. SEVENs are highly independent, spontaneous people who do not like to feel restricted; you want what you want and you want it right now, and it's very easy to slip away from commitment when you feel secure enough to leave.

STRESS/RISK RESPONSE AT POINT ONE

Losing an option is unusually painful and is reported as a SEVEN's most common stressor. You were counting on a job interview, but it was a no-go. You were expecting a raise, but it didn't happen. Your characteristic SEVEN defenses emerge in force: frantic planning, a nonstop schedule, and a fixed smile. Fleeing into pleasant escapism to avoid current difficulty, you try to dislodge unpleasantness from your thinking. When escape doesn't work, you move into One.

The shift to One is promising in the sense that you are now aware of the problem. Distraction doesn't work anymore, so you stand and fight. It makes you angry to commit yourself to a single option. It's infuriating, but in One, you can do it. A deprived SEVEN either criticizes or makes fun of other people. Jealous of the freedom that others enjoy, you chafe at limitations. In the stress of One, your disappointment is someone else's fault. It's someone else's problem. If everyone else was open-handed and broad-minded, you wouldn't be in pain.

When you're stressed, chronic self-blame undermines your usual buoyancy. If the finger points at you, you feel immense inadequacy. When the finger points to others, they should change and give you what you want.

But the upside of One shows you rising to deal with stress. You're single-mindedly focused on the problem, and, like a One, have to take action. When a project is interesting enough or so important that you are willing to make the commitment, things get finished perfectly, with considerable pleasure in a job well done.

HOW OTHERS SEE SEVENS

COMMUNICATION STYLE

If a SEVEN were writing a "position wanted" ad, it might read like this:

> *Effervescent optimist filled with energy seeks constant stimulation and opportunities. Has the ability to find connections,*

parallels, and unusual fits between disparate bits of information. Hardworking and committed while there is a challenge.

SEVENS are convincing communicators because they are fascinated by new concepts. As a result, they are the Enneagram's generalists. Collectors of exciting ideas, they like to network as a way of expanding their breadth of information. This need for new data is compelling; they want to stay informed about emerging trends, rather than commit themselves to a predictable course of action.

> *Their lens of perception produces a mental sleight of hand. Positive options grab attention, while irreconcilable views and other negatives are reduced to vague background elements.*

Because of their optimistic focus, SEVENS can unintentionally shortchange the details. It's not that they are unaware of the time and effort involved in implementing a plan; it's just that a spur-of-the-moment idea seems so brilliant and right that mentally the SEVEN can see it effortlessly already accomplished.

Communications are full of loopholes, contingencies, and backups—all of which are designed to keep their options open. While gathering a herd of options is understandable from the SEVEN's point of view, it sends contradictory and ever-changing messages to others.

Still, the SEVEN approach is a useful mind-set for occupations demanding on-the-spot sorting of information. SEVENS shine as the point men in the field, where fluid data demands spontaneous decision making.

SEVENS make the assumption that other types of people are also multi-option thinkers and equally comfortable with a rapid turnover of plans. Obviously, that is not often the case. As a result, SEVENS tend to reframe problems and recontextualize ideas in ways that can baffle more logical thinkers.

As presenters, Epicures can be masterful raconteurs and story-tellers. They convey their enthusiasm for a product or service in a charming, personal manner filled with metaphors and "imagine how this could be" word pictures. Their speech pattern rarely follows a logical step-by-step progression. Their style is to support the basic premise from a number of different angles, showing points of agreement between each rather than focusing on the differences.

When SEVENs are present, there may be several ideas afloat at the same time, borrowed from different theories, but in their mind all of those ideas are clearly linked.

> *When their approach works,* SEVENs *can synthesize a disparate collection of known ideas into a brand-new unified system that couldn't have come about by proceeding in a lockstep manner. Their minds work by imagining how all the diverse pieces of information fit together in a constructive way.*

It's hard to pin SEVENs down because in their view all the disparate ideas they constantly play with do intersect with each other, and the options for action are constantly changing as new data come in. The question-and-answer period following a SEVEN's presentation. It can be a chaotic scene as the entertaining Epicure, in response to a query, crams several different ideas under one umbrella and makes them all seem logically connected. It can be very appealing if the audience is in sync and willing to switch gears quickly.

SEVENs like to stay loose. Like the best running backs in football, they see the holes in the field ahead and constantly dart about to avoid being tackled by limitations. Besides, when the angle changes and the perspective shifts, it's easier to achieve agreement.

Nonverbal Communication

Epicures are the life of the party. Without saying a word, their bright expression and active body language exudes enthusiasm. Even among old friends, they find something new to talk about and can always bring a fresh look to a long-standing topic of mutual interest. Nothing is static when you're standing near a SEVEN, and that produces a high-voltage charm that's pleasant to be around.

SEVENs invite others to share their enthusiasm, but the message is that it's their party and they get to choose the menu, the entertainment, and the topic of conversation. You're invited and it's great to see you there, but understand that everything's already been planned. If you can't make it, then maybe some other time. Anyone who doesn't like the agenda is perfectly free to leave.

SEVENs are hard to control. They are upbeat, optimistic people who communicate a contagious sense of adventure through colorful metaphors and stories. A listener feels drawn to be a participant in the story; the exciting subtext reads, "We're in this together" and "Wouldn't it be fun?"

There may not be any real intention to mislead, but a SEVEN's invitation to play is naturally promissory. Just don't forget they're delighted to have you involved in their story, but it's the story that counts.

COMMUNICATING WITH SEVENS

- Engage SEVENs' fascination with new ideas and possibilities. They are often the ones who will keep the dream alive and inspire others.
- Draw attention to problems and frame concerns in a positive manner. Help them understand the downside or limits of the situation.
- SEVENs are easily bored or distracted. They prefer that information be delivered quickly. Their attention may

wander during long presentations. Highlight or summarize the major points. Allow SEVENs to respond and comment as much as possible.

- Remember that SEVENs tend to make agreements loosely. They may say yes to the idea or the meeting, then change their minds if another option comes up. Help them understand when you expect a serious commitment.

- SEVENs may evade responsibility for their mistakes. They usually want to make it all okay, and they hate to be pinned down. Expect strong resistance to criticism.

- Be prepared for frustration or sarcasm when limits are set or their ideas are turned down. Don't dismiss impractical ideas outright. Try saying instead: "That's a great suggestion, but we'll have to take it up later," or "It's good to consider all the options."

- Epicures can be the bonding agents that hold an office together, the optimistic figures who see light at the end of the tunnel.

MOTIVATION

Epicures are drawn to imagining the future, to opening new professional vistas. Attention moves quickly from an idea to the mental associations that the idea stimulates, producing a branching out of possible outcomes.

SEVENs can be described as being "monkey-minded." This phrase conveys the image of an agile mind with a far-ranging but easily distracted scope of interest. Monkeys travel along the forest canopy, moving in any direction that promises a tasty experience. But monkeys do not act at random. They search for things that not only help them survive but are entertaining as well. While possibilities stretch to the farthest horizon, committing to a single course of action requires them to descend and to walk along predictable paths on the forest floor.

Fascinated by the adventure of imagined possibilities, SEVENS have their private epiphanies when several good ideas fit together. Those are the glimpses of what the SEVEN mind is seeking, a juncture point for action that will bring all the best options together into one grand plan. They are also motivated by variety. For example, SEVENS working in the accounting profession will reengineer their career every few years, moving from work for individuals to corporations to nonprofits eager to experience different approaches to the same problems.

> *For Epicures, the passion for ideas and the wonder of bold new systems sometimes culminate in a breakthrough moment when synthesis occurs, and a new line of thought is born. The expansive possibilities that they imagine are a source of pleasure that may not be apparent to other types of people.*

Motivated to find work that involves cutting-edge technology, systems thinking, and complex networking, SEVENS are attracted to jobs that model an interdisciplinary approach.

But when this drive is frustrated, when real-life limitations curtail freedom of exploration, Epicures become slippery and evasive, to escape limitation.

At its worst, this frustrated energy can pave the road to burnout. Either exhaustion will finally catch up, or they, like everyone else, will finally reach a fork in the road that requires a definitive choice.

SEVENS will feel immensely frustrated when their desire to be free runs up against real-world limitations on that freedom. When this happens, they are motivated mostly by an ongoing plan to escape those limits at the first advantageous opening.

But burnout can also produce the right conditions to discover intrinsic motivations, which for SEVENS include work worthy enough to deserve full commitment.

SEVENs grow by noting the difference between genuinely productive ideas and interesting diversions.

Understanding the larger picture depends on returning to those special moments when distractions drop away and ideas coalesce into a satisfying plan of action. At such times, SEVENs know the pure pleasure of unifying their widely divergent interests. It is possible to have it all when all the pieces fit together in a course of action that calls out for full commitment.

A first step toward that goal lies in knowing when the mind gets crowded with frantic thoughts. When this happens, the SEVEN may find it helpful to say: "This is a flight into distraction. I may be running from pain." Then, instead of entertaining imagined possibilities, the SEVEN can step back and refocus on a basic priority that can be accomplished one step at a time.

MOTIVATING SEVENS

- Welcome the SEVENs' optimism and positive vision. They are excited by ideas and possibilities, and they excel at creating multiple options. Support them in developing and sharing their good ideas.

- Most SEVENs enjoy contact with people and make great communicators and hosts. Support them in taking on these roles on behalf of the project and using their charm appropriately.

- Help SEVENs match their plans with real resources: people, time, money. Count on them more in the planning stages and less during implementation. Expect that not all plans will be carried out.

- Give SEVENs the room to establish their own rhythms at work. Don't expect them to always conform to set schedules and procedures. Their productivity tends to rise and fall with their enthusiasm. Be clear about expectations for tangible results and time lines.

- Support SEVENs in having fun, as in telling stories, making jokes, discussing new concepts, entertaining pleasurable possibilities.
- Allow SEVENs to maintain a sense of equality. Don't be too heavy on the use of authority. They will resist "command and control" methods. If you're the boss, don't be put off by a superior attitude. If you're the employee, try to tolerate a lack of direction or clear structure.
- Don't ask SEVENs to limit their options prematurely. Support them in establishing their own priorities. They don't commit themselves out of obligation. The work has to be "worth it."

TIME MANAGEMENT

SEVENs play with time. When things are going well, they can reprioritize, reschedule, and stay up all night if they have to. There's always enough time to sandwich in a new experience, and then it's time to move on.

There's an elastic property to a SEVEN's use of time. When they're on a roll, time expands and anything seems possible. By comparison, real time feels slow, circumscribed, and restrictive. Time drags when Epicures have to show up at exactly the same time every day to the same desk and the same familiar faces. A fixed timetable feels like a jail sentence. Without spontaneity, projects seem set in stone and frozen in time. SEVENs are quite aware of clock time, but it's far more interesting to operate as if time is unlimited. Brainstorming and envisioning the future are ultimately freeing, because there are no restrictions on time, space, or consequences. In fact, the power of imagination is so remarkably self-sustaining that a turn of attention from ideas to practicalities feels like a major slowdown. Ideas are liberating and transcend time, but actualizing those ideas seems to take forever, triggering a SEVEN's pattern of procrastination.

Here's how it plays out. Ellen, a SEVEN attorney, describes herself as impeccable during the initial, creative phase of determining a cause of action that will make up the grounds of a suit and of determining the overall strategic approach her client should take. Articulate and charming, she can position her arguments in several dazzling formats, rationalizing any cautionary objections from members of her firm.

While Ellen finds immense satisfaction in breakthrough thinking, she considers the necessary follow-through—doing the research, writing the briefs, filing the motions—a mere matter of details. In her mind she can imagine the completed project, so for her it practically *is* complete.

It doesn't seem like procrastination to think about the Next Big Thing. It seems like extending the inquiry. Why settle for an obvious solution when the next idea could be better? Why stick to the topic? Why follow the outline when you're on the trail of a brilliant new direction?

> *Dynamic and optimistic,* SEVENS *procrastinate at high speed. A deadline sparks brand-new ideas not only for the task at hand, but for other projects as well. This makes it difficult to finish current commitments.*

HELPING SEVENS MANAGE TIME

- Support SEVENs in their multitask approach. They can be more efficient doing several projects at a time rather than being limited to just one thing.
- Build in time for SEVENs to plan their next project while still at work on the current one.
- Help SEVENs stay on track in discussions and presentations. Their tendency toward associative thinking can lead them all over the map.

- Interrupt SEVENs if they fall into talking too much or telling too many stories. Don't make it personal, but rather use content to redirect their attention.

- When the going gets tough or boring, SEVENs may want to escape. Help them stay focused a little longer, and let them know when they can leave or take breaks.

- SEVENs shine in the short run, but are strongly aversive to routine. Organize repetitive work into short sections, each with a "finale" and a reward. Renew enthusiasm for the final goal at the end of each section, then bring the focus back to the next stage.

- Try the "sandwich exercise": A difficult task can be executed between two tasty moments, something fun at the beginning to get the SEVEN in motion and something to look forward to at the end.

NEGOTIATION

Negotiating with SEVENs is like wrestling a greased watermelon—it's slippery and unmanageable. Other people are dazzled by the loquacious SEVEN's barrage of charming talk that tends to blur distinctions between fact and speculation. SEVENs may offer hypotheses that sound like truth and open-ended suggestions that sound like concrete offers.

Getting a handhold on such a slippery situation requires noticing when a SEVEN moves off onto tangents and bringing her back to the issues on the table.

SEVENs may respond to others' concerns with understanding condescension—"You'd get it if you had my breadth of experience." Their first line of defense is the charm-and-disarm strategy. Next comes condescension. Others know they've scored when an Epicure gets angry. The last line of defense for SEVENs is either fight or flight. SEVENs fight with cutting criticism. Flight is exactly that: They're gone and on to the next thing.

The best approach is to meet their charm with a similar pleasing appearance while sticking to the agenda. Remember, SEVENS do not think in terms of binding settlements. They see their world in terms of multiple options, so where others see a single, permanent commitment, SEVENS may see a context-specific agreement. If the context changes, other options come into play and, in the SEVEN frame of reference, the decision looks different.

In negotiating with Epicures, realize that they may not be thinking in terms of specific loopholes, contingencies, or clauses releasing them from obligation, but they may embed those options within the agreement out of habit. Get a handle on specifics: How much? How many? How long? And when's the due date?

TRAINING AND DEVELOPMENT

The computer revolution and the electronic age provide avenues of training and development that are perfect for SEVENS. They're experts at handling huge amounts of data and stimulation, and they're able to put seemingly unrelated concepts together very quickly in a useful manner.

SEVENS can jump right into training material without needing to have it all fit together. They can quickly pick up ideas, and they communicate well, though perhaps in a disconnected, free-association style filled with questions and comments that drives methodical trainers crazy.

The SEVEN's way of sorting information clearly lends itself to nonlinear, associative learning that doesn't require thinking in depth about a single topic. They learn lots of useful stuff this way, but in a haphazard manner, and they may pass with high marks, although they don't appear to be paying attention.

SEVENS show up as serious learners when their minds are engaged. Unlike Nines, who require a comfortable physical environment, or Fours, who want rapport with a trainer, SEVENS can demonstrate amazing indifference to comfort or to rapport. The defining factor in their learning is their degree of boredom or interest. The trick is to make the right amount of effort in bringing them back to focus, without being too controlling. SEVENs are glad to concentrate on something interesting; they are quick studies who like to learn on their feet. Just don't slow them down or frustrate them. These are self-confident people whose attention comes and goes. Trainers should reinforce the goals and standards, but not expect a consistent learning curve.

THE CASE OF THE SEVEN WHO THOUGHT EVERYONE LOVES A WINNER

The senior partner, a Three, is relaxing in anticipation of conducting the last performance review of the day. The previous reviews didn't go too badly, and he smiles when he thinks about talking to the young broker who will be coming in about ten minutes. How easy it will be to tell his most competent employee that she's done a great job—no ifs, ands, or buts.

Since he has a few minutes before the hour-long interview, the Three partner checks his voice mail. He listens with half an ear while he sketches out a letter to a potential investor.

Both tasks done, he pulls the broker's file but doesn't open it. "Why should I?" he thinks. "I gave her the highest score last time, and as far as I know, nothing has changed. There's no reason to go over the form line by line." Absentmindedly he taps her closed file with his pen. It can stay on the desk for reference purposes, in case she has any questions, but he sees no reason to waste time going through its contents. Still doing several things at once, he quickly checks off "excellent" on all areas of the form while he returns some of his calls.

In glancing at the form while he talks, he vaguely remembers hearing about one of the broker's successful accounts from another partner. This young woman, he thinks, projects a great professional image, just right for the firm. She's young and energetic; she graduated from a good school; she's accomplished, articulate, and comes right to the point. He hasn't heard a bad word about her. He has a welcoming smile on his face as he hears her high heels clicking down the corridor toward his office.

TYPICAL INTERACTIONS

The SEVEN broker is indeed young, bright, and articulate. She sits in the leather chair on the opposite side of his desk. Two equally self-assured smiles flash across the cherrywood desktop. The mutual message: "No problems here."

Reading this positive signal, the SEVEN broker is inwardly relieved. She just might live to see another day. She opens the meeting on a confident note with a question that has fascinating implications. Would he advise her on how best to get a piece of the hot new issue the firm is underwriting? Offering the next Microsoft would be just the thing to cement her relations with two big investors she has been courting.

Pleased to share the benefit of his experience, the partner outlines a strategy she can use in approaching the firm's underwriting team. Being a mentor to this broker is a pleasure.

From the broker's point of view, the feeling is similar to the one she gets when a deal is on course and ready to close.

Without a word being said, a mutual projection takes hold in which each sees the other as an admirer.

Taking a more serious tone, the conversation turns to the Epicure's performance since her last review. The SEVEN, now in familiar territory, accentuates the positive features of her client services, but offers no working papers or backup for the partner's review. But, to be fair, he doesn't ask for any. Hard questions about the completion of transactions and the accuracy of her paperwork don't come up in the conversation. In essence he leaves the substance of her job unquestioned.

The SEVEN broker glances at her watch and realizes that half of the sixty-minute session has expired. Her nervousness, which never showed, drops another level. She's counting on his reputation for not being thorough.

"Maybe he didn't even hear about the Watkins debacle," she tells herself. "I bet he hasn't checked."

The broker had failed to meet a deadline in posting a complex transaction, causing the firm to be fined. SEVEN-like, she rationalizes her error: "It wasn't totally my responsibility. My secretary should have reminded me of the due date. It could have happened to anyone."

Grasping for loopholes and justifications, she remembers: "I just got jammed up. A lot of deadlines crested at the same time the week I got back from Hawaii." The Hawaiian trip was business, but she decided on the spur of the moment to stay for a long weekend.

Reentering the conversation, the Epicure sees there are just fifteen minutes left, and the Watkins case drops from her thinking as if it never happened. "It'll blow over. It won't be important after the firm sees how much business I'll be bringing in," she thinks.

The Three partner catches her looking at her watch. "Well, there's no reason to drag this out," he says. "Your work's unusually good. Congratulations."

They both stand and shake hands. Each is pleased that the session ended a little early, and she leaves quickly.

After she has left the office, the partner picks up the broker's personnel file to put it back in the drawer and notices a blue page sticking out of the very front. It's from the legal department, requesting his signature authorizing payment of a $50,000 fine on the Watkins case.

His pulse jumps. "Oh, my God," he thinks. "How could I have missed this?" Now it will all come crashing down on his head. His partners will hold him responsible, and ask which broker was accountable and how he could have allowed it to happen.

Moving very quickly, he shifts the blue sheet to another drawer. Then he buzzes the broker's office and asks her to return. When she arrives, he pulls out the damning sheet and says: "I forgot to bring this to your attention. This matter needs discussion."

THE TIDE TURNS

It is a moment of truth for two committed optimists, each trying to put the best possible spin on the situation.

The Epicure SEVEN, noticeably flushed and gushing with justifications, ducks and weaves as she frantically searches for a way out.

The partner is deeply conflicted. He wants to keep up an appearance of competence, yet at the same time is angry that the broker took advantage of his habit of not sweating the details.

He is also embarrassed that he didn't make it his business to know about the incident sooner. He realizes that, in his effort to get several things done at once, he has missed crucial details. And the SEVEN knows it. Now the Three wonders who else has seen his weakness and taken advantage of it as well.

> SEVENs *avoid pain whenever they can, and* Threes *project a successful facade, but each now faces severe embarrassment.*

The Epicure is racked with anxiety as she hears the critical edge in the Three's voice: "Fifty thousand dollars! Do you realize what you've done? Watkins is an established client. You've put that relationship in jeopardy and damaged the firm's reputation."

When the incident happened, the broker knew she'd let the

company down, but she didn't think much about it at the time. Now she is presented with the fact that the fine was equal to her annual salary.

She now sees that his anger over the fine is greatly compounded by the fact that she tried to put one over on him—essentially embarrassing him and making him responsible for her mistake. She doesn't want to lose his support, but now she may have jeopardized it or even ruined the relationship permanently. She realizes that she should have owned up to the incident in the first place, instead of banking on the Three's lack of thoroughness. Or better, she should have gone to him right after her mistake to enlist his advice.

RESOLUTION

Oddly, the partner feels sympathetic, although he knows he can't let the emotion show. Still a master of appearances, he will keep his image intact but can't help wondering if he wouldn't have tried to hide the same kind of problem. He tells himself yes, he would have, and the insight is suddenly moving. What can he do to help her now and ensure that she learns from this mistake?

"You know this can't happen again," he begins. "I am going to have to put you under strict supervision and make a note of this in your permanent file. There is no way we can forget about it."

Relieved that she wasn't fired, the Epicure realizes she will be facing painful weekly review sessions from here on out. Plus all of her actions, including the cover-up, will have to be accounted for and justified.

When she leaves, the partner sits back in his chair, drained from the experience. He realizes he's been fooled by the broker's image, and thinks: "God, I hope I can stop deceiving myself." "She could have been a younger version of me," he thinks.

The broker's self-presentation does indeed mirror the partner's. But while his attention is on accomplishing as many tasks as possible, hers is on pleasant future options.

A taste for pleasure got her into trouble in the Watkins case. She was in Hawaii and decided to stay for a long weekend, and as a result she missed the filing deadline. The moment she decided to stay in Hawaii, she forgot the Watkins matter.

Self-observation

SEVENS need to be aware when a pleasant option beckons. When a fascinating possibility comes to mind, it helps to step back and ask: "Is this move constructive or another escape from commitment?"

Point Eight: The Boss

Alias: **General, Confronter, The Challenging Person**

Motto	*Never let them see you sweat.*
Mental Model	*The strong survive and the weak do not.*
Lens of Perception	*Who's got control?*
Way of Sorting Information	*All or nothing.*
Blind Spot	*Impact on others.*
Growth Edge	*Learning the appropriate use of power.*
Spiritual Path	*Feeling secure with own vulnerability.*
Vice	*Lust (excess: too much, too loud, too many).*
Virtue	*Innocence (assuming goodwill from others).*
Inspired By	*Truth.*
Managerial Style	*"My way or the highway." EIGHTs are powerful people who don't always realize their impact on others. No news is good news. If someone's doing well, they hear nothing from the boss, but if they're off course, you hear plenty. Employees should expect to be both protected and micromanaged.*
Appearance to Others	*Blunt, take-charge, commanding presence. EIGHTs are larger-than-life people who fill a room all by themselves.*
Typical Conflicts	*EIGHTs can confuse objective justice ("what's right for us all") with their own interests ("what's in it for me"). EIGHTs make others feel that they must either agree with or oppose an EIGHT's agenda.*

One-Minute Resolution	*Stand toe to toe with an* EIGHT. *Match your voice level to the* EIGHT's *and repeat slowly: "I understand your position. These are the points in your argument. Right? I disagree. Here are my reasons." Do not doctor information in order to avoid confrontation.*

The Signals EIGHTs Send

Positive	*Coworkers feel empowered by* EIGHTs, *who are courageous, persistent, fair-minded, truthful, straightforward, and unpretentious. What you see is what you get.*
Negative	*Misdirected sense of justice leads* EIGHTs *to control others. They can be intimidating and intrusive.*
Mixed	*Secure* EIGHTs *move toward the Giver Two's position and become as supportive as a Two, but when angered, they can be punitive and uncaring.*
Security Response at Point Two	EIGHTs *moving into a Giver's need for approval become highly protective of coworkers, employees, and teams. Approval is earned by empowering others to achieve their full potential.*
Stress/Risk Response at Point Five	EIGHTs *retract into the Observer's need for privacy when their attempt to assert direct control is frustrated. Withdrawn* EIGHTs *hang a large Do Not Disturb sign on their door.*
Work Best In	*Jobs where there's competitive juice and a constructive outlet for energy.* EIGHTs *like their own fiefdom and a clear chain of command for redress of grievances. Real estate developer, CEO of their own company, military commanders.*
Have Problems Working In	*Jobs that require protracted diplomacy and shared power: cochair of anything, consumer relations, representative commanders.*

Where Business Wants Its EIGHTs	*At the helm during a confrontation; spearheading an expansion phase; trial lawyer, union organizer, manager of a sports team.*

ARE YOU AN EIGHT?

An EIGHT's focus is on power and control, on securing the territory. You want to know who's in charge and whether they're fair. You push for full disclosure of information, not only to understand the big picture, but also to stay abreast of workplace politics. Your lens of perception magnifies the fact that top dogs are well rewarded, and that those to whom you report are often less than innocent. All of this equips you with an early warning system that triggers internal sirens at any sign of a power play.

Realizing that the strong dominate the weak, you are extremely protective of the people around you, making sure they're treated fairly. You have also developed great respect for those who are willing to stand up for justice. You're attracted to people who don't cave in under pressure, who go toe to toe at meetings, and who look out for their friends. Weakness is appalling and dependency is beneath contempt, but you have a long history of protecting plucky contenders who stand up for themselves.

However, the people you work with may see your interest in justice as provocative. While all you're doing is trying to get straight answers, they are feeling badgered. What you see as eliciting clear and honest answers, they see as starting a fight. Those same people, however, seem quite willing for you to fight their battles for them, and may indeed seek your leadership. Ann, a vice president in one of our large corporations, is a case in point.

Ann keeps her office door wide open so she can survey as much of the action in her department as possible. Everyone knows they can get her attention if they need to, but they better have good reason to take up her time. Although she's a small woman, her presence fills the entire office, so when Bill enters, he has the impression of a powerful force to be reckoned with.

Bill had been feeling worried when he went in to tell her what had happened. As a member of the marketing department, he's used to collecting feedback from other parts of the company, and when Ann's counterpart, the v.p. of sales, made some pointed suggestions about their current campaign, Bill's ears pricked up.

"But then, it was like this guy took charge of the whole deal," Bill recalled the incident to Ann. "He made it sound like we weren't holding up our end of the campaign. He started dictating what we needed to change and was even talking time lines. I felt awkward. I mean, who am I to tell him no?"

The truth was that Bill would benefit if Ann took charge, instead of allowing the project to be dominated by her counterpart in sales. He didn't like the proposed changes for the project, and knew that by exaggerating the picture slightly, he might be able to influence the decision. Yes, Bill conceded to himself as he watched Ann's face change color. It was like watching a thermometer on a hot day: the red color just kept rising.

The more Ann listened, the madder she got. Teamwork was one thing, but abusing her people—and that was the only thing she could think of to describe what the v.p. for sales had done to Bill—was something else. No one, but no one, ordered her people about. No one.

She asked Bill a couple of questions, just to clarify what had happened, and then picked up the phone. When the vice president's secretary answered, Ann asked to be put through.

"I'm sorry," the secretary said. "He's in a meeting."

"Then yank him out," she said in a stony voice. "We're going to take care of this right now!"

HOW EIGHTS SORT INFORMATION

In the spiritual traditions that use type as a factor in human development, EIGHTs are traditionally known as "monks of lustful mind" because they go for what they want. You're at your best when challenged, and are seen as the type of person who rises to leadership when a business is under pressure. In spearheading a turnaround or a takeover, you secure the bunker, tighten the corporate belt, and, after getting the troops to swear undying allegiance, propel them into battle, knowing they have the complete backing of the Boss EIGHT.

However, it's vital that you realize your impact on others. If you're opposed, you raise the ante and escalate the consequences. Focused on the goal, like a horse with blinders, you may not realize you've cleared the field of friends and foes alike. The goal's the thing, and you quickly forget angry words spoken along the way.

It may not compute that what seems fair to you may be unjust in the eyes of others. Indeed, you may initially dismiss other options as ill-conceived, too obvious, stupid, or boring. You brush suggestions aside because it's too hard to shift position once your attention fixates on a goal with suction-cup intensity. You don't intend to deny alternative opinions, but they simply cease to exist once the energy's up and a lusty rush of vitality propels you forward. The physical power of lust and a dead-ahead focus on the goal justify your position. How could this be wrong when it feels so truthful?

Here's what happens when the EIGHT mind-set clicks in. Imagine you're playing center forward in an aggressive basketball game. When you have the ball, the hoop's the thing, and getting there requires tremendous momentum through a human barricade. Once in motion, you lock your mind into an all-or-nothing stance. From the sidelines, you seem unlikely to score, as there are two or three defenders between you and your goal. But that fact barely registers. You've spotted a small weakness in the opposition's defense that's magnified in your lens of perception. Now you can control the game by taking advantage of that weakness. From the sidelines, you look heroic going up against impossible odds. But you don't see it that way. You're so focused on taking the ball to the hoop that you don't see the defense's actual advantage.

EIGHTS AT WORK

EIGHTs are justice-minded people. In going back to the story of Ann and Bill, we see how this is true of Ann. In fact, her tough exterior protects the heart of a vulnerable child who felt unfairly controlled. She grew up learning to conceal her vulnerability and to test the intentions of powerful people, because she expected to be hurt when she showed weakness.

If you're an EIGHT, you'll relate to Ann's focus on fair play. You'll also have a history of defending causes in the name of justice, like this popular CEO of an East Coast furniture chain, who worked his way up the corporate ladder.

> *I've ended up sitting on every grievance committee the company ever formed. I can't stand oppression, and oppressed people who sit around and take it make me angry. The truth is I get so bored at meetings, and so sick of waffling, that I get mad to stay interested.*
>
> *It got to be a standing joke, because I would argue against everybody, just to break the ice. That way nobody had to worry about their image, because I went first. I do not see why anger has such a bad rap. It's supposed to be a divisive, negative emotion, but to me, anger clears the air and gets everyone mobilized and moving.*

The CEO assumes that others also have the ability to assert themselves and back up their opinions. He finds that a fair fight clears the air and is quickly forgotten after everything that should have been said has been aired. If you agree that anger feels cleansing and exhilarating, you're likely to be an EIGHT, who knows that anger quickly reveals deeper feelings. Under pressure, people blurt out what matters most. They speak the truth in anger.

> *Above all, watch your boredom level. When boredom creeps in, trouble swiftly follows. It's a lot more fun to energize and to bend the rules than to sit around waiting for something to happen.*

The trick to staying out of trouble is making sure you stay interested. You like making the rules, but breaking them is just as delicious. Actually, the rules don't really matter. What matters is that it's your call to agree or rebel. To stay out of trouble, increase what you require of yourself, rather than micromanaging or interfering with others just to stay interested.

KEEP THIS IN MIND

EIGHTs on teams have the energy switch either on or off. When a project's interesting, the switch gets flipped, and the energy rises in a few seconds flat. Finally! Something huge and difficult to deal with. A consuming idea. A titanic project that keeps you working late for weeks. What the team may not know is that you're also observing their commitment and calculating their endurance. Positioning yourself as an example of perseverance and fortitude is bound to set things in motion and reveal the line between coworkers who give their all and those who wimp out.

The idea that there are multiple equally valid points of view can be chilling, because you want an unshakable platform for action. Ambiguity, mixed messages, or unclear team communications are threatening because they make you question the truth of your own position.

In your spiritual path, lust for life brings power and charisma to the foreground, dispelling questions and doubts. The blind spot in the picture is your own vulnerability. Yes, you can mobilize quickly and hit the goal harder than other types, but invincible players can also be weakened by denying the good ideas of others. Your growth edge lies in knowing when the desire to control first arises, and learning to use appropriate force. Why use a hundred pounds of pressure to lift a bag of feathers? Why think of justice and blame if the powers around you are innocent?

A FINAL THOUGHT

An EIGHT's mind-set works wonders on the basketball court but is notoriously unproductive when diplomacy, patience, and flexibility are required. Here's where the proverbial "wait and count ten before you answer" really works. Remember Ann the vice president: she had to learn to hear another person's point of view before letting her own opinion kick in.

So wait. Practice listening skills. Use the time while you're counting to ten to really take in what you've been told. Then internally repeat the words that you've heard, even though it makes you feel foolish as you do it. Use your imagination to practice shifting your perspective. If you could see yourself through someone else's eyes, what advice would you give yourself?

During periods of calm, keep checking out your impact on the people around you. Get feedback about how you come across. An understanding of the Enneagram quickly reveals how the other types react to powerful, direct contact. Be skillful in matching different emotional patterns, because what you see as merely expressing an opinion, others typically see as setting up a confrontation.

SECURITY AND STRESS

Dynamics of Change for Point Eight

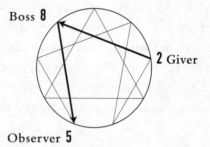

SECURITY RESPONSE AT POINT TWO

When a Boss feels good, so does everyone else around them. You're the office power pack, formulating large-scale plans and following a megawatt schedule. Such a boss is outgoing and gregarious, having a great time extending a protective mantle and making the way safe for staff.

When you feel good enough for long enough, your control needs soften, and you find yourself moving toward people rather than testing them out. In the diagram, this shift shows up as the EIGHT falling back to the security position of a Giver Two. Your guard goes down when you can trust the people around you, and you realize that you need them.

It suddenly matters that people like you, and the same words that would have slid off when you were geared up for action are suddenly piercing. Coworkers may not notice this inner change, but you're easily wounded when you let someone under your skin. It's important to set an example of how you want to be treated, although it may be unsettling to feel vulnerable. Unexpectedly, you'll be pleased to find that others become protective of you when they feel that you need them.

STRESS/RISK RESPONSE AT POINT FIVE

The first signs of stress heighten your EIGHT-like strategy of defense. Your attention narrows to sense the weak spots in an opponent's position, while hiding your own strength until you find an opening. Then you strike, using whatever skills are available. A petite EIGHT woman holds her adversary close through force of will and persistence. A large male can use his powerful voice and commanding personal presence. In either case, the objective is dominance, and it's very hard to shift gears once your all-or-nothing focus of attention kicks in.

What happens if you don't win that fight?

A partial failure makes you dig in, escalate whatever pressure you can bring to bear to influence the outcome, and hold out for the duration. In times of risk, be careful about inadvertently turning your anger on the staff who support you. Your frustration must not polarize the situation further. Once you are entrenched in siege mentality, it will take unusual powers of persuasion to coax you out.

An outright failure sends you into retreat at Five, the place of the Observer. If moving against people doesn't work, then safety lies in strategic withdrawal. You disappear to consolidate your strength and are incommunicado when you're down for the count. Bad times have to be handled alone.

Wanting to be seen as powerful, as leading the charge, you need a while to collect yourself and return in a neutral role. When you do emerge, it will appear that nothing has happened. Ironically, failure is a good time to reach you. Because you fully expect to be crippled when you're weak, an offer of help or a face-saving solution creates a friend for life.

HOW OTHERS SEE EIGHTS

COMMUNICATION STYLE

EIGHTs are direct communicators. Coworkers typically appreciate their blunt and forthright style, knowing that "what you see is what you get." Quick to assign blame when they feel threatened, EIGHTs mobilize energy rapidly by creating a target for action. What isn't communicated is the fact that they are equally hard on themselves when, in seeing their own errors, their anger turns inward.

An EIGHT's opinion is immediately known because he is not afraid to talk about it. EIGHTs speak in terms of justice, pointing out what seems unfair and how to balance the scales. People working for them have learned that the best way to deliver news is straight out, without qualification. They've also learned not to hide bad news. EIGHTs are frequently unaware of their impact; they do not harbor hidden agendas, and won't carry a grudge once their anger has been vented.

It isn't surprising that people leave the chair at the head of the table empty, knowing that the Boss is likely to take over the meeting when he arrives, even if he's sworn up and down ahead of time that he only plans to "listen and learn." Those in attendance know that he will get interested and suggest a course of action, while the rest of them either fall in line or resist.

Those who believe in the EIGHT's position view him as assertive, powerful, and protective. Those who are opposed think he's presumptuous and overbearing.

The people who get along best with an EIGHT make sure to tell him on the spot about the consequences of his proposed actions. They do not waffle, delay, or soften their delivery.

> *The unfortunate consequences of communication by power are the resulting debris of hurt feelings and the time spent in damage control. It's a cyclical loop. EIGHTs respect strong opposition, but confrontation can turn potential allies into opponents who want to retaliate. Fallout is inevitable.*

Consider this report from someone in an unaware EIGHT's communication loop:

> *I recently found out at a team-building session that I'm a Five, but what's more important is the fact that my supervisor is an EIGHT. There she was, complimenting my "instrumental support" for her award-winning publicity campaign, and I'm thinking, "This is crazy."*
>
> *For me, that project was a career low point. I would rather quit than have to fight her every inch of the way again. I had spotted a delivery problem at the very start, but she kept saying we'd deal with it when we got there. Finally, one day I had had it. I got so angry that I didn't care about the outcome. I hate that feeling of aggression—it hits me in my stomach and I feel out of control for days. But for her, my yelling that this problem had to be solved was business as usual. She has no idea what it cost me.*

Nonverbal Communication

People feel an EIGHT's presence without a word being said. Bosses radiate certainty, which can be perceived as potentially challenging, especially by types who repress their own hostility. Loyal Skeptics, for example, succumbing to their own Six-like fears, may see an EIGHT as dangerous and withhold unwelcome information. And Mediator Nines, eager to keep the peace, can wait EIGHTs out for years.

Even when they're physically small, an EIGHT's body language is direct and unpretentious. There's an up-and-out surge of energy that broadcasts an impression of size and determination. These power surges can be highly constructive. We line up behind a Boss during an expansion phase of a campaign, trusting him implicitly because we know he can deal with conflict.

Coworkers also know that EIGHTs communicate poorly when things get quiet. Without the excitement of a constructive outlet or obvious goal, an EIGHT can turn to troublemaking. When they're bored, EIGHTs can fan the flames of minor incidents until they become major bonfires, disturbing a peaceful office.

COMMUNICATING WITH EIGHTS

- EIGHTs are usually assertive about what they want. Meet them directly and be clear with your yes and no responses. If you stand your ground they may not like it, but you will earn their respect.
- EIGHTs can regard having to make compromises as weakness. Let them know you understand their position, using words they would choose for themselves. Then state your case. Avoid escalating the argument and keep returning to the basics.
- EIGHTs can be sparing with compliments and praise. They don't generally seek other people's approval and may underestimate the value of giving approval. Encourage them to think about what supports and motivates others.
- Listen to the content of what they have to say even when they are angry or blaming. Accept that they are angry without taking it personally. If you have made a mistake, say so while maintaining your self-worth.
- Help EIGHTs to moderate their forcefulness when appropriate. They can miss out on vital information or resources if people withdraw from them to avoid anger or

conflict. Reframe justice issues so that all sides are equally heard.

* Give EIGHTs feedback. Challenge their assumptions about other people, or the way things have to be done. They can easily charge ahead with wrong information or without taking the time to consider the options.

* Keep EIGHTs well informed. Consult with them whenever in doubt. Oversights may be perceived as betrayal. Bad news can be handled, but no news makes you suspect.

MOTIVATION

The emotional survival strategy that EIGHTs depend on is called lust, and it means a lust for life—for energy, challenge, and competition—for using the vitality of the life force to get things done. There's nothing more pleasurable than accelerating into a job that demands a huge commitment of time and energy. EIGHTs don't have to be motivated when they feel well used in their work and can finally go full out, instead of feeling like someone who goes through life with one foot constantly on the brakes.

> *Why bother unless you can bring full commitment to bear? Why make an effort unless there's something of magnitude to accomplish?*

Young EIGHTs like to work until they drop and sleep until they wake and go to work again. They can also be extremely lazy when the work's not challenging. It's an all-or-nothing pattern. The energy switch is either on or off because the job's not worth doing unless you can give it your all.

For example, an EIGHT attorney will be highly protective of those who seek her help. She will take charge of dealing with the opposition, the courts, and even the client's family. She may also hector the clients "for their own good." Clients are bound to be admonished, "Don't quit. We've got to fight this." If a compromise or a defeat is inevitable, she will shift gears to manage the death march. Arrangements have to be made, emotions controlled, and grieving people supported.

Our attorney doesn't have to be motivated when the environment provides enough challenge. She would move mountains for someone she believes in, just as she becomes a rallying point for staff in times of stress. Under pressure, she rises to direct and control every response to an emergency, becoming the will of those who tend to unravel in crisis. Perfectionist Ones, for example, prone to freezing for fear of making a mistake, find themselves infused with her confidence, while emotional Giver Twos are steadied by her mastery of the situation.

But when she can't go full out, when her take-charge leadership is ineffective, then her natural vitality turns to anger directed either at herself or others. EIGHTs cause trouble when their need for stimulation is obstructed or when they feel controlled by others. At an all-time low, she is motivated by survival needs and will bide her time until justice is done. But burnout also produces the right conditions for discovering intrinsic motivations, which for EIGHTs is to find a constructive outlet for their formidable energies. To grow, EIGHTs must be aware when loss of control escalates into anger. A first step is to notice when anger rises and learn to refocus on the elements of a job that can be constructively shaped and managed.

MOTIVATING EIGHTS

- EIGHTs demand respect, fairness, and direct communication. Provide all three if you want them as your allies.
- Fair fighting builds trust. EIGHTs will fight with friends and colleagues in the interest of getting to the truth and

working things out. Stick up for yourself and your position, and don't cave in.

- Encourage the natural leadership ability of EIGHTs and help them harness their assertiveness and enthusiasm to the shared goal or cause. Support EIGHTs in using their strength to empower others, rather than to dominate them. Point out the benefits of a cooperative system and the limits of a coercive one.

- EIGHTs mobilize against a competitor and for a friend. They will fight for justice for themselves and others, and will go to great lengths to redress a wrong.

- When they are invested in a project, EIGHTs will work past the point of exhaustion. Support them in pacing themselves and in delegating responsibility to others.

- EIGHTs want the truth and will push until they get it. Let them know where you stand. Schedule regular report sessions and get everything out in the open. Insist on full disclosure from them as well.

- EIGHTs want to be in charge of their own territory, whatever that is. They may test the leadership or try to increase their own control. Support them in establishing clear boundaries in which they can operate with autonomy.

TIME MANAGEMENT

EIGHTs are in control of time. When they're on time, then everyone else has to show up promptly. When they want off, then everyone gets a break. EIGHTs make and break the rules. They control by enforcing—or not enforcing—punctuality.

They also control time by focusing on what interests them, while everything else gets less than full attention.

Deadlines are not an issue for an EIGHT in the printing trade. He meets them. Deadlines signal the culmination of a project in which the EIGHT has invested his experience, skill, energy, and intensity.

An EIGHT printer will often arrive early for meetings (another way of controlling time), but once he is on the job, time does not register. The job fills time. Supervisors cannot easily tell where he will be at any time between starting a project and the deadline. He doesn't think in terms of formal time lines when it comes to completing the project. All he knows is that he has to stay in motion and keep going. The force of his forward momentum will get him to the deadline. He comes and goes, allocating time to what he decides is important. Time is his to control.

The need to control time spills over into how EIGHTs deal with colleagues, because their preferred interpersonal mode is leadership. They get to control not only their own time but also the time of those who work for them. However, an EIGHT's genuine blindness to how others react can result in his time being siphoned away from more central goals while he is forced to backtrack and mend fences.

Working with others, being patient at meetings, and waiting for people to get up to speed are sources of ongoing frustration to EIGHTs. It seems to them that other people are overcautious and deliberately stalling. "Why is everyone wasting my time?"

Because EIGHTs don't run on other people's time—it's the job that's important, not some artificial construct such as keeping track of time—they do not see themselves as procrastinating. If a deadline isn't met, if a project is overdue, blame falls at the doorstep of unforeseen obstacles that took up extra time.

HELPING EIGHTS MANAGE TIME

- Support EIGHTs in effective planning. They can be very impatient with delay and tend to move into action without considering all the consequences or alternatives.

Remind them to listen to other people's opinions and incorporate them when useful.

- When EIGHTs meet opposition, they tend to push even harder. Tunnel vision can set in. Help them take time to evaluate and reassess. There may well be important information that would indicate a change of course.

- Support EIGHTs in taking the time to enroll others in the project. In a self-fulfilling prophecy, they may discount other people's potential contribution. Remind them that others depend on conceptual understanding, group consensus, or personal contact, etc., in order to get into gear.

- Present the idea that working well with others not only increases productivity, but that it's also a great survival tool.

- Encourage EIGHTs to think before they speak, especially when they're worked up about an issue. They won't be comfortable putting a lid on themselves, but it can keep them from having to spend a lot of time on damage control later.

- If you work for an EIGHT, suggest informal weekly sessions to provide both the boss and others with an opportunity to collaboratively explore issues and ventilate concerns. This will help to head off potential explosions down the road.

NEGOTIATION

You will have to speak up when negotiating with EIGHTs. From their side of the table, they come across as self-assured, very grounded, and unaware of any chinks in their armor. Conversely, they are hypersensitive to opponents' weak spots and may probe until they find one. Once they do, they won't let go, even if that isn't the real issue.

For example: An Observer Five goes to an EIGHT supervisor to ask for a raise. The Observer deserves it. He's been working hard, and the company has been prospering from his efforts.

In the course of the Five's argument, he happens to mention that a colleague in the next cubicle got a raise two months ago and that he is actually asking for less than she received.

Don't be surprised if the EIGHT supervisor seizes on that point, ignoring all the others. If the Five compares himself to his next-door neighbor, that quickly becomes the issue. All of a sudden the Five is defending his attendance record against hers, and not talking about his accomplishments.

Conversely, if the EIGHT supervisor wants to give him that raise, the supervisor will dismiss every possible objection as secondary and focus on one of the Five's attributes, minor though it may be, as the reason for giving him more money. Odds are that the Observer will get exactly what he wants when the supervisor has no real preference about the outcome. However, in adversarial matters, when the EIGHT has an axe to grind, one way to negotiate is to shift attention to another option.

For instance, say that a Loyal Skeptic Six knows she is about to be transferred. She will be sent either to Dallas or to Houston, and would really prefer Dallas. The Six may want to argue the merits of the city she *doesn't* want.

The Loyal Skeptic's argument to the EIGHT supervisor could go like this: "You know, I really do understand why you may want to send me to Dallas, but I've made a list of reasons why the company would be better off if I go to Houston." The odds are that the Boss may take the other side and end up "convincing" you that Dallas is the better place.

The advantage of negotiating in this way is that the Six may get the city of choice, and if the strategy backfires, is still in the same place of having to go with the Boss's choice.

TRAINING AND DEVELOPMENT

EIGHTs have difficulty asking for guidance, so offer feedback carefully and fairly. Have regular debriefing sessions to prevent EIGHTs from going off on their own. EIGHTs don't take naturally to constructive criticism or phrases like "You should follow these steps exactly," and will surrender control only if the trainer has proven his own competency.

When EIGHTs are in the class, trainers should set a tone of conviction and provide strong leadership. EIGHTs show up as superb learners when they see the practical benefit of the job and can be enrolled to help other trainees. Keep the sessions interactive. Allow EIGHTs to move around the room; encourage participation, but stay in charge. EIGHTs like to see the big picture and how their piece fits into the whole. But balance theory with practical applications to keep them from getting bored.

Read the following interaction between a One supervisor and an EIGHT trainee for tips on how to help EIGHTs learn new skills.

THE CASE OF THE TECHNOPHOBIC EIGHT

The EIGHT transport dispatcher is up for review. His unit is the largest provider of home service meals in the area, and he's responsible for four hundred deliveries a day.

His distribution system has been so effective that the board has decided to expand service in his area. The EIGHT dispatcher does not yet know of the proposed changes that the board wants kept confidential for the time being. What he does know is that client satisfaction is at an all-time high, despite the erratic requirements of the homebound elderly and ill.

The executive director of the company is a Perfectionist One, and she's not looking forward to the review. She knows about the impending expansion, but the increased kitchen capacity will require more delivery vans, adding to an already troubled transport system. It seems at least one van breaks down daily.

This is the dispatcher's third review, and the pattern looks familiar: Top ratings in all categories except planning, and planning is going to be the key to handling the soon-to-be-increased volume of deliveries. The One director has already given him a computer with logistical software, but the computer boxes remain unopened on the floor of his office. Now it's time to revisit this troublesome subject.

TYPICAL INTERACTIONS

The director is irritated. How can she tell the popular, hardworking EIGHT that his good work isn't conforming to his standard job description? Everybody loves the generous, freewheeling dispatcher. He's the kind of supervisor drivers are willing to switch routes for. The director knows the dispatcher can always get the drivers to pull together when things get too busy.

The Perfectionist director sighs. Why is hers always the lone voice of complaint? Why is she cast as the prissy authority? Still, for his own good, she can't let the dispatcher get away with what she sees as insubordination (ignoring the new computer).

The expansion will blow the current transportation system out of the water. Right now most of the scheduling takes place in the dispatcher's head. There's no way he'll be able to keep everything straight once all the new routes are added. It's clear that the dispatcher will have to use a computer, but how can she insist in such a way that won't rile her EIGHT employee, who periodically goes on the attack? Why does he insist on doing it his way?

The dispatcher loves the controlled pandemonium of his job: telephone in one hand, microphone in the other, several agitated drivers competing for his attention. The job is as much about the excitement of a crowded operations room as it is about getting the meals through.

In the dispatcher's EIGHT-like viewscreen, the chaos and fragility of the aging van fleet is part of his day-to-day challenge. The director sees it differently. Why, she fumes, is the dispatcher not supporting change in the organization?

The Perfectionist director is a worrier, and she does a bunch of it while waiting for the dispatcher to show up for his review. The nonprofit's books are open to everyone, since hers is a publicly funded facility. What if the newspapers discover this mismanagement? She has seen how they can shoot down a public-sector operation. What if a board member dropped in during the morning chaos? The dispatcher makes her feel out of control, and she resents what she sees as his negligence.

Ten minutes late, the EIGHT breezes in with the confidence of someone who knows his way around. The director's rigid posture suddenly makes him feel awkward, so he overcompensates with a hearty "Good morning!"

As usual, the One executive director sits upright in her office chair, so the EIGHT deliberately slouches. It never takes more than three minutes of being in each other's presence before each tries to control the other—the One by making the rules and the EIGHT by breaking them. Unfortunately, they like each other. Open animosity would be easier.

The rebellious EIGHT knows this review is going to center on planning, and he also knows that he does not want to develop any new skills. He takes the offensive and begins rationalizing out loud: "You can only do this job a day at a time. A computer printout won't work, because everything gets changed or screwed up almost the second you write it down. The important thing is that our service is doing great, costs are in line, and the drivers are happy. We've already dealt with planning during the last two evaluations. This is all old news. Besides, I have no time to learn about computers. Better toss that machine."

In response, the director hears her own voice, pinched and high, say: "I sent you a memo regarding your computer literacy. What happened?"

The EIGHT slouches down further, and the One thinks: "Why can't he cooperate?" She remembers that the dispatcher has worked his way up from van driver.

"You are going to need new skills," she says. "Trucks are breaking down because they aren't well maintained." Her jaw clenched with anger, the One knows she's being maneuvered into an uptight, authoritarian posture. Though she's in the right, she's not enjoying herself.

> *What you have is two angry people in a standoff—a One's perfectionistic indignation pitted against the up-front anger of an EIGHT.*

From his side of the desk, the EIGHT is throttling up. Now the director's issue is on the table, and his litany of grievances surfaces.

"This isn't a desk job," he begins, while internally thinking: "I'd like to see her handle those drivers! This job isn't about rules, it's about people."

He considers going over her head to the board. Reciting his list of complaints gives him a sense of control; he can see that she's uncomfortable, and he wouldn't mind escalating the action.

THE TIDE TURNS

In actuality, the dispatcher knows he can't go on keeping everything in his head, using a tiny pocket notebook to jog his memory. But admitting weakness feels like groveling. He's decided to quit rather than go to computer school.

To the outside observer this looks like a standoff, but the

unspoken communication between them is milder. Neither is making much money, but they're firmly committed to the non-profit, and they've worked together for a long time. The director gathers herself. She's just thought of a new possibility, and says: "The board has voted to expand, mainly because of your record."

Caught off guard, the startled EIGHT blurts out: "We can run a thousand trucks if I don't have to use that machine."

The Perfectionist director suddenly gets it. Her hunch had been right, the EIGHT hasn't read the computer manual because he's afraid he might not understand it. It wasn't sabotage or insubordination—it was insecurity and embarrassment.

Thinking quickly, she reviews the budget. "The expansion can fund a part-time data entry technician for the computer. Can you manage all the drivers *and* the tech?" The director thinks, "A tech will be a safe teacher. The dispatcher can ask beginner's questions in private."

The meeting ends with a quick nod, a handshake, and the EIGHT's hearty laughter drifting back from the hallway. Savoring the warmth of the moment, the Perfectionist realizes, "I wouldn't want to be ashamed, either."

RESOLUTION

The Perfectionist director acted against type by breaking confidence with the board. One-like, she would have preferred to attack the dispatcher, vindicate herself through the board's mandate, and rid herself of a management headache. Had she continued in that vein, a seasoned employee would have quit.

Instead she tuned in to her long-standing admiration for the EIGHT and tried to see through his eyes. When she did so, her One-like vice of anger shifted, and she stopped judging him.

From his side of the table, the dispatcher was taken off guard by being appreciated. Temporarily losing his "tough guy" control, the EIGHT admits to his technophobia and, by showing vulnerability rather than insubordination, breaks the impasse. Now they both know what's at the root of his resistance and can structure a face-saving approach to computer literacy that serves both their needs.

Self-observation

Oddly, EIGHTs need to pause when they feel totally right in an argument. If indeed their view was 100 percent accurate, there would be no disagreement. It helps to stand back and internally question: "Am I seeing the full picture?" "Can I exchange places and see the rightness of another point of view?"

Point Nine: The Mediator

Alias: **Reconciler, Negotiator, Arbitrator,**
The Person Who Avoids Conflict

Motto	*Don't rock the boat.*
Mental Model	*Everything has its pros and cons.*
Lens of Perception	*Other people's agendas.*
Way of Sorting Information	*Processing the different angles on a decision obliterates a personal choice.*
Blind Spot	*Own position.*
Growth Edge	*Acting on your own behalf.*
Spiritual Path	*Finding your own path of identity and decision making.*
Vice	*Self-forgetting.*
Virtue	*Action.*
Inspired By	*Unqualified support.*
Managerial Style	*Either mediation-driven consensus agreement, when everybody gets something and everyone's best emerges, or management by the book: "Don't argue with me—argue with the book."*
Appearance to Others	*Unflappable, amiable, and comforting, or stubborn and foot-dragging.*
Typical Conflicts	*Passive-aggressive tactics; the job just never gets finished.*
One-Minute Resolution	*If you are a NINE, remember that anger can clear the air and be constructive.*

The Signals NINES Send

Positive	*Adaptive to the needs of different individuals. Compromising and receptive. Able to draw out what is essentially good in others.*
Negative	*Stubbornly angry, deliberately missing the point, tuning others out, seeing everything as equally important, which makes people feel unimportant. Repeating the known, safe route.*
Mixed	*Outer compliance to keep the peace, mixed with inner rage at missed opportunities. Overt message: "It doesn't matter." Covert message: "I was overlooked."*
Security Response at Point Three	*Here NINES are in action—on target, on schedule, and hopefully on course for a personal choice.*
Stress/Risk Response at Point Six	*Here stress forces choices, and while cold panic can produce paralysis, on the low side of stress, on the high side, uncustomary powers of focus lead to accurate risk assessment.*
Work Best In	*Jobs that require big-picture perspectives and take account of multiple inputs: global planning.*
Have Problems Working In	*Fast-paced, rapidly changing environments that downplay interpersonal communication.*
Where Business Wants Its NINES	*U.S. Postal Service, vice president of administration, office manager, big-picture planning.*

ARE YOU A NINE?

If you're still having trouble discovering your type, you may be a NINE who can see everyone else's agenda while neglecting your own. NINES are aware of all the points in someone else's position, but when you're asked what you want, you're not sure. Besides, you probably feel that you're unlikely to get what you want anyway, so why bother asking?

However, most of the people you work with assume that you've chosen your course of action. To them, the fact that you haven't said no means that you're in agreement. Why? To you, agreement means understanding that X is vitally important to someone else. You get swept up in their enthusiasm for X and are committed to supporting their interests, but your agreement only covers going along with X until you decide how you feel about it.

It can take a long time to decide, because most people have a big agenda, and their opinions sound louder than your own. Here's what happened to Karen, a young associate who shares the NINE predicament of understanding all the warring factions at her law firm.

The office bickering has broken out again, and there's no question in anyone's mind where they'll be taking their coffee break later today in an effort to resolve things. They'll head straight to Karen's office.

The fact that the associates in one of Chicago's largest law firms are squabbling shouldn't come as a surprise. They're lawyers, after all—young ones, to be sure, but trained to argue about everything, including the division of research tasks on a major new case. Much of the work will be tedious and boring and may take weeks. That's the current dispute.

What is surprising is they all agree that one of their own is an understanding, impartial arbiter. With absolute affection, they have nicknamed her "the reconciler." Karen is the one they turn to when there's a conflict to be resolved. She's famous within the firm for seeing the pros and cons of every court decision, and she's known as a natural mediator.

Because she sees the big picture, there's no doubt that Karen will make an excellent lawyer. She can spot many different angles in a single case and argue for any of them. However, her inclination to find a middle ground puts her at a disadvantage when it comes to jockeying for position within the firm. Positioning herself is complicated by seeing the merits of the other people who are also trying to become partner.

Karen's very approachable because she listens without inserting her own opinions and judgments. People don't feel opposed by her or manipulated into giving her something. Karen seems to be in agreement even when she's not, because she's "trying out" an opinion to see how it feels. She likes taking in other people's stories and lending herself to their perspective, but she cannot deal with anger and is very uncomfortable with confrontation.

As usual, everyone at the "Who gets the boring research?" meeting has a strong motive for getting their own way, except Karen, who's too busy listening. It's obvious they need to make assignments, and they're looking to Karen to negotiate a schedule. The only bad moment is when Jim turns and asks, "So where do you stand?" Inwardly Karen flinches, realizing that she is sitting squarely on the fence, so involved with everyone else that she doesn't have her own opinion about the schedule.

How nines Sort Information

After they're gone, Karen holds the real meeting inside her head. If you looked through her lens of perception, you'd see Jim's thoughts about the schedule, and by widening the angle slightly, the other associates would come into focus. NINEs are traditionally known as "monks of lazy mind," people who lose their own agenda. Karen is not at all physically lazy, but she is so occupied by simultaneously processing other opinions that she herself drops out of the picture.

How can Karen decide, when there are pros and cons for each side of the case? It all seems so arbitrary. Why have an opinion when it's so easy to know who's for and against it? Is a research schedule worth fighting for? Soon there will be new faces in the office, and the current associates will scatter if they don't make it to partner. Newcomers will have their own ideas and different opinions. Is this all worth the effort when the context will inevitably change?

The more Karen broadens the scope of her decision, the more burdened she becomes with additional input. But none of this seems irrelevant. By now she's obsessing about the real values of decision making, and her feelings about the research schedule fade. Like a juggler, keeping a complex cascade of balls aloft, she's simultaneously processing everyone's take on the schedule, her own emerging opinions, and the various contexts in which these decisions are set.

After all, doesn't menial research actually fall into the broader context of hierarchical work roles? And weren't the associates really caught in a battle of wills about authority, about setting turf? Was the context of the question merely about getting the research done, or more about equalizing authority? With a slight twist of Karen's lens, the whole context shifts from squabbling about a schedule to posturing about who should make it to partner.

Karen feels herself starting to space out. The research schedule is irrelevant in the bigger context of partnership, and maybe the schedule even has bearing on the far broader context of professional commitments. At this thought Karen's energy starts to die and she wants a cup of coffee.

But Karen does have a knack for seeing all the inputs in a big picture. It's both her talent and her bane, especially when she can't figure out what she wants. She has no problem knowing what Jim or the other associates want, because they're very clear about the context they're coming from. But in choosing for herself, where should Karen begin?

Unlike Epicure Sevens, who see points of agreement between different systems, or Performer Threes, who see the useful aspects of many systems converging on a goal, Karen the NINE is aware of the global context, which holds every system within itself.

NINES AT WORK

Karen has always been good at knowing where people are coming from. She remembers feeling overlooked by adults when she was a child, and eventually she "fell asleep," by emotionally distancing herself from what mattered most. Her thread of connection to the people around her depended on keeping the peace instead of asking for what she wanted, so she learned to numb out, distracting herself from disappointment.

Trying to get her own way was a no-win situation. She either felt overlooked or got pulled into someone else's agenda. So she learned to wait it out. Her emotional survival strategy allowed her to partially agree with everybody, get along with most, and thereby avoid conflict.

If you're a NINE, you'll relate to being distracted from what really matters. You arrive at work eager to get going on a project that excites you, but at the end of the day it hasn't been touched. What happened? How did the main priority get sidetracked while incidentals got done? In retrospect, you were waylaid by calls, distracted by talk, sucked into E-mail, and derailed by secondary projects. In hindsight it's all obvious, but at the time, those choices seemed as important as your own agenda.

NINEs like structured work. Deadlines get you up to speed. When the priority is external and objective, everybody understands the reason when you say no to their requests for your time. However, you are typically challenged by organizational cultures requiring fast-paced, rapidly changing decisions, like David, a

NINE product development manager who had to learn to pick up the pace during Seven-style brainstorming sessions for new product design.

> *I used to go in with my specs already in place. I knew what I wanted ahead of time, but I also knew enough to keep my briefcase under the table and my mouth shut until all the shouting was over. It just moved too fast. I am far too methodical to deal with a bunch of different ideas without some way to hang them together.*

The NINE product manager was stolidly trying to stay on track so he wouldn't get distracted by trivia. He dealt with new product design with a go-slow pattern of fitting each idea into the big picture as he moved ahead.

> *The* NINE, *with an excellent track record, was perceived as someone who always wanted a safe, boring design, whereas the less practical Seven brainstormers were on the cutting edge, hip and experimental.*

The NINE, who wanted nothing more than good feelings among his team members, realized he was a major irritant. To him, an influx of new information signaled a dead halt, right at the point when everyone else was wildly excited and moving rapidly forward. He needed time to mull over one idea at a time, instead of letting them all stream by. He got disoriented at the dreaded design meetings, and he couldn't wait to be alone and construct a framework to save what he knew were excellent suggestions. He did eventually learn to loosen up, but what he didn't know was that in the process, he had learned to pay attention like a Seven.

I finally got it, that I'm not supposed to understand what's happening in those meetings. I start with a design idea, and then let whatever the idea reminds me of run through my head. There is no logic, just mental associations; sometimes they hit, sometimes they don't. Figuring this out was a big relief, because I finally saw why no one felt insulted when their idea wasn't chosen, and it wasn't my responsibility to make sure everyone got equal time.

KEEP THIS IN MIND

If you're a NINE, working on teams may be your natural element. So long as there's harmony, you're able to fully support a group effort. Equipped with the marvelous ability to take in another's victory as your own, you'll be a fair-minded sounding board for disaffected players.

> NINEs *will back a star, as long as the star is quick to acknowledge that team effort won the game. Merged with the ambitions of others, you're the glue that holds a team together.*

You tend to internalize the overall climate of opinions on a team, taking the shape of the environment around you. You're upbeat when that's the prevailing tone, but you get very discouraged on a team that's dissatisfied. At your best, you can draw each individual out, simply by giving them unconditional support. But you'll feel undone if you let yourself be torn by conflict.

Remember, finding your own course of action is the spiritual remedy for people who forget themselves. Your own agenda must emerge regardless of the environment. A good line for NINEs to remember is "I'm not for you, I'm not against you, I'm for what I feel is right." Far from being a moral prescription, acting for what's right is liberating for people like yourself, who tend to sacrifice their own needs.

In the spiritual sense, taking right action means rallying others by example. Speak your mind and don't worry about who agrees or disagrees. When you have an opinion, stay on course and don't get distracted. Nonaction has measurable consequences that can be greater than those caused by open conflict. So don't fall into the trap of waiting too long or decisions will be made without your opinion.

A FINAL THOUGHT

As a NINE, indecision is familiar to you, but it can upset the people around you. If you give the impression of sitting on a fence, people are inclined to push. They want to know where your commitment lies, but additional pressure makes you stubborn, because you don't see inaction as saying no. It's true you obsess over decisions and ask for advice, but you won't be hurried into resolving a problem.

Going stubborn is a passive way of saying no. The message is loud and clear although you've never shouted. You're hoping to avoid confrontation, but your inaction—slowing down and tuning people out—is provocative. There's no overt anger, but it's clear that you're dissatisfied.

Allowing yourself to get angry can be a great relief. Your anger takes a long time to surface, but with it comes a real position. Once a position is taken, the logjam of indecision is broken and commitment swiftly follows. When you're angry, you know exactly what you don't want and you have enough energy to make big changes in a very short time.

For NINEs, anger builds slowly because you're examining all the positions involved. Then there's a further delay for fear of alienating others. Finally, there's a volcanic explosion as all the past grievances spill out. But it's a relief to have the argument over and done with, and the truth is, it feels terrific to have all that energy backing a position.

Remember Karen, the peacemaker who had all the law associates crowding into her office? She knew everyone else's position but tended to forget her own. The trick for Karen would be to notice when she's paying too much attention to other people's ideas. She needs to focus on her own agenda, figure out where she stands on being a partner in the firm, and take the right action. One way she could do this is to see which of the proposals angers her the most, and then work backward to the most innocuous— and possibly the most desirable—choice. This process of elimination helps NINES sort through competing ideas and discern which one matches their own opinion.

SECURITY AND STRESS

Dynamics of Change for Point Nine

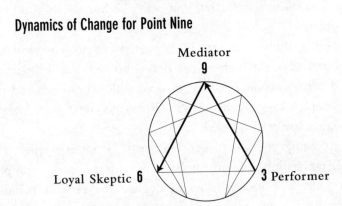

SECURITY RESPONSE AT POINT THREE

NINES operate from the principle of inertia: A body in motion tends to stay in motion, while a body at rest tends to stay at rest. When feeling overburdened by details and decisions NINES are usually sedentary, ruminating about the pros and cons. Everything looks peaceful on the outside, but internally you feel agitated and will not move into action while you're thinking.

However, a good schedule can make a NINE feel secure, and structured guidelines allow you to be extraordinarily productive in a Three-like way, unencumbered by decision making. Now your energy's up and you're in the motion phase of the inertia principle. Moving into Three excites interest in performance, material possessions, social prestige, and a high-profile image—all Three-like preoccupations. But unlike Threes, you want to be loved for yourself rather than for what you do, and you're well able to distinguish between task approval and genuine affection.

Whether the move to Three is useful or not is determined by your focus of attention. In a low-level security response NINEs latch onto someone else's enthusiasm or to a project that looks good but isn't a personal choice. The image is in place, but you're still not focusing on yourself—you'll tend to act by rote, repeating the same procedures that worked last time around.

But when the focus turns to goals that you choose, the energy level stays high, and an incredible amount of work gets done in practically no time. There's no better role model than a NINE who loves what she does. Having recognized a personal calling, you work for the joy of activity itself and the pleasure it gives to others. To stay focused, you have to check in with yourself: "Am I still following my chosen course of action, or am I repeating familiar solutions? Am I moving forward, or am I just running in place?"

STRESS/RISK RESPONSE AT POINT SIX

Conflict is a big stressor and signals the onset of defenses characteristic of NINEs: distract, divert, and digress—anything to buffer open confrontation or having to say no. Mediators can sink into what's called armchair depression, which carries the image of someone slipping deeply into the stuck side of inertia. A body at rest tends to stay at rest: You may be in the office at nine A.M., but are working on automatic and evading action as long as possible.

Eventually, time runs out, and the adrenaline rush brought on by facing a deadline or acting on an unwelcome decision is more than your nervous system is used to. It feels like cold panic. There was lots of time, but now time's up. Obsessive thinking begins: "What if I made the wrong choice? Whom can I ask for advice? Do I really want to be doing this?"

Programmed to follow routine, NINEs who are faced with a task that will force them out of that routine usually won't move until the last minute.

The shift to Six takes place when you start to imagine worst-case scenarios, but the quality of your thinking is tinged with anger. As a Mediator, you know exactly what you don't want in stress. You're fed up—there's no use in denying the obvious any longer. You blame yourself for inaction, but it's also abundantly clear that your goodwill was taken advantage of, so it's really someone else's fault. Blame and rising anger can be turned to advantage if you allow real values to emerge. This is often the point where the tables turn, and NINEs finally become overtly assertive on their own behalf. Your anger can allow a wide-awake, dynamic person to emerge. Now you know exactly where you stand, and coworkers will be happy to see you take a position.

HOW OTHERS SEE NINES

COMMUNICATION STYLE

Because NINEs see the value in most positions, their communications tend to be ambiguous. After hearing them state the case for both sides of an argument, a listener wants to know: "But which side are you on?" The fact is that Mediators hate being the bearer of bad news. Preferring the comfort of neutrality, they avoid conflict and anger at all costs. This deep desire for good feelings on the job, particularly between authority figures and employees, makes NINES pull back from an argument. Their first reaction is to shrug the matter off: "It's not important" or "It's not my responsibility" or "I'll wait this out"—anything to keep the peace.

Ironically, once they establish a position, NINES are remarkably stubborn. They won't budge once they've made up their minds. It takes a long time to decide, but once convinced, NINES close their ears and dig in for the duration.

Mediators can come unstuck at having to choose between alternatives. Choice, they believe, means taking sides and ultimately leads to conflict. Easily pulled into other people's agendas, NINES who can't say no communicate tacit agreement by going along. For example, a consultant will wind up implementing a project he was only hired to design, and may then be so vague about finances that he doesn't get properly paid for getting it up and running. Or perhaps a secretary will slip into organizing after-school activities for her boss's children, even though it's not part of her job description. The NINE's attention easily shifts from essential tasks to inessential work, creating a time-consuming burden of details.

After the initial rush of feeling valued fades, resistance sets in, leaving NINES wondering how to extricate themselves: "I can see what's needed and I hate to say no, but I'm feeling used. How did this happen?" In the workplace, NINES lean on a safe structure to keep the peace. They blend into the organizational climate, suppressing anger, energy, and overt enthusiasm—anything that might create conflict.

This personality style also affects the way NINES give presentations. They are often uncomfortable reaching for the new or unfamiliar, so lectures can be circuitous, as equal time is given to key and minor issues alike. It's as if the Mediator is wandering in a morass of undifferentiated facts, with no real path forward. It's hard to come directly to the point, and the audience loses its own sense of direction as the speaker looks for a starting place.

Once settled in, NINEs adopt an even, pedantic tone that communicates neutrality, rather than opting for an emotional pitch that could polarize opinion. They favor familiar material, road-tested by personal experience, and are extremely convincing when they speak from deeply held belief: "It's best to go with what I know."

Nonverbal Communication

Even when they're distressed, NINEs do not radiate a sense of hurriedness. Apparently placid and unperturbed, they continue their methodical pace even in an office filled with frantic activity. Unlike Fives, who withdraw from pressure, or Eights who try to control the activity, NINEs continue to look stolid and peaceful while feeling overwhelmed. Their inner state rarely shows on the surface. Coworkers should realize that this apparent island of sanity amid chaos may mask the same degree of stress that others are willing to voice.

Coworkers sense a NINE's dissatisfaction when she begins to slow down and sit on the fence, unwilling to give an opinion. NINEs need others to help them shift these emotional roadblocks and allow the project to evolve. Otherwise they are likely to fall into a planted stance, passive-aggressive tactics of delay, and an "I'll wait you out" kind of stubbornness.

It's a strong nonverbal cue that NINEs want change when they gather masses of information to attack a problem. They'll also seek a structure to support decisions: "According to the industry code, regulation 103, subsection (ii)…" There is an overemphasis on going by the book, so it looks as if opposition is coming from the law rather than themselves.

COMMUNICATING WITH NINES

- If you don't hear yes it's probably no. To keep the peace, Mediator NINES can appear to agree, because they haven't said no. Don't assume that silence is agreement.
- If you want a true agreement, frame a conversation in which you state your own interests. Then elicit their need in the project. Establish common ground. Otherwise NINES are likely to buy your agenda up front to keep the peace and then feel trapped.
- NINES flourish with lots of support. Value their contribution. Conversely, they hate to promote themselves. Recognition is paramount. Give it to them. They want it but won't ask.
- Remember NINES like structure. They want well-defined procedures and clear lines of command. They want rewards to be well defined. Keep the lid on sudden surprises. When making changes, acknowledge the difficulties and ask for their cooperation.
- NINES can be stubborn about taking orders. Try to communicate the overall context or the organizational need behind the orders. When possible, reframe orders as suggestions in which the NINE has input.
- NINES have a tendency to talk at length, sometimes avoiding the bottom line. Interrupt them in a friendly way when necessary, and ask for their help in getting to the point.

MOTIVATION

Mediators are motivated by other people's agendas, and are thereby caught in a classic bind. In their model of the way the world works, standing up for oneself means standing against others, so NINES err on the side of harmony. In seeking a no-conflict zone, they often fail to establish their own limits and wind up overwhelmed with unfinished business.

> NINES *try to keep the peace, to see all sides of an argument, and to make people feel comfortable with each other. As a result, they often seem agreeable, but the reality is they've agreed to go along for the time being,* having suspended final commitment until later.

Easily distracted by claims on their attention from elsewhere in the work environment, NINES find it hard to remember a personal priority when bombarded by so much extraneous information. Unlike Sevens, who are true to their own interests, NINES are chronically pulled from their own course of action. And they are never so busy with inessential matters as when they are trying to bury an essential priority or to avoid a confrontation.

For example, as academics at the university level, NINES are aware of the conflicting needs of staff and administration and the divisive potential between political factions. They react to the departmental atmosphere, taking on the tone of the people around them. By trying to steer clear of overt confrontation, Mediators inadvertently absorb the conflict, internalizing other people's problems.

Precisely because NINES internalize the general tone of their environment, creating harmony is very important to them. NINES are known for developing organizational structures that rely on consensus. Structure is a way to cut through conflict; that's why nines are drawn to fields such as banking and law that offer a clear structure—they can always fall back on the rules for common agreement.

But merging with other people's agendas is also a powerful source of pleasure, one that may not be apparent to other people. The benefit for NINES who put their empathy and skills behind a project, a person, or an organization is that they avoid discord while still fully participating in what's going on. When deeply committed, NINES can serve others unconditionally. They need not be stars, because they can experience someone else's victory as their own.

Mediators like defined areas of expertise that build and become profitable over time. They like to stick with an organization for the long haul, refining the system over years. Health care professions are an example of work requiring clear lines of responsibility and communication, clockwork expectations (such as patient care and meticulous record keeping), and protocols for complex medical procedures.

But this approach to work can lead to exhaustion when NINES are overwhelmed with detail and cannot prioritize or say no. When a NINE is overwhelmed, attention spreads to secondary pursuits that drain time and energy from the main agenda. Anything to keep distracted. Burned-out NINES blame others. Having given themselves over to other people's priorities, it must be the other guy's fault when work goes wrong: "I didn't initiate the program; I didn't make this choice; this was someone else's idea."

Overwhelmed, NINES zone out in rote response that stifles any initiative. At their lowest, Mediators go on autopilot, performing just well enough to hold their job and stubbornly refusing to quit or commit. They go through the routine of shuffling papers, but their energy level drops and any truly productive activity is shelved.

But burnout can also produce the right conditions for discovering intrinsic motivations, which for NINES involves finding a chosen course of action. A Mediator's first step toward achieving appropriate action is knowing when she's beginning to let others' needs crowd out her own. NINES should notice thoughts such as "I wonder what he's thinking right now" or "What would he do in my place?" They need to differentiate between choosing for themselves, and when they're motivated by someone else's enthusiasm. When other people's priorities begin to take over, the NINE needs to step back and observe: "I'm taking someone else's position now. What do I want for myself?"

MOTIVATING NINES

- Mediators rely on structural support to stay motivated. Create clear time lines and hold periodic two-way feedback sessions.
- Help them to stay aware of their own needs and priorities. NINES can easily lose personal boundaries. Help them to set limits and focus on priorities.
- NINES are "big-picture" thinkers. They see all sides of a problem and how the parts fit the whole. Use this strength, especially in drafting organizational vision statements and strategic planning. NINES can identify with many points of view and like to be consulted in the planning and decision-making phases of any project.
- When the focus is on application or immediate action, let them know that their "big-picture" thinking will be called on at another time.
- Help NINES to see conflict as a necessary part of processing ideas. Their tendency toward conflict avoidance may lead to premature closure of promising options. Or they may withdraw their participation and contribution.
- NINES will more likely accept criticism that seems fair, that is referenced to the structure of the work rather than the personal reactions or frustrations of the person giving the criticism.
- Mediate your own style or your impatience. Don't come on too strong all at once. Give them time to receive and absorb what you're saying. "We have a problem here; what can we do together to solve it?"

TIME MANAGEMENT

NINEs are suspended in time. Everything happens in its own time: opportunities emerge, priorities gradually surface, and a choice will eventually present itself. Given enough time, decisions sort themselves out. They think, "Why push for closure when the passage of time will carry me to wherever I'm going to wind up anyway? Why act now when things will certainly change by tomorrow?"

Paradoxically, Mediators flourish with structured time lines. A NINE setting out to design an ad campaign, faced with a broad topic and lots of time, can flounder, unable to settle on a vantage point. Where do you start when the pros and cons all seem important, when each idea seems to have equal merit? Given their feelings about time, NINEs find deadlines a welcome focus. They are an external, artificial construct that organizes time, placing the immediate priority at center stage and forcing lesser matters into place. In advertising, Mediator NINEs are among the most diligent when it comes to designing regular magazine copy. The adrenaline rush of meeting day-to-day deadlines keeps them actively creative.

Famous for last-minute saves, Mediators pull out all the stops as the final deadline approaches. Suddenly they make good use of time as secondary distractions drop away.

Mediators are decisive in emergencies and are galvanized by a highly structured external focus. But they're slow starters when it comes to their own priorities.

Where to begin when conflicting priorities all seem equally important? Where to start when time is running out? It seemed like there was plenty of time when the NINE agreed to another commitment, but time accelerates alarmingly when all the deadlines are converging at the same time.

In this situation, the NINE advertising designer pencils the latest assignment at the bottom of the list. Next week there'll be another assignment to go below the current entry. She'll work on each design bit by bit as time allows. No assignment is totally neglected, and there's always something to attend to, because all the articles are progressing at different stages.

> NINEs *need to limit their time commitments. That means learning that no does not automatically create conflict and separation.*

Time can also be used to express anger in a passive way: "I did work on your project yesterday, and I'll get back to it tomorrow." "Yes, I know I said I'll rewrite the report this week, and I will. I'm not holding you up, am I?" Dancing between competing demands on time is as frustrating to NINEs as it is to those who wait for them.

When Mediators shift into automatic mode, their work begins to do itself and time passes without much awareness of what's happening. NINEs are living proof of the extent to which things get done without our conscious participation. There's a flurry of activity; an energetic and successful image is projected. A NINE looks busy, mechanically working to meet deadlines, but feels inwardly numb.

HELPING NINES MANAGE TIME

- Plan. Get an agreement to meet consistently while the work progresses. NINEs like structure and consistent support. Repetition is a must.
- Constantly reinforce the agenda. Once priorities are positioned, take time to remind NINEs of what you are trying

to accomplish together. Keep reinforcing the benefits they will receive from the project.

- Break it down. Present the big picture up front. Then break a large decision into stages. Do each stage sequentially with its own deadline. Don't let time go by, or the NINE's energy will drop.

- Mediators can be drawn out by other's needs. But they are extremely stubborn when "told." (Take time to get an itemized agreement or the job will take forever.) A stubborn NINE moves very slowly and will continue to do so until grievances are heard, blame assigned, and a structure reinstated.

- NINEs thrive in an interactive environment. They appreciate your feedback and approval. Err on the side of too much presence rather than too little.

- Stay on top of problems or mistakes and give feedback all along. Confront problems early on in a friendly way. Don't let things build up.

NEGOTIATION

Mediators are people who can represent warring factions to each other. They come to the table with an ability to see the different sides of an argument, with the obvious liability of potentially sacrificing their own.

Predictably, NINEs feel torn between what others want and what they want. In contrast to Eights, who take what they want, or Fives, who feel detached from what others want, NINEs require unusual precision of attention to negotiate their personal position. In their mental model, everything has its pros and cons, so they face an overwhelming number of decisions that simply don't exist from another type's perspective. To evade those decisions, NINEs typically begin negotiations by "wanting it all or wanting to

walk." They just can't face the prospect of a point-by-point negotiation.

Expect a stalemate until a NINE distinguishes between what
she really must have and nonessential concessions that seemed
equally important at the beginning of the negotiation. Spend time
with them in sorting out essentials from nonessentials, because
NINEs would rather take it all, give it all away, or not play the
game. The decisions are overwhelming.

Introduce "survivors" of previous win-win negotiations, not
only to demonstrate that facing conflict can end in constructive
results, but also to give NINEs a place to air their feelings. Having
said too little for far too long, they must acknowledge how much
they want. Structure the steps of a negotiation carefully and
methodically; when NINEs are involved, it won't be a lightning-fast
settlement.

Here's a suggestion. Set dates for each stage of the decision,
with the NINE's agreement. Admit your concerns: "I understand
that decision making drives you crazy. You need closure, and these
dates will give you peace of mind." The decision itself hasn't been
touched, but at least you've got a structure. Now comes the hard
part: Let it go. Do not call, coerce, or counsel a NINE. If you give
them the freedom to choose, they may come through much faster,
but when you push, they drag their feet.

NINEs appear unflappable and unconcerned, even when decisions create major internal conflict. Don't let them isolate themselves, or they'll take forever to examine every side of the
question. NINEs persevere in discovering loopholes, inconsistencies, and potential points of conflict, but it all takes time. To speed
things up, make sure NINEs have counsel who will formalize their
thinking. The main delay is right at the beginning, in enunciating
a position.

Try this: Ask the NINE to describe each participant's position
in the debate without voicing her own. Ask her to state how each

participant is seen by others, without asking how the NINE sees them. It's obvious that NINEs have tremendous insight into others—they can produce reams of material about everyone else's position, while leaving themselves out. Next, make a list of what the NINE doesn't want, instead of what she does want. This process of elimination can reveal the key elements of a NINE's unspoken agenda.

The negotiation is on course once the NINE articulates a solid position. Remember, at first NINEs may take an impossible position: for example, "I want it all," or "You can have it all," or "I refuse to enter the game." But over time, a defensible proposition will emerge as long as there's enough time for the idea to originate within the NINE herself. The rest of the negotiation will build around that proposition.

TRAINING AND DEVELOPMENT

Along with Eights and Ones, NINEs are people who feel truly competent only when they embody what they know. After all, how can you really be aware of what you want until after you've experienced it? The mainstay of body-based learning lies in repetition and practice. Ideas are important, but NINEs reserve final judgment until they get the feel of a new skill.

As body-oriented learners, NINEs are fundamentally affected by the presence of others and the physical environment. Good vibes between participants are paramount, since NINEs internalize perceived discord. Avoid environmental distractions such as hot or cold room temperature and an excessively high noise level in the hall. Don't worry about repetition. Training described as monotonous by Performer Threes and Epicure Sevens, for example, is predictable and comforting to NINEs.

Easily thrown off track by distraction, NINEs may find it hard to distinguish between key points and ancillary material. Trainers should move cleanly from one essential point to the next. Trainers must also anticipate likely points in the material where tangential thinking could take off. Make the distinctions very clear at those junctures in the syllabus: "Follow path A in your problem solving. Do not consider options B or C." This technique might seem pedestrian to Threes, who always want the quickest route to the goal, or to Sevens, who aren't bothered by unrelated bits of data. But NINES appreciate a periodic restatement of the context, because they need time to reconsider the whole question when a detail doesn't fit.

Mediators stick with each piece of the puzzle until it's coordinated with the other pieces and positioned in the big picture. What seems like a minor detail to trainers may become significant enough to capture a NINE's attention, slowing their learning until they can place the piece in a larger context.

First lay out an overview of the training by listing the course objectives and describing the context in which new skills will be applied in the field. Then move to experiential exercises to anchor each subset of the material. Trainers will see NINES moving into high gear during hands-on practice of skills. NINES learn by building a habit, and they are quick to internalize new learning if they can practice and if they are given positive reinforcement.

THE CASE OF THE NINE MANAGER WHO HELD HIS GROUND

It's a trying moment for the newly appointed Six president of the family-owned restaurant chain. Most of her family's money is invested in the business her brother built up from one restaurant to the five busy places they currently own. Now he's ill, and she, a prototypical Loyal Skeptic, has to finish the negotiations he began.

The restaurants are popular local spots, but their niche has recently been invaded by a regional restaurant chain and the competition is forcing them to streamline in a hurry. As part of that plan, the new Six president is negotiating a sales, service, and support contract with the NINE manager of an integrated computer systems firm.

Neither she nor anyone else in the chain knows much about computers, and this is the most money their small business has ever invested. They would be committing to a system that includes point-of-sale equipment with repeater printers in the kitchens so the wait staff can punch in orders, notify the kitchen, and generate a bill at the same time. She's also ordered scanners for the storerooms and accounting software for the head office. It's a big order.

The Six president wants an agreement that will allow her to sleep at night without worrying about system bugs. She feels secure about the hardware and software she's bought, but service and backup support are still being negotiated.

The NINE sales manager is anxious to close, but the final 10 percent of the contract—the service and support component—will either make the deal or break it. He's spent a lot of time with the president, there's a sizable commission at stake, and this installation could be a deal that attracts other local businesses.

TYPICAL INTERACTIONS

The Six president doesn't know how she's gotten into this mess. She's been in the restaurant business all her life, but now the weight of the family is on her shoulders. In a way, it seems too simple; her brother's research had been meticulous, and basically all she had to do was follow through on his leads. But now the decision is imminent and she's flooded by doubts.

All she can see is an expensive new system blowing up in her face. Once unleashed, her imagination gains momentum and goes wild: "They could discontinue this whole line of computers!" She sees herself scrambling to stockpile bits and pieces of obsolete machinery: "Maybe that's how they make their money—when your perfectly good system slips a gear, you have to buy a whole new machine." She imagines herself in front of a dead monitor with her family hovering.

The NINE sales manager has tried to be supportive. He sent her to a nearby restaurant that had bought the same system. They had also bought the same support package that is now being negotiated, a package that includes telephone technical support as its key component. But the visit backfired, and the skeptical Six president panicked. It seemed ridiculous to suppose that someone on the other end of a telephone line could walk her through the complicated series of commands necessary to get the computer system up and running.

"Who did those guys think they were fooling?" was her reaction once the visit was complete. She started to feel misused. How long, she began to wonder, did it take to resurrect a dead machine? Two hours? A day? "God, suppose it takes a full day," she thought. "We'd lose thousands, let alone the goodwill of customers who wouldn't come back."

Now, alone in her office, she starts to pace, imagining the restaurant is packed with people—there's a huge party going on—and the computer is down. It would all be on her shoulders.

Just then her intercom buzzes. The manager is here for their two o'clock meeting. He's a warm, rotund presence who's hard to read because he's so affable. She'd love to dump her doubts in his lap and pay him to take them away. But she doesn't trust him, and she's wary of any advice he could offer. Why ask for reassurance from someone you don't trust?

The NINE sales manager is painfully aware of both her doubts and her inexperience. He can see she's beginning to scare herself again and wishes he could calm her down. Not knowing what to do, he waits it out. The service contract—as he feared—could turn out to be a deal breaker. If the president insists on a guaranteed on-site technician instead of going for the usual telephone technical support, he'd make the sale, but would lose money on the deal.

As a NINE, he can't stand feeling caught between what a client wants and what the company can deliver. He's been here before, hating the conflict that comes with saying no and setting limits. If he doesn't pay attention, he'll buy her agenda and agree to on-site service.

THE TIDE TURNS

The Mediator reviews what he knows: The president, an ultra-conservative person, bought top-of-the-line software, the most reliable on the market. He didn't even mention the company's cutting-edge technology because it's clear she isn't a risk taker. He played to her conservatism, underscoring the things he was con-vinced she needed to hear repeatedly: "Our company's the most reputable in the entire area; we've done business here for years. The software at the restaurant you visited has been up and run-ning for eighteen months without a hitch." Everything he said is true, but he realizes he can't hold her hand forever. Thinking about her situation makes him feel uncomfortable. He can easily identify with her position and wants to allay her fears, but how can he do so and still make a profit?

A sale to this family would lure other local businesses, so there's a lot more riding on the deal besides the $15,000 com-mission. He's sure she's not going to do better anywhere else, so he must reestablish the Six's confidence in the package before she loses her nerve and bolts. The NINE manager knows where she's coming from. New to her job, she's stuck with a big decision right out of the gate. He remembers his own professional baptism—he felt the whole company was depending on him to salvage a deal that he wasn't sure he could handle. Maybe she feels that way, too. NINE-like, he sympathizes, seeing himself from her perspective—

to her, he's just some large and anonymous stranger trying to cut a deal.

Seeing the problem through her eyes clears the logjam. He no longer feels divided and knows how to move the negotiation forward. Rather than opposing the president's need for security or pushing the telephone support, the Mediator opts to address her fears. She hasn't winced about price so far, so he'll offer the maximum coverage possible—a set of spare machines and on-site technical support. Then he'll repeat his offer of the far more reasonable standard telephone technical support. Maybe they can compromise somewhere in the middle.

Oddly, the Six brightens at the prospect of owning extra machines, although she acknowledges that the cash outlay is far more than her restaurant can afford. The idea of having that much backup makes her feel safe, even though it costs a lot. As the president relaxes, the sales manager feels better. He's struck a creative compromise that doesn't sacrifice his own agenda.

RESOLUTION

During the initial negotiations, the Six president holds out for guaranteed security, while the NINE manager stolidly repeats his litany. "You're going to have to find a comfort level with something you can afford. This is a good deal. Nothing in life is a hundred percent certain. We won't strand you without help."

The skeptical Six latches on to the word *help*. She trusted her brother's research; that was helpful. This computer company has a strong reputation; she can trust that. She's sure the machines will break, but she can get help. The company will rescue her.

The sales manager sees that she's now examining the problem, and he lets her ride her doubts. Inwardly, he feels certain of a positive outcome. Sure enough, she shuttles back and forth: "How do I know? How can I be sure? Who do I go to when the system breaks?" The NINE reassures her with comforting phrases: "proven track record"; "solid reputation"; "we've done business in this area for years."

When the president finally runs out of steam, the NINE sales manager presents his compromise. "If the tech can't deliver on the telephone, I'll have a live body to your place within an hour." His initiative goes to the heart of the president's anxiety. She hears "rescue within an hour" and is encouraged by the image of a physical presence to nurse the ailing system.

From his side of the bargaining table, the sales manager hears that a technician will be sent only when there's dire need. Telephone backup remains at the heart of the contract, so it's a good deal for his company.

As this scenario shows, NINEs are called Mediators for good reason. Once the sales manager picks up on the Six's key concern about safety, he structures an elegant compromise. He creates a win-win situation by using the magic words "We won't strand you without help" and does it without abandoning his own position.

Self-observation

NINEs caught in a conflict need to remember their own position as they draw on their talent for empathizing with others. Aware of his tendency toward self-forgetting, our Mediator remembered his company's needs, weathering the discomfort of a potentially disappointed client. Instead of spacing out or distracting or prematurely compromising, he includes his own position in the picture while maintaining a sympathetic bond with his client.

Epilogue

There's often a certain comfort in discovering your Enneagram profile. It's immediately obvious that you are not alone, that your outlook makes sense and is validated by millions of people throughout the world who share the same perspective. That understanding was traditionally reserved for spiritual aspirants, who turned attention inward to discover the barriers to their progress in meditation. Every world tradition has something vital to say about the monk of judging mind or lustful mind or doubting mind, yet most people have no idea how radically different the world seems through someone else's glasses.

For example, it doesn't take much imagination to transport history's monks of judging mind to a high-rise office complex, where in modern dress they monitor themselves, coworkers, and their job through a lens of perception focused on error. Likewise Enneatype Sixes, today's monks of doubting mind, perceive their world in precisely the same way as their spiritual predecessors. A Six's mind automatically poses questions, not out of choice, but because doubt is a corner stone of their emotional survival strategy.

Imagine a Six, seated at adjacent desks in the same office with a Performer Three, historically seen as prone to self-deception. Both look up as their Nine manager heads in their direction. The amiable manager, a monk of lazy mind, is feeling comfortably laid back, looking forward to a relaxed morning undisturbed by pressing decisions. There are no clients scheduled, a major report that is due tomorrow, is well under control, and the office feels relaxed, just the kind of ambiance he likes.

As he appears, the doubting monk's antennae activate, scanning the manager's face and body language for signals. "Why now? The report's not due until tomorrow. What have I done?" But from where she sits, the monk of deceptive mind sees a chance to impress the manager with her efficiency and enthusiasm. She gestures for him to come to her desk, and with a smile produces the group report that he didn't expect until the next day. His eyebrows raised in pleasant surprise reward her for a task well done, so she doesn't notice the shock waves spreading through the office. Once again, she's stolen the credit.

Left alone, this interaction is likely to repeat on a daily basis. The Three will keep calling attention to her value. The Six will vigilantly anticipate difficulty, and the Nine manager will continue to compound the problem by remaining comfortably oblivious. But if this trio knew about the Enneagram, the outcome could be different. If each borrowed the other's glasses and could see each other's intentions, their view of the workplace would shift.

The Six would be pleased to find that the Performer Three doesn't intend to attack him. Even her disturbing deceptions seem quite plausible from another angle. After all, every contributor signed off on that report, so they did get credit. Did it really matter that she was the one to bring all that diligence and effort to the manager's attention? She had worked hard. The manager was satisfied. Didn't everybody win?

Looking through her glasses, it's clear that getting the manager's approval fills her lens. She's not intending to injure her coworker's feelings. Not at all. In fact, she's so focused on the manager that feelings don't enter the picture much, either her own or anyone else's. If the Six looked further, he'd be surprised to find that she even wants his approval—whenever he figures into her thinking.

Seen through her eyes, the Six will know how reactive he

seems. He questions her intentions, but doesn't suggest a better course of action. The Three sees herself as proactive and positive, while he's feeling attacked, but doubt prevents him from speaking up. He could figure out an honest way to give her the approval she needs, but will she respond? Would she ever learn to spread the credit? Should he take the risk? Insight alone won't change the situation, if the main obstacle to change lies in his doubtful thinking.

Likewise, by seeing herself through a Six's lens, the Performer Three would realize that her sense of efficiency is coming across as ruthless, unfriendly behavior. Instead of dismissing him from her thinking, she could become an ally by publicly crediting everyone who works on the next report. Knowing that Sixes are demotivated by competition, she might also encourage him to present the next report to the manager on his own. Given Enneagram insight, she would know that doubt vanishes when Sixes trust the situation. Yet the major barrier to achieving the high performance teamwork she wants lies in her own desire to excel over others.

From his place in the triad, the manager—history's monk of lazy mind—will have to take action. At the moment the Performer demands his attention, while the Loyal Skeptic is in retreat, widening a breach between the pair. Good management requires that he equalize credit for the report. But that decision could lead to conflict.

If the manager saw himself through the eyes of a Three, he'd see a man who doesn't make waves. The manager could well agree with that perception—Why bother when the problem might take care of itself? The manager might also guess that he's being manipulated by his Performer employee, but will bide his time, sidestepping conflict and hoping the Six will eventually come forward on his own. But the manager's preoccupation with weighing the pros and cons of the dilemma won't register in the

Six's lens. The Six will see a gullible manager, flattered by an aggressive coworker, all of which confirms his doubt.

Knowing that he should take action, the manager may still hesitate out of habit. Nine-like, he could succumb to routine, spending time on paperwork instead of solving the problem. Insight alone won't heal a management hurdle that lies deeply buried within himself—a Nine's belief that his actions won't make a difference.

In this example and in our own professional lives, it's easy to misread our coworkers' intentions yet we easily comprehend their logic once we see a coherent pattern. Rather than feeling ignored or manipulated by a different agenda, we see instead the limited focus of Threes, who single-mindedly pursue their goals, and Sixes, who create safety by questioning, or Nines, who cushion disappointment by wondering if their efforts make a difference.

Yet insight isn't enough to change deeply seated habits that serve a protective function. Now that we have seen how habits of heart and mind determine our outlook, what would be a useful step toward getting out of the box that we're in?

Most of us wouldn't ordinarily think of going to work every day as a spiritual exercise, yet our patterns are constantly triggered by the job and the people around us. Once you know your type, you may become increasingly aware of times when your habit engages. Eights will notice when they've begun to blame someone, Sevens recognize a barrage of interesting plans. Nines suddenly wake up to realize they've been spaced out, while Fours report painful attacks of desire.

All of this is encouraging. There are two of you in there. The box of habitual thinking and an observer that can watch you think. When you notice your type pattern emerge, instead of letting it run, take a pause. Give the habit a name: "blaming" or "planning" or "forgetting" or "I am desiring." Step back and observe instead of engaging your thoughts.

In our time, there is practically no education for inner observation, yet you used the observer to look inside and discover your type. The Enneagram was originally designed as a map to assist self-observation, and its power still lies in pointing to the part of ourselves that is already free. The observing self that can witness what we're thinking.

The observing self recognizes habitual thinking before the pattern fully engages. Naming your habit will reinforce the difference between the observer and your thoughts, so naming is a vital first step. Stepping back and introducing a pause allows you to shift perspective and get a reality check on what other people are doing. More important, the pause interrupts habitual thinking so you don't go on automatic.

All of this calls our own bias into question, giving us enough flexibility to see other points of view. But the spiritual agenda lies elsewhere. In the traditions that use type as an agent of spiritual change, the agenda is to leave the box of habitual thinking entirely. Using the inner observer to discover your type, sets the stage for the vice to virtue conversion. Now you know what you're looking for and will be less distracted by secondary patterns.

The vice is the emotional survival strategy that energizes habitual thinking, so quieting the vice is the way out. A frightened Six naturally seeks the virtue of courage, and Threes, caught in a cycle of deception, will prize the power of honesty, the freedom to just be themselves. While anyone can become fearful for a reason or deceptive upon occasion, the emotional vice that energizes your type is more like the way that you're wired.

In the ancient world, cultivating the virtues, or constructive ways of being, was seen as an ethical choice. Learning to step back, take a pause, and name your pattern of thought as it rises is a more effective choice than letting the habit run. Any fixed pattern has its limitations, yet mysteriously we seem to be seeking the virtue of our type whether we know it or not, because the search is lodged in our own emotions.

In the previous chapters, we've seen how the different points of view described by people today, are much the same as when systems like the Enneagram were developed. Anger is the same as it always was, and the vice of Envy won't have changed much through the centuries. Everyone has a personality type, because it is rooted in a survival strategy that can be discovered by self-observation. The age-old explanation of why people do what they do is that we're simply trying to survive. Yet despite ourselves, humanity seems lifted from its own crude defenses as each survival strategy becomes a source of suffering.

One commonly asked question about the Enneagram is "Which type is most suitable for a specific job?" or "How can we build an ideal team?" And the answer is "Find mature human beings." People are hired for their skills, creativity, past experience, and whether they act like grown-ups, rather than for their lens of perception. Yet that lens affects teamwork, management style, problem solving, decision making, and interactions of all kinds.

We have seen how each type communicates, uses time, negotiates, and can best be motivated and trained. Yet the greatest advantage in understanding how other people see themselves, lies in standing back, taking a pause and naming our own habit, before we go on automatic. In practicing that pause, we can dedicate both our thinking and observing selves to living our full potential as borh productive and spiritual beings.

A Brief History of Enneagram Contributors

What the West knows of the Enneagram began with George Ivanovich Gurdjieff (1872–1949), a spiritual teacher of enormous personal charisma. Gurdjieff lived and taught while Freud's ideas about the unconscious had yet to be popularized. Claiming that he received the system from traditional spiritual sources, Gurdjieff introduced the nine-pointed star, which even then included the internal flow patterns that unite the points in specific ways. His teaching about type was called "chief feature," and the diagram that we use today became the signature of his work. Gurdjieff-based schools still function in most major cities in the United States and Europe.

Anyone working with the system owes a great debt to the work of Oscar Ichazo, who initiated many of the seminal ideas that have perpetuated the Enneagram system's psychological and spiritual merit. Without doubt he is the major modern contributor to the system. Ichazo's teaching is promoted through the Arica Institute, 145 Palisade St., Suite 401, Dobbs Ferry, NY 10522. The ideas represented in this book about human personality and its relationship to aspects of higher awareness are different and distinct from those expounded by Mr. Ichazo.

Claudio Narnajo, M.D., is another major contributor. He provided the rosetta stone that aligned Ichazo's personality descriptors with current psychological thinking about type. He also initiated the panel method—a teaching style in which representatives of the nine types speak for themselves.

Helen Palmer has shaped and refined the panel teaching method for over twenty years. Her contributions to the Enneagram lie in the area of intuition, placement of attention, and the vice to virtue conversion, through which the types access their higher potentials. Together with coteacher David Daniels, M.D., she trains professionals in the use of the system throughout the United States and in Europe.

Helen Palmer's office will furnish information about all areas of her work. These include oral tradition workshops, professional trainings, and organizational consulting.

You may also request information about Enneagram educational groups, with referrals to graduates of the Enneagram Professional Training Program throughout the United States, in Europe, and in Australia.

The *Nine Points of View Video Series*. Illustrative graphics and speakers who represent their own type explicate the themes of her books. An eight-hour audiocassette seminar on the Enneagram produced by Sounds True is also available.

To have your name added to the mailing list so you may receive the current international teaching schedule, please contact:

Helen Palmer
1442A Walnut St., Suite 377
Berkeley, CA 94709
Voice (510) 843-7621
Fax (510) 540-7626